CONTEMPORARY *Details*

CONTEMPORARY

Details

NONIE NIESEWAND

SIMON & SCHUSTER

New York   London   Toronto   Sydney   Tokyo   Singapore

SIMON & SCHUSTER

Simon & Schuster Building

Rockefeller Center

1230 Avenue of the Americas

New York, New York 10020

Copyright © Mitchell Beazley Publishers 1992
Text copyright © Nonie Niesewand
All rights reserved
including the right of reproduction in whole or in part in any form.
SIMON & SCHUSTER and colophon
are registered trademarks of Simon & Schuster Inc.
10 9 8 7 6 5 4 3 2 1

Library of Congress Cataloging-in-Publication Data:
Niesewand, Nonie.
Contemporary Details/Nonie Niesewand.   p.   cm
ISBN 0 671 74958 7
1. Interior decoration accessories.
2. Interior decoration-History – 20th century.
I. Title.
NK2115.5.A25N5 1993   747- dc20
91-40408 CIP

Edited and designed by

Mitchell Beazley Publishers, part of Reed International Books Ltd,

Michelin House, 81 Fulham Road, London SW3 6RB

Simultaneously published in

Great Britain by Mitchell Beazley Publishers, London

Design Director **Jacqui Small**

Executive Editor **Judith More**

Design **Town Group Consultancy Ltd**

Editors **Jonathan Hilton, John Wainwright**

Editorial Assistants **Jaspal Bhangra, Catherine Smith**

Production **Ted Timberlake**

The publishers have made every effort
to ensure that all instructions given in this book are accurate and safe,
but they cannot accept liability for any resulting injury, damage or loss
to either person or property whether direct or consequential and howsoever arising.
The authors and publishers will be grateful for
any information which will assist them in keeping future editions up to date.

Typeset in Trade Gothic Bold Condensed,
Trade Gothic Light and Garamond 3 Italic by Town Group Consultancy Ltd, London W3
Colour reproduction by Scantrans Pte Ltd, Singapore
Printed in the Netherlands by Koninklijke Smeets Offset b.v., Weert

Page 1 Steel railings punctuate a mezzanine balcony in a conversion of a redundant power station into a recording studio by Julian Powell-Tuck.
Page 2 & 3 Wooden boards, white walls and glazed screens are the sparest of contemporary details in an interior by the former partnership of Claudio Silvestrin and John Pawson.
Right Venetian blinds filter light across the mezzanine floor in a house by David Wild.

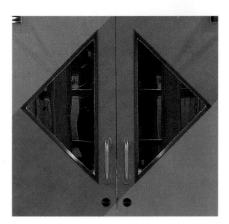

Contents

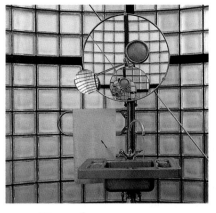

Introduction

The first international guide to contemporary details is an invaluable source of ideas and innovative products for anyone interested in 20th-century interior design. Contemporary Details presents design innovations and technological developments that have made it into the mass market because of their usefulness and good looks. Form follows function in designs for the clean-cut, contoured interiors of today, where period pieces are as out of place as a Victorian fireplace aboard a space shuttle. This is a book for homeowners who want to live in the present and who look forward to the future. It is not the book for people who wish to disguise their radiators with trelliswork or hide their televisions under skirted tablecloths, or for those who believe the builders left early if they do not see moldings on every wall. Intensive sleuthwork among the top manufacturers in Europe, the United States and Japan reveals patented inventions: armorplated

security doors that masquerade as friendly tongue-and-grooved front doors, door pulls that can store both daylight and artificial light to glow in the dark, the high-heat

ceramics pioneered by microwave cookery transformed into slimline, wall-mounted heater panels or sculpted into geometric firebricks for smokeless fires. The original and unusual ideas on show include an oven with a curved concave front that turns corners gracefully, slimline ceiling-mounted loudspeakers built into acoustic tiles in bathrooms to beam music in while showering, battens profiled like dado rails that hide wall-mounted tube lighting to delineate stairs with a lit handrail and photo-sensitive lights that turn on when people enter the room. Less obvious in their technological attraction, but no less innovative, are products like energy-conscious window shades that store sunlight and release it during the night to warm the glazed areas or energy-conscious ovens that steam cook as well as convection fan heat.

Innovations in manufacturing bring back hand-made techniques that are in reality machine-cut and mass-produced. Mosaic tiles or parquet patterns arrive on site already

4

assembled, pasted onto templates, to fit geometric configurations. Art is translated into wall-to-wall carpet with the newest Timbrelle acrylic yarns, so finely tuned to carpet weaving that artists' and architects' artwork can be reproduced accurately by the yard and less expensively than linoleum flooring. Tooling up a factory to make new products

5

means they are effectively marketed worldwide, and consequently less expensive than one-offs or customized finishes; although Contemporary Details also examines these specialist areas so popular with contemporary interior designers. There is nothing mechanical about all this mass production. Rather, a lot of thoughtful comment about the expressive new designs that shows how functional form can be good-looking. Take the ordinary door pull as an example, and note the comments of designer Jasper Morrison: "Few products are so closely involved with architecture as the door pull. As soon as it is fixed it becomes part of the building and

6

7

will have an influence on how the building works." Yet this attitude is not accompanied by grandiose flourishes: "If the user is aware of the pull every time the door opens, something is wrong."

So, containing a place for the forefinger, the thumb, and the convex arch, these door pulls are high-touch, rather than high-tech. Style does not take second place to technological innovations: there are traditional kitchen white goods colored black with simple-to-follow electronic controls by Roberto Pezzeti for Wizard; thermally insulated aluminum window frames clad with "Clima" wooden façades; ceramic-clad stoves in the traditional wood-burning shape fired and wired for

8

top-heat gas, and triangular bathtubs that tuck into corners while offering whirlpool massage techniques.

The story of modern furnishings and fixtures dates from about the mid-19th century when products began to be made in factories by machines, instead of by hand. As the bentwood café chair began to roll off the assembly line at

4 Lighting is the interior designer's most exciting tool – from built-in wall, floor and ceiling background lights to theatrical spots that pivot and move to decorative task lighting, uplights and modern chandeliers. Tadao Ando employs all of these in his sparse interiors.
5 Extendable chromed mirrors and marble surfaces are typical of the minimalist style of John Pawson.
6 David Chipperfield combines different flooring materials – slate, granite, wood – to demarcate areas of an open-plan house.
7 Arata Isozaki's design for an ascent to a bunk-like sleeping area frees floor space.
8 A spider's web of metal is strung together for a dramatic staircase by Eva Jiricna.

the steam-pressed timber yards of Thonet, the era of the artisan came to an end. The cabinetmaker, stonemason and gilder rapidly found their skills obsolete as technology developed in response to scientific discovery. By the 1880s, while machines continued to mass-produce furniture and fixtures, an esthetic revolt was brewing, led by the Arts and Crafts movement in Britain but quickly taken up elsewhere in Europe and in North America. Designers wanted a return to the deliberate craftsmanship and simple design of the Middle Ages,with stained-glass door panels recalling ecclesiastical windows and giant pewter hinges replacing Victorian brass fittings. English artist and social reformer William Morris pontificated on simplicity, fine craftsmanship and the belief that good design should be available to all, regardless of their social standing. His sentiments were admirable but doomed to failure—in a machine age, any solutions to the problem of machine esthetics must work with, not against, the machine.

One offshoot of the movement was Art Nouveau, which drew its inspiration from Nature. Samuel Bing's Paris shop, La Maison de l'Art Nouveau, opened in 1895, spearheaded the style with Tiffany glass, Beardsley posters and Lalique jewelry in room settings by Henry van de Velde. The movement incurred Le Corbusier's epitaph: "an intolerable period, Art Nouveau—a time of crushing bourgeois values sunk in materialism bedecked with mechanical decorations." In Vienna, by contrast, designers confronted the dilemma of the machine age head on. "To each time its art, to each art its freedom" was carved above the door to the Secessionist Gallery where Adolf Loos and Josef Hoffmann led a designer

Right Philippe Starck's designs for the Royalton Hotel, New York, are now available for the domestic market. The "Royalton" collection's signature horn motif appears as light fixtures, door pulls, vases, fenders and even fire tongs.

protest against the pompous, historicist Ringestrasse style of the Neoclassicists. Hoffmann's style evolved in a geometric and structural direction and his door pulls and light fixtures made for the Palais Stoclet in Brussels in 1905 — a landmark of residential modern architecture—are still in production.

In Germany, the School of Arts and Crafts changed its name to the Bauhaus (literally "building house") in 1919, when Walter Gropius, the father of Modernism, became its new director. Adopting the American architect Louis Sullivan's principle "form follows function," the immensely influential Bauhaus group aimed for high-quality machine production, bringing industry and art together to create prototypes for mass consumption. New techniques and materials made this possible, and Bauhaus members went on to pioneer a series of world firsts, from the cantilevered chair to the transparent armchair and shelf. When Le Corbusier applied the same principle to domestic architecture, describing the home as a machine for living, the worldwide reign of modern style had begun.

Between the world wars another style, known as Art Deco, or French Moderne, also flourished. The hit of the 1925 l'Exposition des Arts Decoratifs in Paris, Art Deco was at first modernistic rather than historical in its inspiration. Plastic, shagreen, tinted and frosted glass were used for interior fittings and Jacques-Emile Ruhlman and Pierre Chareau came up with practical solutions to seating and storage. However, in the 1930s Deco designers borrowed from pop culture as well as Bauhaus. The iconography of transport, jazz and the movies were central to Art Deco, but when excitement about the exploration of King Tutankhamen's

tomb led to the adoption of sun-ray motifs and other symbols derived from Egyptian papyrus scrolls, the sheer geometry of the style made it difficult to clasp a door pull, let alone turn it.

In the early 1940s came organic curves from Scandinavia and the Finnish architect Alvar Aalto. Simple but bold fabrics, curvaceous glass, bentwood simplicity and sleek, stylish steel bath and kitchen faucets and mixers are still associated with this movement.

Meanwhile, in Italy a rationalist organization called Gruppo 7, founded by Guiseppe Terragni, designed structures that mirrored the simplicity of form pioneered by Alvar Aalto, with exposed new brick, timbered beams and the lengthy glass panels that larger kilns could now produce. The exposed technical elements – for heat and light – were a forerunner of Minimalism in the 1970s.

The Case Study House experiment that Ray and Charles Eames conducted at the Cranbrook Academy in the United States in 1948 mixed materials in a thoroughly modern esthetic in order to construct an inexpensive, livable house out of standard factory parts. Wood and leather took on shapes like airplane wings; the pressing and molding techniques of the aeronautical industry combined to make furnishings that stacked, flexed, folded and rolled.

All over the world, mid-century modernism evolved against a background of interior stone walls or mosaic tiles, with terrazzo floors replicated in linoleum, lit by recessed lighting, or three-in-a-row hanging lamps, while spindly legged furniture sat on brushed-pile rugs in neon colors and the television took pride of place.

Alongside the flowering of a counter-culture in the 1960s came a loosening-up of form, encouraged by the fluid new materials – molded plastic, fiberglass and wire mesh. The Italians began to develop their sleek modern style. There was less wood around and new lamp sources, primary colors and molded forms became important features.

After such exuberance, the Minimalism of the 1970s was inevitable. Designers worked with attenuated lines, making things smaller, lighter and more moveable as they explored materials such as carbon fiber. Pressed metal came into its own for stair treads and chair supports, its industrial punch-card imagery relating to the new high-tech look as cladding was ripped away and the inner organs of a building – its air-conditioning and heating, its stairs and elevators – became adornment on the outside.

As the pendulum swung again, 1980s designers turned their attention to volume and mass under the banner of a refined classic Modernism. A more playful pop imagery was allowed. Suddenly surface finish was all-important, with polychromatic glass panels, silk-paneled laminates and gilded accessories. Function is there in the detailing, but power-dressed as chairs sprout wings and fireplace fenders resemble Viking helmets. Robert Venturi ripped off Chippendale for Knoll International in two-dimensional form and Ettore Sottsass launched Memphis with its overscaled, colorful pieces.

While the Post-Modernists turned the skyline into backdrops for playschool, the 1980s also saw the emergence of the architectural interior designers – the graduate architects who have transformed the way we look at interiors. How do they differ from the decorators of old? One of them, Pierre d'Avoine, sums it up like this: "The interior designer

Right Every detail in Sir Richard Rogers' London house – from faucet to cabinet, balustrade to floor – has been chosen for ease of use and maintenance.

plays with spaces, the decorator with camouflages." Good-looking, fashionable but lasting interiors are no longer a question of moldings, dados, skirting, paint and flounce – all those age-old decorators' tricks of camouflage. They are functional, technologically advanced and, above all, they follow an idea that has been drafted along architectural principles. The innovative new young modern designers seek to throw out artifice; they prize the intrinsic integrity of the structural material. Throughout Contemporary Details examples of their work underline this approach. Their conversions within chapels, warehouses and office blocks have created homes out of space that had no relevance in today's world. And the result? Homes will never look the same again.

By using products designed to make life more comfortable and more leisurely, the products themselves have come to represent not a style, but an attitude. Set in the context of vernacular materials—corrugated metal panels, steel girder steps, plywood walls and ceilings of wavy plastic, flake-board and corrugated carport aluminum – contemporary detailing allows for individual expression.

Products reflect the way in which we want to live today, with far-sighted views, generous spaces and lyrical light. British architect Julian Powell-Tuck believes that: "Attitudes reflect the fact that there are more women at work than before." So the latest appliances used in kitchens can do most things, and they have provoked "a new break-down of space within the home, with one long room combining dining, cooking and living, and clusters of cells off it for study, sleep, bathing."

The architectural legacy of the Modernists has altered forever the shape and purpose of the home and its new practitioners value honesty, simplicity and integrity. After all, the elaborate swags and festoons that are still reproduced from "retro" decorators from 100-year-old pattern books were devised when draperies were the only way of making a house draftproof.

The challenges for today's designers include how to heat the space efficiently, how to light it without cords and how to climb a level without taking out great chunks of the room in what Pierre d'Avoine calls "B-movie architecture." Indeed, with property prices in cities making floorspace so expensive, the question is, quite simply, how to save space. Market research has encouraged manufacturers to produce slimline kitchen appliances, for example, that suit the small kitchens and families in today's cities. And with social awareness one of the givens, the solutions have to recognize our anxiety about the environment.

Every decade of this century has brought increased mobility and income to the industrialized world as a whole, and the ideals expressed by William Morris at the turn of the century are a little closer to being realized. "Good design for all," is the maxim of Philippe Starck, France's most celebrated architect/interior designer. A commission from President Mitterrand in 1978 to design a private apartment at the Champs Elysées propelled him far ahead of the mainstream matte-black design crowd, but Starck still cites as the best example of contemporary design his pack-flat furniture at low prices for the mail-order catalog company, Trois Suisses. "Functional, accessible, appropriate" is the criterion upon which all the innovations shown in Contemporary Details are judged.

Walls & Ceilings

The spaces within which interior designers prefer to work all tend to have certain characteristics in common: unbroken, long expanses uninterrupted by openings and space-inhibiting walls. Gallery space is the most enviable, and many architects working on domestic interiors strive toward a "flow of space" by removing walls. To achieve this, load-bearing internal walls are replaced by the modern "rafters" that dissect ceilings – the reinforced steel joist (RSJ). The additional space created by this simple ploy often means that the dividing walls become more shapely as architects rethink the linear grid upon which so much of modern box housing was developed. Planes and angles and sinuous wavy lines insinuate their way into interiors, just as they did at the start of the 20th century with Frank Lloyd Wright's exploration of "organic" architecture in the vernacular. Wright threw out this challenge:

"Americans, in seeking culture, could not accept that posts and beams could be thrown away in favor of folding or 2

Previous page
Architect Steven Holl's interiors reflect his fascination with materials. Here, he contrasts blue-stained wooden storage fronts with the milky opalescence of perspex shielding the light tubes.

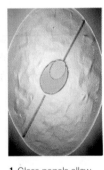

1 Glass panels allow light to filter through. This "Polifemo" glass tile by R. Lucadamo for MITO has, additionally, the chromatic variation that makes for an interestingly textured surface.

2 Modern architects favor the removal of boxed-in walls to create the feeling of free space. In their place, they tend to prefer sliding partitions that can be positioned to seal off an area when needed, or slid back to reveal an uninterrupted expanse. In his own home, architect Sir Richard Rogers used industrial roller systems, grooved and tracked, to clamp opaque glass partition walls in place.

3 Rooms seen only in artificial light, like the busy professional's drawing room and study, warrant dramatic wall treatments which might appear bold or even shrill in the harsh light of day. Malcolm Last painted the walls in this jazz club in pink and eau-de-nil, which transform to purple and chartreuse under night-time lighting.

3

4

4 Tadao Ando's trademark is his use of poured concrete walls. Unadorned, they represent the perfect foil for this Japanese architect's reinterpretation in modern glass of traditional shojis – translucent floor-to-ceiling panels, which allow walls to become doors. Bare concrete, coarse-seamed and studded with holes at regular intervals, becomes a canvas for evolving light patterns as the sun strikes the walls.

5 Clearly, East meets West in these concrete stud wall panels in David Chipperfield's offices. Chipperfield enjoys contrasts, of concrete with stainless steel or marble, for example. He will also set painted steel frames filled with panels of sand-blasted glass into areas of concrete wall.

5

1 & 2 These examples of John Pawson's work reveal something of his challenge to modernism. Slender white walls (above) flanking the stairs show how in this passageway nothing interrupts the flow. In his monolithic wall (above right), slab-like partitions hover over the floor, while a slender column appears to support the ceiling in an otherwise empty space.

3 In David Wild's interior the corrugated zinc roof, more commonly associated with carports, undulates sinuously across the room to bring unity to this dining space, in which the cantilevered Bauhaus chairs help to replicate that directional flow.

4 Normally the atrium is the widest glazed opening in a building, but Frank Fitzgibbons reverses this order with a monumental ascent using massive wall volumes that narrow and thin toward the top, while the tubular rails and guards emphasize the stages of the ascent.

5 Ron Brinkers uses the adobe approach in this curvaceous wall, which appears to end in a triangular dovetail at the corner. This is emphasized below by a triangular plaster shelf. Slender ceiling-to-floor glass panels enhance the dimensions of the plasterwork walls.

movable planes, nor that organic architecture could derive from the tall grass of the mid-western prairies."

It was Frank Lloyd Wright who challenged the traditional subdivision of the home into separate rooms. In his houses built around Chicago in the first decade of the 20th century, each space was linked to and integrated with the landscape outside, as walls made way for the large, unbroken living room, with cells for bedrooms, studies and bathrooms fringing it. Modernism, that catch-all name for a panoply of styles since the Industrial Revolution, has seen a shift from the early moderne of Le Corbusier and the Bauhaus school of the late 1920s and 30s to the frankly flamboyant façades and wall finishes of the post-modern school, to the new simplicity of the late-modern movement. From glass to gloss to gleam in 20-year periods, the shift has come about through an interest in materials.

Fascinating materials are in use today: light-sensitive filters like camera lenses, opening and closing according to light levels, with which the French architect Jean Nouvel fronted his Arab

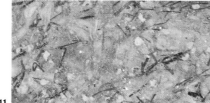

8, 9, 10 & 11 Id-Ekor specializes in wallcoverings. Their "Sajade" material is made from cotton, mineral and plant fibers. A special water-proofing solution is available.

12 "Plastline" from Id-Ekor, is a marble and acrylo-synthetic wall-covering that is resistant to temperature change and abrasion. It also keeps out damp.

13 Charles Rutherfoord blocked out a ziggurat basement wall with this softly flowing one to house a flue and slate hearth, echoing the shape of the piano to be housed in the room. To emphasize the theatricality of the effect, he rubbed red pigments into the polished plaster.

6 The novel use of modern building materials, usually clad with plaster, serves, like exposed beams, to structurally adorn this interior. RSJs inverted at right-angles delineate the change of wall direction and demarcate the unusual base-boards. Even the door jamb is a solid pillar of rough-hewn stone, and the flooring changes from boards to slate.

7 Charles Rutherfoord describes himself as an architect/designer. Unclad, the macho materials of the building site become surfaces for his interiors. As a theatrical touch, pigments were rubbed into the panels, which, with the well of light above, have a surface play of light and shadow in steely pewter.

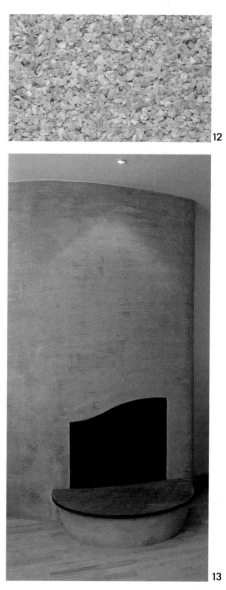

Institute building in Paris; reflective glass that becomes transparent when the lights are turned on at night to reveal the interior. In his vision of the future of London in the year 2066, the British architect Nigel Coates predicts that by the middle of the 21st century buildings will be a series of pods or cells created from DNA membranes that slide into load-bearing frameworks to form partitions that vary space according to need.

Although Coates propels science-fiction materials into his prediction, the principle of creating rooms within rooms using mass-produced components already exists. Partition walls, a trunking system of flooring that includes raised platforms, and ceiling panels, all of which interlock, are features of some current buildings. The ability of steel frames to span large distances without support means that the wall can be reduced to a mere in-fill between structural elements, providing thermal and acoustic insulation. How curiously lacking in imagination it makes the published pronouncements in Vogue in 1961 in an article entitled "Fashions in

WALLS & CEILINGS

1 The fashionable decade for paint finishes, the 1980s, launched many methods of paint application, including period-style rag rolling, scumbling and sponging finishes. As the 20th century concludes, there are new applications that involve metallic finishes and spray-gunning. Ingrid Stegmann is among the many contemporary designers applying specialist finishes such as this one, which involves layers of metallic bronzes shot with gold

2 The citric yellow of Vico Magistretti's "Sinbad" sofas, inspired, he claims, by horse blankets, is sharpened by the soft swirls of paint rubbed on the walls. This is allowed to dry before other colors are sponged over it. The result is reminiscent of vellum papers.

3 Abet Laminate has colored patterns running like geological seams through the material. Abet's "Serifragia" swatches for wall finishes, shown here, are popular with architects. Alessandro Mendini specified Abet Laminates for the exterior of the Groningen Museum in Holland, with interiors designed by Frank Stella, Philippe Starck and Michele de Lucchi.

4 Charles Rutherfoord lowered a ceiling in a narrow room with curved plywood panels. Special paint effects enhance the walls.

5 A wild effect here from Ingrid Stegmann, creating a sunset of colors illuminated with flashes of gold. This artist employs a team of craftsmen and women to apply gilded finishes. These owe nothing to mannerist fancies of another era, which is why you see them only in contemporary interiors as a background to modern furniture and lights.

6 A column is given an etched relief with the dado panels in Abet's "Straticolor" laminate, which, when engraved, shows another color beneath the original finish.

7 The ceiling molding, a narrow, glazed vertical strip above colored walls, with a ridged aluminum ceiling apparently supported on a single column, brings light from every aspect into architect David Wild's own house.

8 Charles Rutherfoord uses a collage of old manuscript papers and polished plaster to achieve this abstract art wall. Specialist decorators and designers, Nobby Clark and Partners, achieve many of the special effects for Rutherfoord.

Living" that recorded the decorator Esteban Cerda at Green & Abbott as saying:

"Even in an empty room, wallpaper transforms the walls from a mere architectural entity into something new." In the modern interior, architects use light, the architectural fourth dimension, to highlight walls and thus reduce their apparent mass and volume. The simple trick of recessing fluorescent lights just above the floor and below the ceiling makes solid walls appear to float on a sea of light. So, too, does recessing the plaster at base-board level, and then painting a dark strip in the recess. This creates the illusion of the floorboards slipping away beneath the walls and thus contributes to the sense of weightlessness.

Lights also affect ceiling plans, since low-voltage lighting requires transformers. These are hidden in the ceiling, which is lowered and insulated to muffle noise and save energy. Dotted with prismatic recessed lights, the ceiling is at once freed from the single light bulb and shade suspended from a central ceiling medalion.

9 A pillar, boxed in by plaster panels rubbed with pigments, and then deep etched and lined with metallic strips by Charles Rutherfoord creates a startling effect.

10 Architect Franklin D. Israel creates a cool, subterranean approach to the garden with scumbled blue walls that curvaceously lead to the glass exterior walls, and a low false ceiling adjoining at only one point.

11 Midnight blue rippled with gold-foil swirls creates a dramatic background in a modern room, illuminated by a single uplighter that plays light on the luminous paint finishes from Ingrid Stegmann.

1 Between an entrance with a leaning screen that inclines at an angle on steel rods, architect Stefano de Martino inserted two screens in the middle of the building before the gable-end wall. De Martino uses screens to define different areas in more flexible ways than solid walls would.

2 Artist Terry Flowers cast these screens in clear fiberglass, and they take their patinated shape from the mold. Architect Stefano de Martino has a great interest in the true nature of the products he uses, especially so in a world where so much is artifice.

1

2

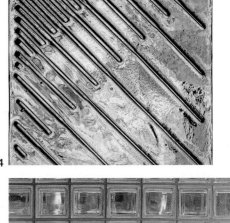

4

3 In these offices, architect Stefano de Martino chose clear-glass walls. Within, sliding partition walls never really cut into the space like a barrier. Slicing through the false computer grid floor and into

3

the concrete beneath means the partitions are freed from the building, and since they do not meet the ceiling they appear to float loosely in space.

The glass industry has provided architects with new ways to optimize natural light, from glass that changes its opaqueness as the light intensity varies, to frosted glass blocks that transmit filtered light in attractive ways. When it became possible in the 1950s to build large, frameless glass walls, glass lost its horticultural associations and became a symbol of the clean, fresh lines of modernity.

Mies van der Rohe, who produced an idealized version of the "house without walls" for the Barcelona exhibition in 1929, perfected his style by 1959, at Farnsworth House. Here he used large sheets of clear glass as walls to make the entire structure invisible in effect. For more solid structures, the harmony of unbroken wall space is refined with spray-gun-lacquered finishes designed to reflect light or, in kitchens and

4 All the colors of the sea and sky can be seen in these glass tiles from the Venetian glass blowers A. V. Mazzega, designed by Massimo Rioda.

5 Glass bricks have been developed by Pilkington to create large wall spaces in the nominal sizes of tiles that include the joint width. Gwathmey Siegel here lines up a full panel of glass bricks with a view to an inner courtyard.

5

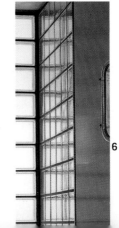

6 A submarine viewing window set into a steel hatch door is flanked with glazed bricks in architect Eva Jiricna's own apartment.

6

7 Framing glass bricks with panels or matte-black produces a grid-like formality, as architect Jo Crepain realizes. Frames can exaggerate the horizontal or vertical – omitting them effectively "knocks-back," visually, a glazed brick section without delineating each brick.

8, 9 & 10 The "Heroes" collection from Mito, designed by Fraboni, uses layers of glass molded in relief to suggest the effects of unpeeling, fracture, splinter and curl. The designs here are "Tebe" (far right), "Itaca" (above right) and "Cartago" (below right).

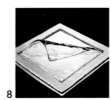

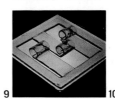

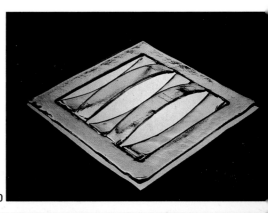

11 Armstrong Associates use glass walls in this interior for architectural fittings company Elementor. The advantage of glass is that the passage of light through a building is not impeded by partitions. Technological advances in the manufacture of glass, with larger sheets being produced, and in fittings (see picture **12**), have given today's architects more flexibility in the use of glass for walls.

12 Pilkington's wall planar structural glazing system is one of the most versatile wall clamps available. Flexible silicone-sealed joints between panels provide a structurally glazed envelope without frames or mullions.

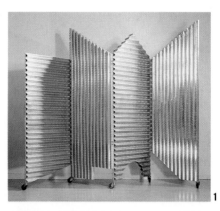

bathrooms, paneling of tiles or veneers of marble, granite or slate.

Fashions in tiling move from the most obvious contrasts, such as black gloss with white grouting, to the more subtle matte tiles in tiny squares that achieve the effect of a mosaic. You can achieve a subtle sheen from concrete walls, unadorned but for dry powder paint rubbed into the mixture before application. This appeals to those impressed by the patina of age on such a modern material.

While colored walls work like an abstract painting in some instances (Jean Michel Frank's colorful early Art Deco interior in Paris sported one pink, one pale-blue, one sea-green, and one yellow wall), pattern has been the decorator's preferred choice. But bold backgrounds are back in business, with patterned laminate panels by Abet in

1 Corrugated aluminum on castors makes up this innovative paneled screen. Jacques Borris creates his designs on the "backs of envelopes" and then finds people willing to produce them.

2 Twenty square tiles make up this screen, called "Paravent," in the Mito collection. The screen can be placed wherever needed, as a room divider or window screen.

3 & 4 With this collection of glass, Dimensione Fuoco glamorizes an ancient craft. "Notte" (left) and "Giardino" (right) were designed by architects Afra and Tobia Scarpa in a limited series of ten pieces and are set into leaded panels.

5 Open-plan living has never been the same since architect Michael Hopkins revolutionized building practices with his own

house that has no conventional walls. The exterior walls are glass and room dividers throughout, except for the minimum of rigid wall to carry bathroom and kitchen plumbing, are Venetian shades from Faber.

6 This wall system of colored luminous listels, "Colora," is by Carlo A. Urbinati Ricci and Alessandro Vecchiato for Foscarini. Its mounts enable the glass slats to be changed to modify the composition.

7 A four-paneled screen effectively blocks out one of the glass walls facing the garden in a house by Franklin D. Israel.

10 Japanese interiors traditionally use shoji screens – translucent paper "walls" in a wooden frame – to divide up space. The Japanese theme inspired this bedroom in America, by architect Gwathmey Siegel, where even the bed is a simple futon on the floor.

11 Pierre d'Avoine created six small houses that manage to look light and open. The kitchen folds away behind a screen, stairs to the galleried upper floor are hidden, and the low ceiling height beneath the gallery and on the upper floor are all part of a clever juggling with space.

8 A thin, opaque sliding screen by architects John Pawson and Claudio Silvestrin serves to pace the space differently, without severance or intrusion.

9 The heavily ornamented paneled screen of Piero Fornasetti's "Pompiana" reproduces classical architectural elements. Despite its size, it can easily be moved about on its industrial castors.

Italy, who gave the Italian maestro Ettore Sottsass Jnr. the opportunity to color them in, and then pioneered a way of diffusing light through the panels in a collection known as "Diafos."

It was Sottsass who introduced at the Museum of Modern Art in New York in 1972 his "Habitat", a structure made up of movable blocks, each of which had a different function. All of the blocks could be opened, closed, packaged, even warehoused, and "Habitat" certainly did away with the concept of conventional load-bearing walls as we know them.

The architect Alessandro Mendini, speaking of his intentions for both interior and exterior walls for his Groningen Museum in Holland, declares his love for artistry in assembling color and pattern across such large surfaces: "Brick, aluminum, concrete and laminates, colored delicately in pale blue, ocher, yellow and pink, gold and silver combine in an unusual way reminiscent of cubism."

Materials more often associated with design and sculpture rather than architecture, such as laminates,

12 From Zanotta, this three-fold screen "Paramenta" by De Pas, d'Urbino and Lomazzi, stands on four feet. Its central panel has irregular wavy fine lines, replicating the same waves on the flanking pair.

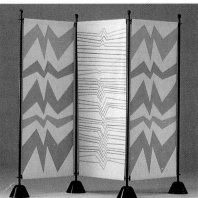

13 Inlaid marquetry fans proclaim the Spanish origins of "Abanicos" as boldly as the traditional Valencian cabinetry on the six-paneled screen, by Jaime Tresserra Clapes.

27

1 The Fendi collection of double-fired wall tiles, "Astrologia," draws its inspiration from the 12 constellations of the Zodiac.

polychromatic silk-screened paneling, mosaics and aluminum, are becoming decorative wall claddings.

Modernists, who would not think to give house room to those ornamental moldings that are so often produced today in polystyrene, are using "Cornice", a design by two Spaniards, Ramon Bigas and Pep Sant, since the moldings work as a contemporary detail rather than as a crown running along the top of a wall.

Their system of architectural moldings is designed like a segment of cylindrical tubing in which there are lights, either metal-halide or fluorescent types, installed within its slim profile, as well as glass shelving. Thus, it does multiple duty in different areas of the home: as a stair rail following the line of the staircase; as an architectural feature at dado rail or ceiling height; or as a source of illumination for bathroom storage.

2 Modular wood wall and ceiling panels by Tilo can be positioned and colored to influence optically the proportions of rooms. The finishes available include oak, antique oak, ash, mahogany, beech, teak, cherry (shown here), larch, spruce and pine.

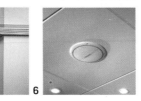

3 Molded borders by Orac Decor create a classical wall finish. The moldings are polyurethaned, lightweight and simple to glue in place.
4 The "Domino" system from Glass Design uses three acid-etched patterns in a panel of nine sheets of reflective glass.

5 Innovative and brilliant in concept, the "Cornice" is a multi-purpose system of moldings designed by Bigas and Sant.

6 Within this ceiling from Svedbergs are built-in hi-fi speakers, waterproofed and ready to connect to your stereo system. Also available are low-voltage light tiles with four halogen lights, complete with transformer.
7 The sunray effect ceiling in ash wood paneling from Tilo accentuates a particular area and so helps to create rooms within rooms – such as this library introduced to a drawing room.

8 A narrow space carved out of a landing for an office in a mews house by Peter Wilson, displays wood panels arranged like a checkerboard according to the grain of the veneer. And a scooped billow of a ceiling, painted orange, echoes in its grandiose curves the desk designed by Royal College of Art Professor Floris van den Broeke.

9

10

9 Ship-like wooden panels cover a curved corridor wall in a house by Peter Wilson. **10** Orac Decor make medalions, ceiling and panel moldings, corners, columns, capitals and plinths to dramatize pedestrian walls and ceilings. Their high-density polyurethane moldings easily adhere to surfaces, as in this Art Deco revivalist room, where a dado rail with two columns and white moldings create ziggurat wall panels to frame pictures.

1

1, 2 & 3 Frost- and skid-resistant paviors from Blockleys would make unusual textured facings for walls. The "Rope" pattern pavior (**2**) was specially commissioned; patterned bricks can be designed and fired to order. "Corduroy" directional guidance paviors (**1** and **3**) are graphically ribbed.

2

3

4

4 Blockleys' "Tactile" paviors can be used for walls although they were designed to be installed at traffic crossing points as a valuable aid to the blind.

5 A pre-cast, matte-gray concrete panel system on the walls of Tadao Ando's house is complemented by polished concrete panels on the ceiling, the latter designed to reflect natural light from the large window down into the room.

5

7

6 Contemporary designers like Ron Resik use brick for interior as well as exterior walls. Some build walls of brick, while others face concrete on breeze-block in slim brick-tiles.

6

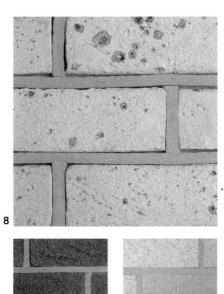

8

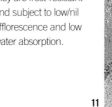

9

10

8, 9 & 10 Facing bricks from Blockleys – "Saffron Yellow, Mellow Grain" (top), "Black Mixture, Wrekin Briar" (above left) and "X Mixture, Wirecut" (above right) – are suitable for interior and exterior use because they are frost-resistant and subject to low/nil efflorescence and low water absorption.

11

7 & 11 Original industrial surfaces are stripped back and left in the raw in a domestic conversion of a power station by architect Gary Cunningham.

12

12 Charles Rutherfoord has built small alcoves into a bedroom wall to provide useful display and storage areas in a confined space.

31

1, 2 & 3 "Metropolis" from Gianfranco Salvi's "Reflections of Italy Collection" are embossed vinyl wallcoverings.

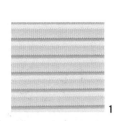

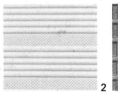

4 "Pergamena Intarsio" from Riflessitaliani sets geometric patterns of hand-made parchment into washable vinyl with a soft, velvety finish. Gianfranco Salvi developed "Intarsio" from his "Karta Pergamena" paper (see **9**) to create a version with wider applications.

5 From the "Heavy Metal" collection by Riflessitaliani, "Pyramid" is a metallic finish vinyl. These deeply embossed wallcoverings have substantial acoustical qualities.

6 For "Graniti," Riflessitaliani have developed a special manufacturing method to obtain a wallpaper that is comparable to real granite. It can be used on walls that are not suitable for the weight of granite facing.

7 & 8 "Rivet" is a metallic vinyl wallcovering from the "Heavy Metal" collection by Riflessitaliani. In renovation work, simulated metal finishes pose none of the grounding problems for electrical outlets that real metal would bring.

9 Riflessitaliani is renowned for its "Karta Pergamena" collection of flame-resistant hand-painted papers in 21 different shades. The most striking are dusted with pure gold and silver. The product is also manufactured as a "Museum" floor tile by saturating it in melamine and backing it with PVC.

Floors

There is no quicker way to direct attention to one part of a room than by covering it with pattern. Long ago, Venetians used bold pattern on the floor of every interior, with mosaics made from marble and terrazzo, while the Spanish used Moorish tiles in turquoise and orange to delineate the courtyard at the heart of their houses. In softer materials, the French spun delicious sherbet colors like lime and raspberry in the flora and fauna carpets of Aubusson; while in Brussels, weavers stretched Gobelin tapestries into enormous hunting scenes. The English perfected the art of needlepoint, the Moslems worldwide used handstitching and disciplined geometrics to establish regional variations, while in Holland, the patterned oiled floorcloth became fashionable. Bokhara kilims, Berber rugs from the Sahara, dhurries in Indian cotton woven in stripes, Peruvian woven rugs and Mexican serapes – all these names read like a travel guide and conjure up the magic carpets of fable while offering color and pattern underfoot.

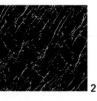

Previous page Art by the yard is now available from famous artists and architects at affordable prices from Vorwerk carpets. The carpets closely resemble the originals in color, line, brushstrokes and shading. This "Dialog 2" design is by graphic designer Milton Glaser.

1 A glazed tile in monochrome grays with a bark-like relief is by Rex Ceramiche with Trussardi in Italy.
2 From the "Grofisimi" collection comes "Negro" by Azuvi – a tile veined like marble. Its single-fired glaze gives it a textured effect, though smooth-surfaced.

3 Limited edition hand-knotted carpets with a pure wool warp on a cotton weft are the work of young artists and famous designers for Elio Palmisano. Beppe Caturegli's "Magdalena" has dance steps in a galaxy of color. Processing methods have been perfected with the aid of advanced craft technologies.

5 The "Marie Antoinette" pattern on hardwood flooring from Rowi Parket is laid on foam underlay to help absorb sound. Interchangeable square boards allow designers to create unique, customized patterns and achieve a variety of dramatic effects.

4 A King Kong view of London's Thames is on show from a penthouse apartment by architect John Young. Its rooftop steel walkways to the terrace and circular, reinforced opaque-glass inlets visually enhance the shipdeck image while allowing portholes of light to filter through to the floors below.

6 Vinyl flooring replicates any hardwood or stone surface. In their "Perspectives" collection, Amtico's "Alabaster SM 6," with green strips and "Florentine NM 7" borders, looks handcrafted.

7 Another Vorwerk carpet, this design is by artist Gerhard Richter and repeats his 1970s paintings in which he experiments with paint manufacturers' color cards.

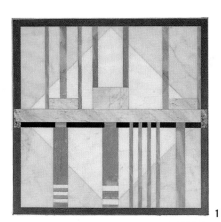

1 Conventional, medium-ash-brown strip floorboards have been inlaid with a cube of marbled mosaic using brown, white, black and gray stone to break up a long run of regular flooring in this house by Roberto Serino.

2 Kentucky wood floors have hardwoods from lightest ash to darkest zebrawood. Felled in temperate zones, American hardwoods do not endanger the rain-forests. This medalion of mixed species is the focal point of the room.

3 The classic parquet pattern from Tarkett is only 7mm thick consisting of three layers of bonded veneers. The flooring is available in oak, ash, beech, birch, maple, red oak or fumed oak, and is laid in long strips.

4 This bleached beech floor whitened with pigments to shipdeck brightness is from Junckers, a producer of solid, hardwood flooring, whose specific-purpose floors include those made for gymnasiums.

5 Oiled beech wood, less than 1 inch thin, from Junckers is factory-sealed for stain resistance, which makes it suitable for use in kitchens. Other wooden floorings with an oiled finish that are available from Junckers include ash, elm and oak.

6 An acoustically sound maple floor re-placed concrete slabs in a conversion of an electricity generator plant for a music lover. In the recital room, adjustable shutters make the space virtually tuneable, or "acoustically bright" according to architect Gary Cunningham.

In early American houses the lack of these rich materials led to the intro-duction of a new technique. The floor's surface was given a rubbing of colored pigment as a background to stenciled patterns of holly leaves, birds and flowers. This decorative device has recently been revived in the modern in-terior as a way to introduce individuality to the room. Patterns are used either as a border or as a centerpiece.

It was the modernists who eventually laid the patterned floor to rest. Suddenly it became fashionable to have every-thing in plain board, cement or white tiles. Stone flagstones were permitted, according to the availability of locally found stone. Redbrick, that innovative building material of the 1960s, was also encouraged.

No wonder contemporary architects spend so much time—and clients' money —considering flooring, sometimes even designing it. Flooring is one of the largest expenses in a house, so choos-ing colors, textures and patterns is vital to the overall scheme. When planning flooring, an important point to bear in mind is the structure of the building

7 In a compact, city apartment, converted from a period house, architect Ron Brinkers simply stripped back and sanded the original beech floorboards. They provide a roughened contrast to a small, black wooden bridge that leads to the informal seating area.

9 A realistic wood strip floor in a bathroom is in fact vinyl from Amtico. This type of material will cope with condensation, always a problem in bathrooms, far better than the washed teak it copies. Accurate reproductions of 19 different woods are available in the range.

10 Red-oak, plank flooring from Rowi can be laid over an existing wooden floor or secured directly over concrete.

8 Maple parquet flooring from Tibbals Hartco in Tennessee is laid in slabs of horizontal and vertical strips to create an intricate flooring pattern simply.

itself. Solid concrete floors can support any type of flooring, but before laying something like quarry tiles on the average domestic wooden suspended floor you should seek advice on load-bearing from an expert.

When the looms at Axminster began to punch out wall-to-wall carpet, the world of uniformity began. Wall-to-wall beige or brown anonymity transformed hotels as far apart as Cairo and Kraków into identical clones of each other. And it became a domestic status symbol to have wall-to-wall carpeting everywhere at home, except the kitchen. In this room, flagstones by the yard became available in prepackaged vinyl that replicated hard flooring.

As the machine-age broadloom carpet asserted autumnal swirls wall-to-wall in rooms throughout the world, the contemporary designer left floors un-adorned. The result, a good wooden floor or, in hot climates, a tiled one. Narrow, tongue-and-groove beechwood planks became the ubiquitous flooring favorite, together with matte-gray or white ceramic tiles for bathrooms. Sometimes planks were laid diagonally

1 Regular, hard-edged marble slabs have been laid diagonally, point to point, and then emphasized by cordoning off a large area with a fine, black travertine inset inlaid at an angle to the slabbed floor.

The effect, created by architect De Maria, is like a theatrically positioned rug thrown down on the floor. Marble is an exceptionally hard-wearing flooring material and, if well-sealed, impervious to staining. Cold to the touch, it is particularly suitable for homes in warm climates.

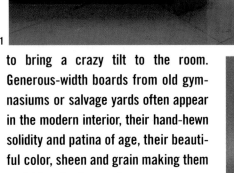

2, 3 & 4 What is commonly referred to as marble can, in fact, be precast material composed of marble chips bonded together with rosin. This reconstituted material by Reed Harris is competitive in price, sold by the yard as floor tiles, whereas true marble has been called the ultimate natural building material.

5 A narrow corridor could be dark and confining, but Ingo Maurer's trapeze lights strung merrily across doorways and ladder-like black and white marble and polyester rosin floor tiles from MARBO give the space light as well as a dramatic, geometric configuration. A place to pause in rather than simply stride through, the design is by Studio Epton.

to bring a crazy tilt to the room. Generous-width boards from old gymnasiums or salvage yards often appear in the modern interior, their hand-hewn solidity and patina of age, their beautiful color, sheen and grain making them matchless backgrounds.

Stained wood went through a revival in the 1970s. But when color fashions change, sealer coats make such floors difficult to adapt. Painted wooden floors – using yacht deck paints – bring a certain nostalgic reminder of psychedelic colors, but it is fair to say that today's wooden floors are plainer. These are made from a softwood, such as spruce, fir or pine, tongue-and-groove or butt-jointed; hardwood blocks in herringbone, basket or brick patterns; or the relatively inexpensive and flexible alternatives to solid wood – plywood and particle board. Particle board, 5

6

6 Kirkstone is a light-sea-green volcanic stone obtained from England's Lake District. It is a popular, hard flooring now only produced since new diamond-cutting processes have made the stone quarriable.

made from shavings of wood chips set in a rosin, can be laid in squares of varying thickness, sealed or unsealed. One of the undeniable facts of present-day hardwood floors is that they are not soundproofed, and it may therefore not be possible to use this material in an inner-city apartment.

If wood is not to your liking, then there are ceramic floor tiles, made of clay and fired at high temperatures, some with a nonslip finish. Tough, waterproof and impervious to staining, tiles can be heated under floor in colder climates, but really they are better suited to warmer countries. And the assertive patterning with which ceramic tiles are often decorated

7 Large scale slate squares, shot with a narrow, triangular sliver of travertine here and there, act as pointers – to the exit, the furniture, the hearth – in this wittily appointed room, by designer and architect Philippe Starck, at the famous New York Royalton Hotel.

8 Conventional wisdom has it that for small floor areas you should keep to a continuous run of the same material underfoot. This is in the belief that changes of pattern and texture visually decrease the feeling of space. But architect David Chipperfield successfully changes direction – and materials – matching slivers of oak, slate and terrazzo on the floors in the kitchen and dining area of a compact house.

9, 10 & 11 "Quartz-line" floor covering by Id Ekor is made of colored quartz pebbles set in rosin. The rosin-and-pebble mix is applied over an existing floor surface.

7

8

9

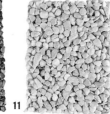

10

11

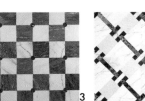

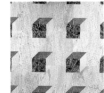

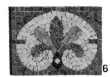

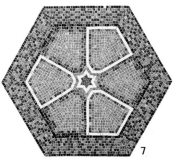

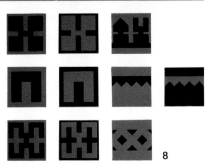

makes them less popular than quarry tiles as a background flooring. Made from high-silica clay fired to an almost glass-like hardness, quarry tiles can be laid in square or rectangular slabs and are available in buff, amber, terra cotta, dark blue or black.

A new hard-flooring product is a mosaic sold in patterns mounted on paper to make them easier to lay, or terrazzo marble chips, plain or colored, set in cement and then ground to a smooth finish. Sandstone, granite and lime-stone slabs are also all hardwearing flooring materials, and slate is an ex-tremely popular, heathery colored alternative, but it is really only suitable for use in a small room because of its high cost.

One of the interesting inventions of this century is without doubt the vinyl tile, or

3, 4 & 5 Ceramic tiles from Matteo Baldini come in a range of rich and sophisticated finishes. "Impallinato" (above left) is by Michele de Lucchi; "Intrecciato" (above right) by Adolfo Natalini; and "Cinque" (left) by Andrea Branzi.
6 & 7 Little tesseras of marble and stone assembled in mosaics are now delivered in

1 Outlined in pale borders, with wide, gray concrete tiles to the wall, Sergio Puente uses patterned tiles like a rug, each tile featuring a diagonal cross in pastels, edged with a spiraling ribbon pattern, like a brushstroke hand-painted on the white ceramic glaze.
2 Andreas Weber uses large terra cotta slabs grouted with pale gray cement in a regular pattern, which he then rearranges by placing a cream rug diagonally, as well as a low-slung platform bed at an angle to the floor tiles.

pre-cast patterns on backing papers with numbered joints for easy assembly on site. "Lux" (above) is in the series Gemmae by SICIS. "Nerone" (below) is a mosaic by SICIS made with marble and granite tesseras. The system reduces cutting and laying time.

8 "Scritture" by Ceramica Bardelli uses Grecian key motifs and Egyptian hieroglyphics to recreate a distinctive series of terra cotta and black designer tiles. The complicated geometric designs match up with borders.

9 These white lime-stone flagstones – just over 1-inch thick to make them practical indoors – are from Paris Ceramics. The tiles can be cut into special shapes, though regular sizes are nearly 16 x 16 inches. Their decorative patterns are highlighted by soft color washes or special distressed finishes.

10 Within the confines of a severe, iconoclastic architecture, Andrew Holmes has laid an interesting motif on the floor. The design replicates the semi-circular window casting its light on that motif, and extends the pattern of light within a grid made up of black squares identical in size to the panes of glass in the window.

11

11 Cool, gray-stained wood laid in large panels resembles flagstones but has the advantage of being warm underfoot and suitable for laying over a wider range of floor surfaces.

12

12 Ceramica San Agostino's "Tiffany" range of single-fired tiles are frost-resistant and strengthened with hard Stratos glaze, which is rich in aluminum and quartz.

13

13 Mexican terra cotta tiles by Corres are marketed worldwide. The lime-rich Coahuila clay is recognizable by its mellow, pinky beige coloration.

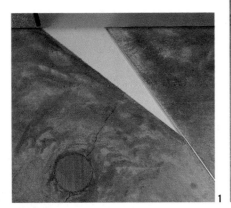

1

3

1, 2 & 3 At this house Studio Epton has used the most sophisticated combinations of materials underfoot. Basic concrete is rubbed with pigment and inlaid with glass and wood patterns that are immaculately outlined in brass. Semi-circular glass swirls and splinters create a decorative scroll, while a stud of wood, like a bolt beside a sliver of opaque thickened glass, amusingly explores the idea of cabinet-makers' traditional joints. And a structure of fineline metal inserted in the concrete, in the manner of the Muslim countries' craft of *bidri-ware* (below), creates a six-runged ladder.

embossed sheet vinyl, a hard-surfaced flooring that changes its face to suit the company it keeps. Parquet, marble, terrazzo, brick, ceramic tile and flag-stone are but a few of the materials that vinyl can simulate. Vinyl first came to the fore with the checkerboard, black-and-white-tile floor, a simulated version of the classic marble pattern, that rapidly became a decorating cliché. Nothing is as versatile as vinyl. Wood-grain vinyl or tiles in the rambling outline of flagstones or a herringbone brick pattern can be unrolled to suit the surroundings. Laminates include the genuine materials — wood veneers, cane, pebbles, mother of pearl — encased in clear vinyl to allow the original texture to be seen beneath a hard, sleek protective surface.

Cork tiles, made from cork granules and a binding agent, compressed and then baked, were the common 1970s floor for the then young modern. Now these tiles are more often replaced with linoleum, a good, natural material made from ground cork, wood, flour, linseed oil and rosins on a jute or hessian backing.

2 Rubber flooring laid in sheets, and

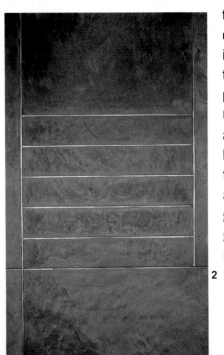

4

4 Trenches cast in the polished concrete floor were originally used to carry power lines in this old electricity generation plant. When converting it into a home, architect Gary Cunningham used the trenches to carry the domestic electricity cables, covered with triple-laminate armored glass to – figuratively – shocking effect. The table on castors reinforces that tramline imagery.

5 This metal landing, looking not unlike a diver's platform on top of an oil rig, has narrow cable grips conjuring all the thrills of the trapeze artist's ascent. At rooftop level, steel walkways give the security of additional support underfoot.

2

5

ribbed or studded, was a high-tech favorite in the 1970s. Modern tiles of synthetic rosins mixed with a vinyl binder are important pattern makers, often replicating the grand piazzas found in Italy, and sometimes producing a giddy *trompe-l'oeil* effect.

An exciting innovation in contemporary floor covering is the wall-to-wall patterned carpet revitalized by the German company Vorwerk in collections commissioned from artists, architects and fashion designers from around the world. Using conventional broadloom mass-production machines, and a new ICI thread known as Timbrelle, any shading of color can be controlled by

6 & 7 Jan Kaplicky of Future Systems used aluminum sheet on particle board panels for a false floor laid above the existing 19th-century floorboards in this city apartment (see detail left.)

The view through the space-shuttle doorframe, rendered in wide steel, shows the effect of the burnished floor and its black walkways, leading to a Rietveld chair beyond. Underneath this platform floor, gas, electricity and water pipes are concealed. Because the floor is metal, the electricity supply has to be grounded on it for safety.

8 Like a stage set from Hertzog's film "Fitzcarraldo," this weird jungle home in Mexico, by Sergio Puente and Ada Dewes, makes a totem-istic room arrange-ment. Rough-adzed tree-trunk architraves against the regular grid pattern of modern window panes are replicated in the floor, with reinforced opaque glass blocks set into colorless concrete.

9 The sloping eaves, with a huge skylight to bring necessary light into the interior, make it impracticable to walk into this attic space, so the architects Munkenbeck & Marshall caused the floor to fall away to allow the light to find its way below. A strategically placed steel walkway, ringed with tubular-steel railings, creates a strut wide enough to accommodate the television.

1 Architect David Wild has laid pewtery gray-blue, rubber sheet flooring here in his own house. Being hard-wearing and practical, it provides a dramatic, workman-like home office floor that is flexible enough to withstand things toppling over onto it.

2 Subtle smudge colors of the Dutch 17th-century master class are accurately used in sheet vinyl by Tarkett, whose sunburst "Eminent" is also available in borders, friezes and decorative edgings for designing grand floors in a contemporary material.

3, 4 & 5 As more architects discover, linoleum is more than just a hard-wearing floor covering – it is an extremely versatile material that can be

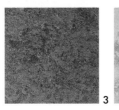

cut to produce unique designs. Krommenie "Marmoleum" sheet linoleum from Forbo Nairn can be hot-welded to give a seam-free surface.

computer to produce a result that accurately reflects an original work of art. The low ceiling, the bugbear of contemporary apartments, is offset by these striking designs, which direct the eye firmly down, rather than up. Only a seriously wealthy collector can afford a Hockney these days, but with this new carpet technology you can afford to trample one underfoot.

More conventional contemporary interiors are turning to the anonymous naturals, such as rush matting, coconut and coir or sisal, backed with latex for easy laying. Those softer, golden colors of sea-grass, jute or fiber matting are a splendid background to a collection of rugs, each one a work of art in itself. The new mobility of today's society makes these rugs a realistic investment, since monied nomads can roll them up and take them away when they move

6, 7 & 8 "Metro" synthetic rubber tiles from Gerland are available in a choice of stud relief patterns and thicknesses – 2.5 mm thick in round, square and pave, and 3.5 mm thick in either round or square. A wide range of primary and neutral colors are available to suit most decorative schemes.

9 Forbo Nairn's "Diamond 1036" vinyl material, in subtle shades of lilac and gray, is a stylish as well as a practical option for kitchen flooring.

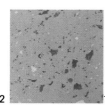

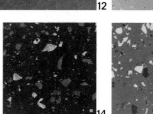

12 Linoleum provides the base for dramatic designs by Forbo Nairn. The material is made from linseed oil, rosin from pine trees, wood from deciduous trees and cork, mixed with fillers such as clay and chalk, calendered onto a hessian back.

10 In his home, architect Andreas Weber has rubber flooring, in discreet cream for his dining-room, which he then accentuates by an exaggerated sense of scale – the low radiator, an oversized console table, the furniture in general. But throughout, the material is an anonymous, sound-proof background.

13, 14 & 15 "Prism," smooth-surfaced rubber tiles from Gerland, have an inlaid chip decoration and are tough enough for use in high traffic areas.

16 RIAB rubber floor tiles are a "green" product, since they are made from recycled auto tires. A selection of colors is available, all in dirt-defying speckle patterns.

11 Subtle gradations of natural brown and gray shades are combined in "Rocky" – a domestic vinyl flooring from Tarkett's "Manhattan" range – in order to impart an appropriate impression of weight and solidity, as well as an all-important sense of comfort and warmth to a room.

home, in much the same way as people have always done, ever since pre-historic times.

In rooms where the architecture is bland and the furniture simple, a richly patterned rug, in relief, brings the decoration down to earth to focus interest and attention on the floor and to define a scattered furniture grouping. A simple, striped rug can visually make a room appear to be much wider or longer than it actually is; a circular rug, in addition to determining the configuration of, perhaps, a seating or dining group, also gives tables and chairs a more compelling background. The flamboyance of the colors and the scale of the pattern are deliberately calculated to initiate a dramatic and vibrant scheme in a neutral room, in much the same way as the addition of an enormous abstract painting does.

17 A high-quality vinyl flooring from Amtico, whose simulations of genuine materials combine natural beauty with the practicality of a man-made product.

1 Ege Art Line's "20th Century Masters Collection" (see **3**) includes "Woman/ Femme 1923" by René Magritte.

2 "Peau d'ours" rug by Pucci de Rossi for Neotu is made of hand-tufted wool, outlining the undulating shape of a polar bear. Ironically, black studs on big slabs suggest hard flooring, an illusion sustained all in wool.

3 Ege Art Line produce the "20th Century Masters Collection" – 48 pure wool rugs to designs by world-famous artists. This example is "Composition-1952" by Gunnar Aagaard Andersen.

4 This design, "Blue Eye," is by Gianni Veneziano of the Oxido group for the Sisal Collezioni, which is in the forefront of Italian contemporary furnishing.

5 Christine van der Hurd's memorable collection of elegant floor coverings is reminiscent of the luxuriant 1920s and 30s. This design is called "Earth."

6 "Rustic Ruins Number 2" is by Liz Kitching, whose designs are painted on canvas floorcloths, worked into tufted wool rugs or made into hooked rugs, which are created entirely of recycled textiles.

7 A tendency to break up smooth surfaces and regular lines is evident in all areas of design. Cartoonist turned interior designer Javier Mariscal created for Mariscal this artwork of the slinky Pink-Panther-like creature called "Leon."

8 Pascal Mourgue's "Espace du Temps," for Toulemonde Bouchart, refers to the origin of the species, he claims. His technique, even here in wool, reflects his training at the *Ecole des Arts Decoratifs*, and wood-carving skills at the *Ecole Boulle*.

9 "Yuyuka" by Sergio Calatroni for Sisal has a biscuit-colored ground with cabalistic signs, blue arrows and a red and green border.

9

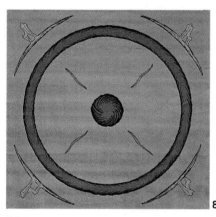

8

10 Christine van der Hurd studied in Britain and worked alongside Jack Lenor Larsen, Angelo Donghia and Kenzo. This rug, called "Present Moods number 3," is a jazz piece in lilac and yellow on a gray ground.

10

14

13

11 Princeton architect Michael Graves, famed for his post-modern classicism, designed "Rug Number 2" for V'Soske, whose "Visions" collection features limited editions of art in the medium of hand-tufted rugs.

11

12 "Au bord de l'eau" by Sergio Calatroni is a jigsaw of squiggles in fine, black erratic line, with a cream square, tending to bunch toward one perimeter, like the ripples piling up in a gust of wind.

12

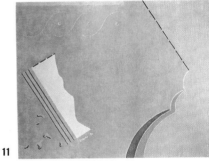

13 "La Natura di Oxido" by Oxido for Sisal shows two hands: one palm-up with a man-in-the-moon face; the other is palm-down and tattooed with a harp. Although not touching, they are the positive and negative fusion of each other.

14 Christian Duc's "Correspondance" with V'Soske Joyce uses a subdued palette and contrasts between light and shade in a self-confessed obsession with balance and symmetry.

"Dialog 1," "Dialog 2" and "Classic" are collections of wall-to-wall carpets by Vorwerk. Using the designs of artists, architects and fashion designers, these mass-produced, affordable acrylic broadloom carpets closely resemble the originals in line, color and shading.

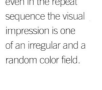

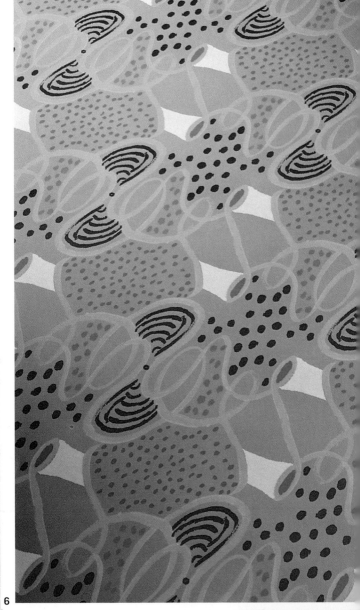

1 Concurrent with their "Dialog" collection, Vorwerk also produce masterpieces in their "Classic" collection, like this carpet from Josef Hoffmann, a member of the avant-garde Vienna Secession dating from 1898 to 1903.

2 Pop artist Roy Lichtenstein demanded absolute pure white as a background, an impossibility in carpet manufacture. Vorwerk managed to overcome the problem in their reproduction of his small-scale squared design in which the black and white diagonally striped squares break the bounds of their form.

3 Artist Gerhard Richter uses both brush and palette knife to apply glowing color. This effect is reproduced in his design for Vorwerk, which consists of squares in six different colors, a reminder of the artist's 1970s experimentation with paint manufacturers' color cards. The pattern repeat consists of 5.5 x 7.5 inches, within an overall repeat size of 39 x 36 inches, which totals 255 squares, with the result that even in the repeat sequence the visual impression is one of an irregular and a random color field.

4 Zaha Hadid is an architect whose dizzying viewpoint of urban planning – and building – can be seen in this blueprint of a design for a hillside recreational club above Hong Kong's harbor.

5 Architect Richard Meier's fascination with geometry – his buildings are based on a clearly defined stuctural grid – is immediately obvious in the blue-printed façades and street plans he created as a carpet pattern for Vorwerk.

6 Painter David Hockney transfers his constant variations on a paintbrush line to his carpet design, with brushstrokes that appear almost to be randomly placed in optimistic colors. Vorwerk have managed to transfer this sense of the rapid application of small spots of color to their carpeting reproduction of Hockney's work.

7 The dodecahedron, which O. M. Ungers uses as the base for his carpet design, makes the polyhedron within appear to shift from being closer to the viewer, to farther away. As a result, this puzzling block pattern literally shifts perspective. Like Italian Renaissance flooring designs, *trompe l'oeil* banding alternates dark and light to give an unsettling, visual effect.

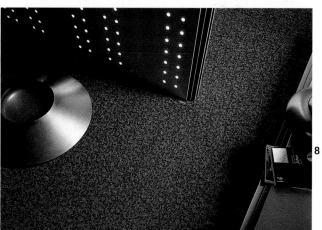

8 Architect Arata Isozaki's carpet design was inspired by Japanese period kimono dye patterns, which break down geometric, cosmic and floral elements into dots for an interwoven, pointillist effect.

9 This design is by architect Jean Nouvel, whose Institut du Monde Arab in Paris responds to the moving sun as light-sensitive lenses on the façade open and close in the manner of camera shutters. This preoccupation with light and shade is shown here in his dazzling carpet for Vorwerk.

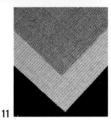

8

8 Ruckstuhl believe in giving their floorings a clear identity in terms of both color and tone, yet never allowing them to dominate other furnishings. They claim that this "diagonal/transverse" weave in natural coir and sisal fiber is a perfect background.

6 & 7 Crucial Trading's "Natural Seagrass" floor covering, available in 13- and 6.5-feet latex-backed widths, has a thread of bold color interwoven with the plaited, natural seagrass.

6

7

4

9

1, 2 & 3 Hard-wearing and anti-static sisal, coir and seagrass from Saraband are all available with latex backing, in 13-feet widths to be close-fitted like traditional carpeting. Or they can be supplied as a loose-laid mat or runner to virtually any size. Herringbone (above), bouclé (middle) and standard (below) weaves are available.

1

2

3

4 All Japanese houses are built around the standard-sized tatami mats, which blend so well with modern design. The Japanese pioneered modular building, since all timber sizes follow the mat-sizing procedure.
5 Bosanquet Ives popular herringbone jute, 36 inches wide, is joined by jute in basket weaves, also 36 inches wide, either in all-natural or crosswoven with scarlet-, emerald- or Baltic-blue threads.

5

9 As well as carpets in coir and sisal plant fiber, such as the "Pianelle" design shown here, Ruckstuhl make flooring in pure new wool, goats' hair and natural fiber wools. Styles range from wall-to-wall installations to edge-bound area rugs, throw rugs and even carpet tiles.
10 Crucial Trading's "Candy Stripe" sisal collection combines tonal colors and contrasts them with two-color weaves on the diagonal.

10

11 Loose-laid coir and sisal tiles from Crucial Trading measure nearly 20 inches square. Produced in bleached or natural finishes, they are hard-wearing and ideal in heavy traffic areas, with effective thermal, acoustical and anti-static properties.

11

Doors

The door is both the first thing a visitor sees on entering your home and the last thing when leaving. We all have doors—front and back and internally for the division of space. Yet most of us seem to take no particular notice of them, choosing to live with the doors supplied in modern houses today. There they stand, a standard 6 feet 8 inches by 2 feet 8 inches, either paneled or plain and usually equipped with a door pull. This is why most homes, even those that are imaginatively decorated inside, look boringly the same when seen from the outside.

However, there are many good, interesting alternatives to experiment with, all of which are fully functional and meet the requirements of excluding drafts, sound and light, as well as offering necessary security.

Making an entrance that is dramatically different yet in keeping with the house's style, character and architecture can be as simple as changing the door proportions. These were laid down in the 18th century when the rules dictated that the door height should be twice, or a little more than twice, its width. More varied in their ratio of dimensions, contemporary doors can significantly alter the apparent height of rooms by slimming down or stretching further the door itself. Architects Trevor Horne and John Pawson both use this visual device to increase the appearance of height in low-ceilinged rooms. They use custom-built doors that are taller than normal and that operate on pivot hinges within the frames

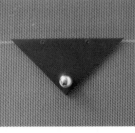

Previous page From architectural practice GMW, triangular glazed insets set into double doors highlight the position of the door pulls and provide a tantalizing glimpse into the space beyond.

1 & 2 In this apartment restoration, Studio Epton's fastidious attention to detail frames each door with ornamental pulls, either in pairs or singles, which reduce the bulk and display a geometric rearrangement of everyday, domestic functionalism.

3 One of the greatest views in California is here framed by a pair of folding doors at the Villa Zapu by the former team of Powell-Tuck, Connor and Orefelt.

4 Irregular but geometrically configured black-wooden frames outline glass doors. Three stone steps mark the ascent into this house by architect Sergio Puente. Inside, an evenly paced wooden staircase set below a horizontal skylight is on view in this entrance.

5 Corrugated acrylics in four folding panels casually yet effectively screen an office with interiors designed by Stefano de Martino. Slimline hinges clench the sinuous panels together.

6 Architect Jan Kaplicky's space-capsule approach to an apartment conversion, set within a 19th-century townhouse, has a normal-sized door covered in steel-mesh and set in a widened, reinforced steel frame.

DOORS

1 & 2 For a custom-built Majorcan villa the former architectural partnership of Claudio Silvestrin and John Pawson used a pair of monumental folding doors on the inside, mirrored in mass and volume by the exterior set which lead out onto a sunken tennis court.

3 With the marketplace in the US driven by demand for period architectural styles, the modernists are left to fend for themselves, says architect Mark Marcinik, whose new company created these bi- or tri-folding doors in hardwood veneered plywood with an aluminum trim.

4 A pair of beech doors, made from American hardwood and set in a monumental architrave, are lightened with a checkerboard grid of glass panes.

in order to avoid revealing unsightly hardware.

As large houses are carved up into smaller apartments, which are then adapted to contemporary living, unbroken wall space is what every architect dreams of. This explains architects' common obsession with eliminating unnecessary entrances. Their aim is to reduce the impact of those entrances that remain with unassuming doors. Sometimes, they alter proportions by widening the gap and lowering the height. In such a case architect Pierre d'Avoine always frames the broader

5 This old wooden Japanese inn was reassembled on a small suburban plot. Inside, the room dimensions are based on the sizes of four, six or eight tatami mats. Shoji screens and mud walls are new, built to open on only two sides, instead of the traditional four.

6 Lynn Davis designed this beech door with two squares on the top corners, which replicate the rosewood inlaid cube and narrow arrow slit.

7 These doors by Rehabitec Y Diseno are made of beech with inset glass keyhole-shaped windows acid-etched, and framed in stainless steel. Architects normally remove doors to free space, but this corridor effect has an interesting theatrical impact.

8 A stylish entrance door to an apartment in American white oak veneer shows off the ash inlay used within the grooved and imposingly wide frame. The US has huge hardwood resources, with some 6 million soft- and hardwood trees planted daily.

11 Armstrong Associates give a substantial entrance a light treatment by splitting two panels in the wooden door with a glass border, through which the giant-sized floor-to-ceiling tubular-steel grips used on either side can be clearly seen.

7

8

view glimpsed through the space with dark-wood mahogany or oak posts either side to support the architrave. The way in which doors fasten is another troubling issue, since the plain, modern doors of today, uncluttered with paneling or finger plates, key rings or any extravagant and unnecessary door furniture, must silently and unobtrusively pivot or slide in their frames. Often the door frame is made of wood, fireproofed and burglar-proofed since it is by breaking the door jamb that most forced entries are effected. Entablatures with pilasters and Venetian heads flanking the door in the classical manner – a style still enforced with grandeur by neoclassicists – are no substitute for the security offered by a strong frame and a well-hung door. In terms of security, front doors in Italy are armor-plated with large, mirrored, bullet-proof glass that allows light into the home while offering occupants a clear view outside. A polyester finish disguises their invulnerability behind care-free color.

Sliding-panel double internal doors, which pull back on either side of an

9

9 Trompe-l'oeil lattice detailing created by skillfully inlaid woods brings a classical façade and an impression of three-dimensionality to a flat wooden door. John Outram is a Post-Modern architect whose work employs the decorative flourishes of the 18th-century cabinet-maker to create a refreshing alternative to period-style moldings.

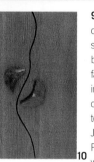

10

10 Wooden doors do not have to be straight-edged, as this curved jigbit in American oak proves. Its organically shaped pulls serve to emphasize that timbered fluidity.

11

opening to flank it like Japanese shoji screens, are a popular alternative to conventional doors. They depend, however, on unbroken wall space at the sides to accommodate the doors as they slide across.

Without paneling and decoration, doors in modern homes are usually hot-spray-painted to give a continuous, smooth surface, either matte or gloss. Mass-produced modern doors are lacquered or made of fruit woods burnished to bring out the patina of the material. Exciting alternatives include doors designed by De Pas, D'Urbino and Lomazzi which are both concave and convex – a sinuous curve like a bow

1 "Radar" by Tre P is a reversible door, made from lacquered wood. Tre P's modern, linear design can be fixed to open either left or right. Patented hinges are well camouflaged.

2 Three little purple glass panels set into the circular glassed stairwell echo the purple front to this door, with its semi-circular grips that are lit for night time.

4 Specially curved glass doors in John Young's riverside home lead to the laundry and bathroom. They are flanked by steel lift doors.

3 Dierre's "AT 4" door pleasantly conceals the fact that it is armor-plated, with a tongue-and-grooved paneling in electrically galvanized, reinforced double-steel plate. It is painted white and set in a black frame with a special, safe-type lock concealed behind high-density polystyrene to give perfect heat and sound insulation.

5 Medieval castles have portcullised entrances reached by a moated fort. This house with red-brick ramparts has a glass-block grid that replicates the ancient portcullis above a human-sized door with a spyhole.

6 This front door within an inner courtyard is convex, with a red-painted frame. It is surrounded by clapboard paneling that is asymmetrically arranged with narrow boards on one side and wider ones on the other. Designed by architect Eric Owen Moss, this external door opens inward and its red frame effectively delineates the entrance.

7 Another view of the unusually shaped design by architect Eric Owen Moss, shown in picture **6**.

8 The Lualdi door, "Super," by Luigi Caccia Dominioni, is the world's first polyester lacquered door, with a horizontal, slimline steel grip emphasized by the scarlet background.

10 Tre P's "Rever" door, designed by architect Cini Boeri with Laura Griziotti and Guido Nardi, is made of wood with a hollow core. Its design allows the opening direction to be decided at the last moment.

9 The angularity of this pair of doors, set within a corner, is offset by the triangular sky panel above. Architect Lynn Davis's design replicates the light that falls between these two doors, exaggerated by the red triangular door pulls.

with polyurethane-foam injections sandwiched between. They feature four dots at eye level, inside which a night light is inserted to make it easy for people to find their way at night.

Also available are silent sliding doors in red lacquer that fold flat like the wings of a butterfly against the wall, leaving only the black lacquer door frame around the entrance. These take up very little room and they are reversible so that they can be hung to the left or right.

Sometimes a small, overall pattern proliferates, like the Braille punch-card pattern in the "Egizia" collection designed by Toso and Massaria, the quiet pattern of which won't overpower the interior. Custom effects are sometimes used – architect Alessandro Mendini stenciled a leaf pattern in shades of green on exterior doors of an

1

2 Too often, garage doors bear no resemblance to the house they adjoin. Here, an inner, open courtyard with glazed walls is shielded from sunlight by louvered, horizontal shades from Faber, that display a distinct relationship to the ridged aluminum garage doors to the right. The design is by architect Robin Spence.

1 A breakfast bar in tubular steel is flanked by a pair of French doors that open outward onto a balcony. Large, vertical tubular-steel pulls on the outside and inside mirror each other. Brick, steel and glass are appropriate in this contemporary make-over of a riverside warehouse, designed by architect John Young.

3

3 Front doors from the street to this apartment have two-storey height glass doors inserted between floors with a semi-circular steel-mesh balcony girded with railings. The doors, in fact, are four double doors, the divisions between them hidden by the balcony. Ten panes of glass on each door form a lattice. The pulls operating on the nearside of the doors are lockable from the inside or out.

4

4 This multi-fold door from Wing Industries flattens against the wall like a screen when drawn back, yet provides privacy when pulled across the entrance without blocking the light.

2

Italian lakeside villa to bring the garden closer to the structure of the house. In older houses it was often necessary to insert fanlights above the door, leaded or in stained glass, to allow light to filter in, but the nature of modern interiors obviate this necessity. Stained-glass door panels designed by the American architect Frank Lloyd Wright at the turn of the 20th century, in the style he termed "Usonian" (US-onian), have now been put into mass production. At a time when the Arts and Crafts glassmakers in Europe were producing the sinuous lilies and vines of the Art

5

5 The Simpson 15-lite beveled French door in the "Mastermark" series has thermal panes.

7 & 8 Three glass screens, one in the middle hinged so that it opens into the dining room, hide the working kitchen from the dining area very effectively, without blocking the light or separating these two related rooms. The house is by Gianfranco Cavaglia.

Nouveau period, Wright's stained-glass door panels show an angularity and geometric formalism — as do his buildings. In rectilinear designs and primary colors, his doors mirror the type of home he pioneered: suburban houses that spread outward, instead of upward like the terraced houses of a cramped Europe. Wright used concrete breeze-block latticed screens to form that vital link between inside and outside.

Inserting light panels in doors is the nearest the modern architect comes to pattern-making. In contemporary doors there are the blocks of opaque glass

6 Customized, glass floor-to-ceiling French doors have been laser cut to a wavy template.

9 To create his own London home, architect Sir Richard Rogers gutted and combined two 19th-century terraced houses and removed most of the doors to create a soaring space that is full of light. To hold the light that streams in through 16 windows, the opaque glass door, with its simple vertical, tubular-steel grip, creates a partition without making the doorway into a set piece.

DOORS

1 In a warm climate the door doesn't have to insulate the home. This tubular-steel door by Franklin D. Israel is appropriately open to the elements, yet still secure with a grill reaching top to bottom.

arranged like Josef Hoffman's stacking grids, two-thirds of the way up the door—esthetic as well as illuminating. Now that brass hardware in period styles is clumsily irrelevant to door fastening, the modern door pull has been the subject for architects and designers to sculpt new shapes and banish chrome anonymity. The newest pulls incorporate light-sensitive materials that glow softly in the dark. To humanize technology it is necessary to have a high-touch, not a high-tech approach. Organic, root-like door hardware by the Spanish architect Antonio Gaudí is still produced today. The designs go back to 1904 — proof indeed that door design can become a classic and play its part in the modern home. Generally, casement and panel doors have fallen from their pedestaled architrave, since their broken fussiness

2 This perforated stainless steel entry door, at mid-level in a tri-plex penthouse in New York by architect Steven Forman, swings open from the vestibule at the touch of a finger. Made by Treitel Grätz Inc, the vertical light troughs that run the length of this long, narrow house are made of opaque glass brick and block from PPG Pittsburgh Corningware.

3 In this former factory, architect Ben Kelly uses a steel front door with a contemporary fanlight above it. Unusually, the steel door is set within a wooden frame – a reversal of traditional roles. The steel is acid-etched to give a mottled, rubbed patina. This play of textures is picked up in the horsehair matting and small block parquet on the floor, set against a rough-adzed, dark-stained wooden wall.

detracts from the simple entrance favored in the contemporary home. The louvered door, behind which most storage took place in the bedroom and bathroom, has also fallen from favor. Bi-fold doors, pivoted at the side and centrally hung on accordion tracks, are now more popular. The newest mechanisms for wooden folding doors are ones that concertina across large spans, dividing dining from living spaces, for example, or dressing from study areas, when necessary. These doors are as versatile as a screen, while practically eliminating drafts and noise, and they take up less space than an ordinary door. Since they are for interior use, these doors are usually made from high-density particle board faced with a range of wood veneers or water-resistant vinyl.

An insecure door lets in drafts, noise and, worst of all, intruders. Magnetic fasteners on interior doors preclude drafts and noise and, for the front and back doors, there are secure door-jamb and mortise-type locks (one set into the full thickness of the door), or the slam-action door lock with a strong, dead-locking bolt.

A door chain and viewer, with front bolts for outward-opening doors, give added protection. On outward-opening doors where hinges are exposed, there are hinge bolts that engage every time you close the door. Two bolts fitted in each door within a few inches of the hinges help to form solid protection between the door and frame.

4

5

4 For a city apartment, architect Eva Jiricna uses steel doors that are reminiscent of submarine hatches, with a glass peep-hole at eye level, and silvered pulls.

5 Irish-born designer Clodagh, working in New York, favors patina finishes, such as unpainted plaster. This blue patina door in painted steel, by David Johnson for Clodagh Design International, has a Harrison door pull and copper lock. Clodagh's interior designs rely upon the good looks of the basic materials of the construction industry – glass, plaster, concrete and steel.

6

6 Stainless steel lift doors provide an interesting surface alongside a steel security door that has a surveillance camera and entry door formula installed by Castle Security Services.

DOORS

1 Unlike most metallic fittings, Hewi's nylon-covered steel pulls and grips do not become uncomfortably cold to the touch during the winter.

5 A lever pull from Ambrose Mortez's "Baia" series for Mandelli. The special shock-resistant "Fluxcoat" finish enhances the brightness of the brass.

2 "Sarissa" brass pulls, from Valli and Colombo's "Casual" collection of decorative door pulls and fittings, are available in polished brass, chrome, white, black and opaque matte-black finishes.

6 Philip Hearsey's scarlet lacquered internal doors are crowned with a pair of heavy-duty, front door ring pulls, their brass finish patinated with ammonia fumes.

3 Designed by Stephen George, these polished "Best of Brass" pulls can either be bolted directly to the chosen door, or else affixed with a round or rectangular backplate.

4 Angelo Becchetti knobs, hinges, door pulls and knockers are made of polished, lacquered brass. The "Erika" pull was designed by their in-house BAL studio.

7 FSB commission door pulls from famous designers. Model "1184," by Franco Berg, accords with the company's belief that "one can only grasp a thing of substance."

8 Looking like a patch of blue sky, the square-plated "Modric" unit from Allgood incorporates a horizontal lever designed to sit flush like a simple door pull.

9 A choice of brass, chrome and polished black metal finishes is available for these door pulls designed by Josep Llusca and produced by the Sellex foundry in Spain.

9

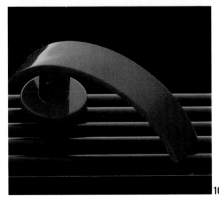

10 Neo-baroque door knobs and pulls designed by Gerard Dalmon and gilded or bronze-patinated by avant-garde company, Neotu.

11 & 12 "Vienna" 1 and 3 are from a collection of solid brass door hardware, finished in polished brass or matte black. They have been designed ergonomically for easy handling, by Ivo Pelligri for RDA.

13 Exact reproductions, both in form and in hand-polished solid brass, of eight original designs from the turn of the century by the great architect Antonio Gaudí, include this unusual vertebraic door pull, engraved with his signature, by Bd Ediciones de Diseno.

14 Christian Cirici used twirls of congoy or coral wood clasped in polished or chromed brass for the bracelet-like pull from the graceful "Herrajes Bd" range he designed for Bd Ediciones de Diseno – a series which also includes a door knob, a catch for a sliding door and a furniture knob.

10

11

12

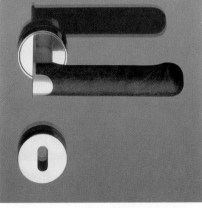

13

14

15

15 Briarwood pull with brass rosette and escutcheon from the "Otto F" series by Gianfranco Frattini for Fusital.

16 "Bridge" pull, by Guiseppe Raimondi for Eurobrass.

17 Frascio's brass "Piramide" pulls, by Paolo Nava, are made impervious to corrosion.

18 "Cormorano" brass hardware from Valli and Colombo's "Classic" collection.

19 "Fenix," a sinuously shaped, solid brass pull designed by Guiseppe Raimondi for Eurobrass's "Design Collection" of door furniture.

16

17

18

19

1 This smooth operator, a satin-finish, stainless steel bolt designed by Alan Tye for Allgood's "Modric" series, is suitably reinforced to slot into a steel door frame, as may be required for reasons of security.

11 Fire-door hinges need to be made of reinforced steel and have strong fastening bolts, like the stainless steel model designed by Alan Tye for the "Modric" range and manufactured by Allgood, the architectural hardware specialists.

12 A doorstop designed by Knud Holscher for Carl F. Petersen's stainless steel and polished brass "d-line" range.

2 Hewi's colorful "625" sprung-nylon doorstop offers a smooth, silent action and minimizes the risk of accidents.

6 A solid-looking, suitably angular chrome lever pull complements the thick custom-made glass and black door frame in David Wild's house.

7 The human hand meets mechanical component in the mellifluous fluidity of Mario Botta's door pull design "1104" for FSB.

13 The "M" lever pull designed by Knud Holscher for Carl F. Petersen's "d-line" range features an anti-vandalism fixing plate.

3 Design "1138" from Dieter Rams' "rgs" range for FSB. The combination of gray aluminum and black plastic underlines his philosophy that simplicity surpasses complexity.

4 Design "1102," by architect Alessandro Mendini for FSB, is a re-design of the lever pull famous Bauhaus designer Walter Gropius created for the Fagus Works in the 1920s.

5 Designed by Alan Tye for Allgood's "Modric" series of door furniture, the "Unilite" is made of a luminous PVC that glows in the dark and is re-charged by either natural or artificial light. It is ideal for bathrooms.

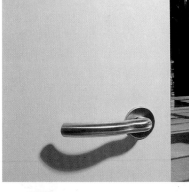

8 & 9 FSB lever "1144" and knob "2374" are "unassuming and usable products" by Jasper Morrison.

10 James Hong's aluminum plate door-pull for CDI is designed to fit any sliding glass door.

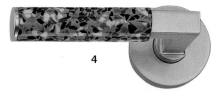

14 Hewi conceal their colorful fixings with nylon caps and covers. One intention behind this is that even when a door is open its hinges will still look OK – which is not always the case with painted hinges.

15 The Stuttgart Design Center awarded a prize to the stainless steel "WSD 88" by Walter Schnepel for Tecnolumen, who produce original Bauhaus designs as well as hardware by today's designers.

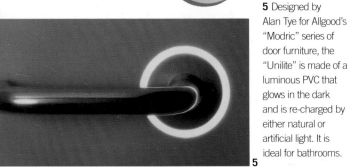

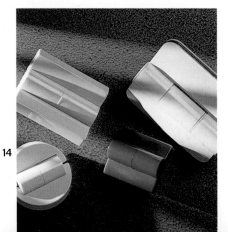

Windows

G lass is the most innovative building material of the 20th century. Architects are constantly exploring new ways of using this one medium that is intrinsic to both the interior and exterior of the building. Windows open the home to light and air; they are its eyes and lungs. But as they rapidly transform into its skin, their role is changing from being simply windows to being the walls themselves. These glass façades have brought their own problems, however, as inhabitants seek to muffle them with draperies to give privacy as well as protection from sunlight.

As the century draws to a close there are signs of a revolutionary new development in windows for contemporary housing. Technological developments within the glass-making industry have produced a type of glass that allows those on the inside to see out but presents an opaque surface to those trying to look in. This glass is also photosensitive, darkening as the light intensifies and lightening once more at dawn when light levels are low. The French architect

1 Wood technology prevails in this Gwathmey Siegel house, which has a formal grid of different shaped windows creating a pleasing pattern while bathing the interior with light.

1

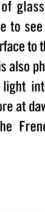

2

3

Previous page
Bigger panes of glass, stronger sealers and fittings that can hold great spans of glass have changed the shape of modern windows. They open outward, pivot inward, flap up, batten down and slide. The lines of this window's metal frames are echoed in the slats of the Venetian shades hanging inside. The design is by David Wild.

2 & 3 The former partnership of Claudio Silvestrin and John Pawson designed these windows. Their placement at the end of a long, tall corridor creates an unusual effect – the rectangular strips of glass catch the sun as it tracks across the sky during the day, casting a moving pattern of light and shade on the concrete floor below.

4

4 An entire wall of glass, braced with a metal gantry, has been built into architect John Young's riverside penthouse apartment. The effect is spectacular while, at the same time, demonstrating the remarkable industrial platecoil heater disks placed near the windowed wall for the best circulation of warmed air. Every third window on the second level can be opened, and three windows at the far wall act as a door onto the balcony.

5

5 In this view of John Young's riverside apartment, four floors above street level, his bathroom tower protrudes from the roofline. Its glass-brick walls double up as its windows. The bathroom tower, made of a braced-steel frame infilled with translucent glass blocks, has a clear glass roof.

1 Even the tubular-steel gate has been designed by architect David Wild to frame this line-up of windows, an arrangement of clear-glass blocks stacked to form a horizontal pattern above an amber slab of recessed wall. On the ground floor, visible from the street, frosted-glass cubes have been used, while the second floor features large panes of transparent glass screened by Venetian shades.
2 Just a few doors away, another David Wild design has produced windows that pivot open, like the wings of a butterfly.

Jean Nouvel dramatically illustrated, in his Arab Institute building in Paris, just how to clad a structure in this photo-sensitive material. The net effect is like a camera lens, which can admit more light as day dims toward night or less light when the sun is high and the light is at its brightest. Chameleon-like, these glass surfaces interact dynamically with the climate to meet the users' needs, as well as to make optimum use of energy.

The British architect Richard Rogers, who already describes as a dinosaur his technically advanced and controversial Lloyds Insurance building in London's financial district – the only landmark to be built this century in the capital – observes that constructions will "dematerialize" as architecture is no longer a question of mass and volume but of lightweight structures with superimposed transparent layers.

Such radical advances are all the more remarkable for their relative novelty. For centuries, loosely fixed waxed skins across gaps, or narrow apertures on crenelated walls, were the only way to bring daylight, and a view of the outside, into dwellings. The Iranians and then the Romans discovered how to

5 A grand piano, the Lloyd Loom wicker chairs, exotic flowers – every detail in this music room has been designed by architect Rick Mather to escape from the feeling of a conservatory addition. The giant incline of glass above, and the evenly paced windows below, create a space of light, yet cozy, intimacy.

6 Alexander Gorlin has employed three monumental sheets of glass, divided by square pillars, to allow light to stream into the building during the day and to flood out at night onto the swimming pool.

3 This house, designed by Lustig, has a perfect symmetry. The glass wall conforms to the geometry of the house, using square panes of glass that extend right up to the extravagant swooping eaves at roof level. The symmetry is confirmed by the room's focal point, a centrally located fireplace, as well as by two steel, cylindrical flues forming columns that are visible both inside and out.

make panes of glass, rolling it out like pastry when molten. But this product was cloudy, thick and shattered if made larger than a tiny pane. Nonetheless, the process lasted until the 19th century, with great banks of small panes in leaded surrounds creating the oriel window. A ubiquitous architectural feature for four centuries was the window seat, which provides a clue as to just how little daylight filtered through into the interior of houses. It was only as recently as 1959 in England that molten glass was poured out of a furnace up to 11 feet wide and was capable of being shifted onto building sites. The evolution of glass became a revolution as monumental sheets of glass up to virtually any length were produced that were sufficiently strong to be supported on steel frames.

Planning restrictions on buildings from earlier ages are designed to preserve the original façades, which accounts for the many diverse window shapes and sizes on the market. Conventional windows need restoration and dressing, according to the age of the structure. Older windows can be in the form of

4 The window range "Inoxfinestra" by Industrie Secco has been chosen by Spectrum for an office development consisting of a soaring stack of windows fixed in rectangular stainless steel frames.

7 Glass bricks bring light into David Chipperfield's inner city architectural practice, a building without the benefit of a view. For balance, there is a window panel of evenly paced square panes.

8 Two solid, immobile sheets of glass make up the corner of this living room in a David Chipperfield design. Selective openings reveal only that which the architect intended to frame, such as this courtyard.

1 Modern windows such as these are usually found in aluminum casings, but Gwathmey Siegel amusingly converted the contemporary style by using wooden frames, varnished like rosewood, in a wooden façade stained a metalic silvery gray.

2 In the Trump Towers, New York, Gwathmey Siegel's use of wooden frames links a classical material to a modern building and helps it to stand out from the crowd in which metal and concrete predominate.

2

3 The porthole, once banished to Art Deco architecture, enjoys a revival as a focal point in an avant-garde makeover in this house. Hinged to open irregularly, it can be secured from inside.

little outward-opening casements grouped in pairs; bays or bows; sash windows; arched windows; vertical dormer windows; or the porthole windows typical of the Art Deco period. Glass doors, known as French windows since their debut at Versailles in the 1680s, are casement windows carried to the floor where they open like doors, usually onto a patio or terrace of some description.

The clerestory window, the peaked, two-storey window in the A-frame house or post-modernist villa, and windows that turn the corner, such as those that the British architect David Chipperfield placed in the home of the fashion photographer Nick Knight, are some of the special casement windows that have made their appearance in the new architectural grid.

3 The loft or attic, which can be a third of

1

4 The south façade of the Villa Turque by Le Corbusier features this porthole, which, on the outside, is ringed with bricks and, on the inside, with an octagonal wooden template and lattice by Andrée Putman, the interior designer of the project.

5 Dovetailed corners in the cabinetmaker's fashion on a modern window fitting by Metall Kommerz are finely detailed with traditional brass hardware.

4

5

6 Metall Kommerz patented a window system called "Clima," which has perfect thermal insulation between the aluminum support and Canadian hemlock façade.

8 A stacked trio of wooden rectangular frames are set horizontally but open vertically, in this house by Gwathmey Siegel. A grid of glass blocks filters in additional light.

10 Pella Rolscreen frame windows and fixed skylight have been installed in an A-frame, with a ceiling fan suspended from the central crossbeam.

11 This sunroom features the vented Pella Rolscreen skylight and traditional french sliding door, which has double-glazed panels and insulated glass.

7 Architect Arata Isozaki has a reputation for designing some of the most beautiful modern art galleries. In this domestic setting, his windows are designed to bring maximum light and ventilation into the kitchen/dining area built beneath a pitched roof space.

9 The Pella Rolscreen entry door shows the circlehead fanlight in insulated glass – a fixed unit with glazed lintels – which brings a formal opening, and light, to a new residence.

12 Small, square, modern windows such as these are often eschewed by architects in favor of more grandiose schemes. But window manufacturers Metall Kommerz show how a plain, white-painted window can be elaborated upon with a Georgian fanlight stencil. Replicating that image below the window as well as above makes an ironical, post-modernist joke of the scheme.

the total potential floor area inside a building, is being opened up to ease the squeeze on space. Roof windows providing light and ventilation in pitches angled as low as 15° have become popular. These windows open outward with an accessible pull on the sash and provide unobstructed views for anybody standing. On steeper inclines the windows open inward operated by a sash pull.

Whatever the style of building, there are frames to support the panes in metal, wood or plastic. Changes in buildings at both the functional and technological levels in the late 1960s and early 70s affected fittings such as windows, which traditionally had the merit of integrating craft skills with new innovations. Windows have always been manufactured, and often assembled, off-site. For centuries wooden window

13 Rolled-steel products for windows and doors from Industrie Secco combine the strength and economy of steel with polyester finishes, such as these frames from their "Seccolor" series.

1 A stunning window, designed by architect Peter Wilson, breaks up a glass wall with an acid-etched, delicate ribbed pattern on a background of frosted, opaque glass. This individual definition of a window brings plenty of light indoors while blocking a rather uninspiring mews courtyard view outside.

2 Stained-glass windows are heavy and this octagonal, domed rooflight had to be composed by Goddard and Gibbs in sections, supported by strong bars set in the roof.

3 Designer Philip Hearsey explores angles on squares with a sandblasted pattern of tiny squares on a vertical glass pane, which is mimicked by the mosaic pattern of the stair carpet.

4 Goddard and Gibbs created this glass panel, spiraling in warm colors, to emphasize and enhance the coppery tone of the wood on the stairwell.

5 The thick cut glass in this window design by Jo Crepain distorts the light and the view outside. The advantage of this type of glass is that it forms the illusion of a translucent wall rather than of a definite window.

6 A modern interpretation of leaded glass by Jochem Poensgen uses float glass, mouth-blown opalescent, semi-opalescent and antique *danziger* glass.

7 An old electricity substation confronts its origins, and its conversion into a spacious residence, with this façade by architect Gary Cunningham. The supporting girders and the ceramic pylon contacts that clad the black-framed window emphasize and reinforce the electrical nature of the building, just as the owners intended.

frames dominated, but during the late 1960s there was a worldwide push for the mass production of windows to meet the need generated by the boom in housing, and other materials for frames, such as aluminum and plastic, were specified. Thus the first windows arrived from the standardized production line. Instead of windows being a craft product, external frames were transformed into just another building component. New materials – synthetic rosin seals, treated aluminum sections, PVC (polyvinyl chloride) with alloys and steel, and all the impermeable plastics – joined forces on the assembly line to meet the new housing requirements. Frames today conform to a series of precise requirements imposed by building specifications. Windows must match standards for dimensional stability, fire safety, mechanical solidity, sound and heat insulation, lightness and long-term resistance to weather conditions. Energy saving is now being recognized as important, especially since windows are a major source of heat and energy loss. Resource conservation is also having an effect on windows. A campaign to halt the desecration of the Earth's tropical forests, without reforestation and controlled logging, has made hardwoods such as teak an unpopular material. It is more likely, however, that hardwoods from temperate regions come from managed plantations. Window dressing has always been an important interior consideration. According to the mood and manner of

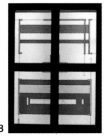

8 Rectilinear music symbols were the inspiration behind this stained-glass window by Patrick Ross-Smith. The lower panel was acid-etched from blue opal glass, the green panel is leaded.

9 Rashid Din of Din Associates designed this stylish assemblage of blue-smoked-glass and frosted-glass windows, which are emphasized by all being set in recessed molded frames.

1

3

2

4

7

1 & 2 The popularity of plain roller shades has receded in the wake of shades with a ridged profile, such as those in Levolor's "Newport" range (**1**), and "Lyverscreen" solarscreens (**2**).

3 Faber's 16mm wide "Microlite" louvers fit into door panels and glazed room dividers with space-saving neatness.

4 Sunlight UK's "Light and Shade" shades in pleated polyester come in 140 colors across five ranges. Opening and closing is with cordlock controls on overhead wands; a fully motorized system is also available.

the times, windows have been covered in every conceivable fashion, from the earliest draft-excluding tapestries to the lightest sheers, or the more substantial alternatives such as wooden shutters. In the 21st century, contemporary details will render window dressing obsolete as the new generation of photosensitive glass does the job automatically. Then there will be something new under the sun.

Meanwhile, textile drapes are still under review in the contemporary interior. Architects are frequently asked to judge textile designs but they find draping a building in swathes of pattern, the way that a decorator does, something of a challenge. They can select patterned rugs for floors, but a piece of fabric is anathema to most modern architects.

In the contemporary interior, most rooms have a radiator panel placed under the window. But this cuts out the opportunity for long drops of fabric to cloak the window. As an alternative, the new wire mesh, paper, plastic laminate and fabric shades offer an uninterrupted view when rolled up and some

5 Opaque shutters, opening inward, veil the windows of this converted powerhouse, yet allow diffused light to enter when closed. While open, a complex hinge system lifts the shutters away from the windows.

6 The "Jalousien" range from Fönstret covers the walls and sloping, glazed skylight in this studio space by Anne Idstein. Louvered wooden slats, angled to any configuration, let in as much light as is required.

7 Timbershade Venetian shades have Western red cedar 2-inch or 1-inch slats tinted in an extensive range of colors.

9

privacy and light when required. The techniques for designing these window coverings vary from the Austrian or festoon version, much-loved by decorators and generally considered vulgar by the design conscious, to the roller shade, which behaves exactly as its name suggests. Also included are the Roman type, which pulls up into accordion pleats on a cord; slatted wood or metal shades on a roller with a spring mechanism to set them at any desired level; and the architectural favorite, Venetian shades, available with plastic, metal or wood slats.

On the outside, further details may be added. For example, the trellised metal grill, which pulls over the window and locks in place, is making something of a comeback in this security-conscious age, as is the exterior shutter.

8 Opaque glazed bricks at garden level are topped by a grid of small panes of glass outlined in simple black frames in this custom-built house by David Chipperfield.
9 Robin Spence used horizontal Venetian shades from Faber throughout this house.
10 Vertical shades are the obvious option for awkwardly shaped windows. Developments in tracking systems offer arched head, twin head, trapezoid and curved shades, and these from the Louvre Blind Company show how the drawing mechanism works.
11 Franklin D. Israel's wide stretch of horizontal shades leaves the eaves of this A-framed window wall free to allow unfiltered light to pour in, while offering privacy at street level.

10

8

44

11

1 Marimekko's 100 percent cotton prints make excellent Roman or roller shades for contemporary homes, as the Finnish designed patterns are uncompromisingly modern. Designs shown here are "Sikerma" (bottom), "Ratamo" (middle), "Viikuna" (top).

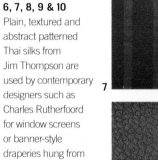

1

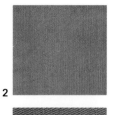

2, 3, 4 & 5 Zimmer & Rohde produce a high-quality range of plain, woven textured and geometric fabrics that are particularly suitable for the windows of contemporary homes. Shown here are Thai silk (**2**), "Camelot" (**3**), silk canvas (**4**) and "Square Root" (**5**).

2

3

4

5

6

6, 7, 8, 9 & 10 Plain, textured and abstract patterned Thai silks from Jim Thompson are used by contemporary designers such as Charles Rutherfoord for window screens or banner-style draperies hung from simple steel, glass or metal poles. From the "Atmosphere" collection are "Luna" (**8** & **10**), "Pegasus" (**7**) and "Omega" (**9**).

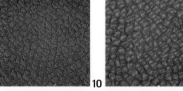

7

9

8

10

11 Graphic stripes are the only pattern many contemporary designers allow. Sahco Hesslein produce a huge variety of stripes in a wide range of fibers – even the latest man-made mixtures – including "Zeno," a self-striped sateen; "Fontain," a multi-colored sheer and "Ebro" corded velvet.

12 & 13 Jewel-colored suede-like fabrics from Alicantara's "Master" range are suitable for heavy insulating draperies. Matching fabrics are available for covering walls and for upholstery.

12

13

11

14

14 Sahco Hesslein's crisply striped fabrics (see also picture **11** for variations) are available in a wide range of contemporary colorways.

Stairs

The movement afoot today in architectural interiors reveals itself in the structural simplicity of the staircases shown here, which resolve aspects of function in their sculptural form. As Nikolaus Pevsner put it so succinctly:

"In twentieth century architecture, the staircase assumes a new significance as the element in a building which is most expressive of spatial flow."

Skillful design solutions pace climbers, as well as acclimatize them to the lower ceilings and cramped quarters typical of buildings today, while deceiving viewers into believing that the space soars and that the ascent is simple. Since neither the Greeks nor the Romans were particularly interested in staircases in their villas, and the Medieval Age saw only some rudimentary ladders, it was not until the Regency period in England that the staircase sweeping upward from the hall became a focal point in the house.

The last grand period of wooden-paneled staircase design was the Gothic revival of the late 18th and early 19th

Previous page
A steel balustrade and metal landing panel add contemporary detail to a wooden stairway by architect Pierre d'Avoine.
1 & 2 Stairs that look very different from each angle in the ascent by architect Michael Carapettan make best use of minimal space. Diamond-meshed iron risers, which support the reassuringly stolid wooden treads, filter light through the perforations, and bring to a long run an almost transparent quality.

1

2

3

centuries. Illuminated by shafts of colored light refracted through stained-glass window panels, the staircase swept heavenward in imposing splendor. Today, however, with space at a premium, the context for such statements would be quite wrong. Generally, there is no hall and all available space must be freed for living – even the spiral stair requires an area of about 6 feet square to allow for wide, comfortable treads.

Prefabricated spiral stairs are designed to telescope upon each tread. This

3 This loft was originally part of an arcade with arches, pilasters and columns. Using the grand height available to him, architect Luigi Ferrario added two platforms in industrial iron grating reached by a ladder-like arrangement of metal stairs.

4 & 5 Within this architectural staircase even the landings have been transformed, projecting like diving boards into the lofty space carved out of the interior of this magnificent house. Above the staircase, a glazed roof allows light to fall freely through the perforated mesh variegated grid patterns.

5

1 This detail of the staircase in picture **2** shows how the arched handrail is supported above the glass, protectively enfolding it at the landings.

2 Glazing the space between the tubular-steel handrail and the narrow wooden treads on this mild-steel staircase sounds risky, but safety glass is capable of both sustaining assault and holding the light. The staircase was designed by Armstrong Associates for the headquarters of the architectural fittings company Elementer.

3 "Buildings will survive only if driven by ideas" says David Chipperfield, whose innovative staircase frees the risers and treads from paneling. The exposed ascent is flanked by metal flattened into a long handrail. Chipperfield exaggerates the distance between the treads and balustrade in a witty exploitation of scale and proportion.

allows them to be easily adjusted, since the positioning of the landing on the second floor will depend on the ceiling height – by no means a standard dimension in older houses that are undergoing renovation.

Spiraling stairs in the 1970s were often taken from old exterior fire escapes, freed of rust and repainted for use in domestic interiors. The spiraling ramps favored by Frank Lloyd Wright in his Guggenheim Museum in New York, or Frank Gehry in his Vitra Chair Museum in Germany are capable of making possible a gentle ascent for throngs of people, with the added bonus of being suitable for wheelchair access.

In the contemporary home, however, design features such as these take up too much space. Mass-produced lines are adjusted in scale to account for reduced ceiling heights and the lack of space for landings, while the best staircases are still custom-built on site using prefabricated parts. Aluminum

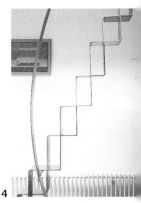

4 The owners of this custom-built staircase by the inventive Ron Arad of One Off call it "a steel waterfall." The house was built in the 1850s, but was gutted and then custom-designed for the current owners. For example, both are very tall, and this staircase paces the treads accordingly.

5

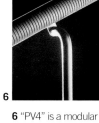

6

5 Without the central fireman's pole, a spiral staircase takes a twist in form from Dimes, using the "Modula" black metal backbone to support the treads.

6 "PV4" is a modular handrail, ribbed in anti-slip black rubber. It is made by Dimes and can be paired with a range of staircase components, including the "PG500."

7 Hewi modular handrail systems produce corner designs, angled balustrades, connections and end fittings designed to hold securely clear protective acrylic sheets. Rails are in nylon with a steel core – a strong, easy-to-clean material that is never too hot or cold to the touch and which is non-conductive to electricity or static charges.

8 & 9 Steel braces clip together like a child's toy to make a self-supporting staircase angled for any twist or turn. Albini and Fontanot mass-produce Roberto Molinazzi's design in polyurethaned steel. Geometric line and well-studied proportions accentuate the scale of the staircase.

treads snake along a gradual incline, as rigorously pleated as an origami cut, uncluttered by finicky balustrades, since the wall acts as the backdrop. The effect is theatrical – an unbroken line like a caterpillar uncoiled. On a practical level, it intrudes very little into the room below and provides the viewer with an interesting profile. The concept is based on Palladio's flying staircase in the Academy, Venice, which spirals upward without any visible support other than the bonding of the steps into the outer wall.

Another neat architectural device to take the eye visually upward and apparently lengthen rooms with low ceilings and meanly proportioned staircases, is to double the length between treads. This gives the appearance of elongating the ascent without actually taking up any additional space. This "visual stretch" is often used by the architect Pierre d'Avoine to make a narrow studio – even one just 10 feet across,

10 Dimes produce stairs that fold, spiral, or fit together in modular pieces. This versatility means that Dimes components will create a staircase to fit most spaces. Shown here is their metal-cast spiral model, the "PG 500," which is polyurethaned in scarlet, with its fan-like treads lined in rubber or carpet. It can be matched with a variety of handrails, like the "PV4" (see **6** above.)

11 Architect Rick Mather achieved a staircase of Hollywood grandeur, with curves like a Cresta run and handrails that resolve their angular differences in a clever cross-over of a quarter turn with winders, to front the entrance to this top-floor studio apartment.

11

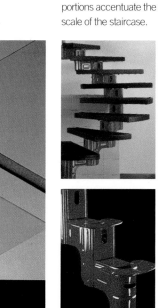

7

8

9

10

1

2

3

1 An unfurled ribbon of steel extended from the top of this office by architects Von Gerkan, Marg and partner provides an airy, deceptively lightweight, open staircase with flattened handrails attenuated as finely as tagliatelle.
2 Narrow steel treads, evenly paced with a fine, nonslip carpet lining, are given a curved edge on one side of the staircase, known as the nosing. Architect Lustig has made full use of illumination in this space by backlighting the sloping back projection that follows the incline of the stairs.

4 Albini and Fontanot's narrow 3/4-inch diameter hand-rail is made of metal treated with rosinous polyurethane. The handrail can be conveniently attached to any balusters from the newel, or principal post, found at the foot of the stairs.

5 Colin Gold of Aukett Associates has brought neo-classical flourishes to the plain geometry of this mahogany-stained staircase, with its steel ziggurat bannisters, which links an upper studio with the lower-floor kitchen.

6 Downtrodden winders rarely get a decorative treatment, though with a spiral staircase very often the view from below is of these wedges wending their way upward. The solution from architects Tsao and Mckown is to splay these fan-shaped, ribbed treads within a well of light so that they cast a pattern on the floor below.

3 Though all but impossible for a modern architect to build himself a new house in central London, Sir Richard Rogers, Britain's most fashionable architect, carved out a contemporary interior for himself by combining two 19th-century houses. Where there were six rooms, now the dazzling space has a galleried bedroom floor reached via a dramatic, perforated stainless steel staircase and, above, this suspended ladder walkway on the top landing. The flapped theatrical lights battened to the landing cast light down the large distances covered.

wall to wall – appear less confined. Safety is a vital factor when planning stairs, but one of the unusual aspects of stair design is to use an unexpected material of the correct tensile strength. The stair treads here, for example, can be disquieting, yet they are made from safety glass laid like slats on iron supports. Today the laser cutter can shape glass in many superior ways, losing sharp edges altogether.

Freedom from timber technology, alongside a more controlled spatial manipulation as living spaces shrink, produces dramatic ascents, with staircases that are not even encased but sculptural walkways that slice through space, turning corners precipitously at the same time as they open up the view. Other senses, as well as the visual, are challenged. The British architect and designer

7 Looking up through a steel mesh platform, architect David Wild's dogleg staircase sets the honeyed color of wooden treads against black tubular-steel handrails and silvery steel uprights.

8 Albini and Fontanot delineate with a spindly lineup of balusters the gracious curve of their matte-black, high-tech staircase, "Xnodo".

9 The "Stonington Stair" in steel with cherry-wood risers and treads, by McBride and Horowitz, is a good resolution of a modern staircase in a 200-year-old salt-box house in New England. Its sculptural simplicity echoes the puritan spirit and rigorous functionalism of the original architecture.

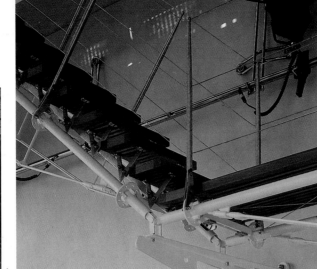

1 In this house, the wooden treads and landing are parquet for a superior finish. Wooden staircases were traditionally built to the standard quarter-turn or dogleg pattern, employing lathe-turned newels, risers, treads and balusters. Since the Industrial Revolution and the relative ease with which cast-iron or mild steel can be made into staircase components, the mass-produced wooden staircase has become a dull reproduction piece reduced in size to fit today's rooms. The best contemporary wooden staircases are those which expose the treads like vertebrae, elevating the planks of solid wood visually and simply in a free-standing staircase.

2 In this staircase, by Albini and Fontanot, laminated beech or walnut wooden risers fan out from a central wooden newel post. The result, a staircase that takes up the least possible floor space.

3 & 4 Riverside warehouses, while providing spectacular views and large rooms, are notoriously difficult to convert to living space. Architect John Young fitted a vertebraed, yellow, buttressed staircase with slatted teak treads on rollerball bearings so that it can be swiveled around to take advantage of the vast floor space. The staircase's lightweight mobility and structural strength makes it as flexible as airport landing steps. The steel gangplank leads to a bedroom on a concrete platform supported by steel rods suspended from the roof.

5 The background to stairs can make a standard run appear more dramatic, as architect David Wild proves in painting this ascent midnight blue. The vivid color stands out against the mellowed tones of wooden treads attached to black metal risers.

6 The design of the spiral is important when the interior has not been revamped as open, flowing space. Here, refurbishment was limited to the standard little well between the floors, where the meanly proportioned old stairs once ran. The solution, the "L 20" by Dimes, pays tribute to its Bauhaus origins in the style that harks back to Walter Gropius and his 1914 designs.

7 When only occasional access is required – to a roof terrace in this case – space-saving designs like this flat steel staircase with oak treads, by David Chipperfield, can be brought into play. The central metal pole serves both as support and handrail.

Ron Arad, whose work in metal includes voluminous stainless steel sofas and chairs, made the staircase in his original shop, which was appropriately named One Off, in London's Covent Garden. The staircase was formed from giant timbers wired to a Moog synthesizer. Everybody walking or rushing along these stairs made their own rhythmic music with each footfall. Arad's first commissioned staircase in a house was made from two continuous strips of metal crossing each other at right-angles to form rectangular picture frame shapes when seen in profile. The stair rail was a single sweep of metal curving like a bow across the structure, which has been described as a "steel waterfall."

You can make simpler staircases of course, using iron building brackets supporting metal mesh treads, or mahogany steps buttressed to joists without bannisters. Sometimes the winder, a tread wider at one end than the other, starts off the staircase ascent and leads the climber upward.

Newel posts, the principal posts at the ends of a flight of steps that support

7

1 Beech is the silky smooth wood favored for "Parisienne," the spiral staircase by Dimes which evokes Art Deco style. When different flights of stairs are not in the same line, the change of direction is achieved either by landings or, as here, by winders. Winders are steps, the treads of which taper for left or right turns. By contrast, landings are constructed as small floors and may be either half or three-quarter landings according to the angle between flights.

2 Laminated beech or walnut treads, protected by a transparent veneer, fit on a central metal support in red, blue or black. Made by Albini and Fontanot, and designed by Molinazzi from Index-studio, Milan, each tread is pierced by balustrades in primary colors.

3

4

4 & 5 Peter Wilson, working with Chassay Wright, created a private gallery above an office. The gallery is reached by an open stairwell with a balustrade forming a slinky seat, as if a giant dragonfly had alighted on the wall. The curve in the balustrade above it echoes the point at which the sitter can relax.

5

the handrail, can be in contrasting material, such as steel with wooden treads, or vice versa. Pierre d'Avoine believes it is important to have a rough-hewn honesty to stair rails in cramped, modern spaces, that same quality Hawksmoor sought with his lathe-turned posts on lectern stairs.

The ironwork traditionally used for balustrades at street level presents the designer with an opportunity for splendid neo-baroque flourishes or more practical uses. One example of such an application is a staircase by architect Pierre d'Avoine, a swooping lectern

7

3 A central stairwell is evenly paced by Gwathmey Siegel in American hardwood. The staircase begins with two flights meeting at a central ascent and then bifurcates to serve two separate wings on the landing.

6

6 This cherrywood staircase at the end of a combined eat-in kitchen/ dining area is by architect David Chipperfield. It brings a clarity of light and variety of tone within a simple structure in this tiny house.

7 Strands of twisted wire marshaled between steel joists, painted pastel yellow, form an unusual barrier for these simple wooden stairs, framed by a large, white display base, in a scheme by architect Frank Fitzgibbons.

STAIRS

1 Engineering feats are possible with reinforced concrete, which allows a more fluid ascent than either wood or stone. Within a corner, a sweep of stairs curves upward with balustrades in five bands of tubular steel to follow the twist like music sheets.

2 Stair treads are often viewed from the back, which in a triangular stacking exercise leads to boring uniformity. But this ascent of molded stairs, each cast individually and arranged with little overlap, makes a feature of the risers.

3, 4 & 5 A reminder that humble concrete is the sculptor's medium is seen here, in a design by architect Charles van den Hove. Double stairs within a central stairwell frame a blond wood door on the upper landing. The handrail that swoops above the stairs replicates their oval form. On the handrails, epoxyed to resemble antique pewter, the capping piece on which the hand rests when ascending or descending the stairs is usually rounded like this, and fixed about 2 feet 6 inches above the line of the nosing. The opposite view from the front doorway is toward the dining room and the open space of the garden beyond.

6 From Cecilia and Ottorino Berselli comes an example of rigorous straightline geometry. Their whitewashed concrete stairs are given a silvered lining with marbled veneers on the treads, set in relief against a natural stone and mortared wall. Designed for a house in Italy, traditional local materials are used in a contemporary way.

6

attached to the bannisters on the landings – thereby improvizing a small reading space in a tiny house.

Cunningly exploiting the sheer narrowness of the rooms and their lack of height, these structures in geometric configurations have handsome safety features, such as an overscaled handrail in marble. Architect David Chipperfield used this as a method of enticing the newcomer to look beyond

7 Simple precast concrete forms unravel like a helter-skelter course on precipitous curves supporting generous treads, evenly paced, covered along their entire width in elephant-gray carpet. Few verticals delineate this spectacular piece of engineering by Rick Mather, who illuminates his design with natural light from a glazed roof panel above the stairwell.

7

the cramped entrance to the studio upstairs. Scaled more appropriately for a hotel lobby, he set his gigantic, gray-marbled handrail against a cavernous main wall to create a real flight of fancy in a simple setting.

Stairs are more than just a means of getting between levels, according to Japanese architect Ryoji Suzuki they are "a device which obliquely traverses space." Slicing diagonally across interiors with stone, wood or steel mesh treads supported on tubular steel columns or rigid rigging, contemporary architects produce designs for staircases that are dramatic to look at, yet safe as houses.

1

4

1 & 2 In his dramatic black staircase, Albert Bardawil emphasizes the turns it takes by lining the concrete stairs with black travertine. The balustrade is a flat black metal twist. The space in Bardawil's apartment was so restricted that he commissioned a structural engineer to work out the exact dimensions required for his staircase.

3 Ron Arad's original London shop, One Off, featured this staircase cast in concrete with wooden railroad-sleeper treads wired to a Moog synthesizer so that each footfall created its own music. The guard rail, in mild tempered steel, blow torched with patterns by Arad, also served as a loud-speaker for the staircase synthesizer.

3

4 A narrow concrete staircase beneath a bricked vaulted ceiling is open on one side in the Mediterranean style. Architect David Chipperfield accentuates this imagery with blue sliding doors and panels and a cobalt colored tubular-steel frame.

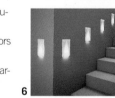

6

7 Western in appearance, Eastern in spirit, Tadao Ando's buildings in Japan are stark and spare but also refined and serene.

5 These stairs, on the 25th floor of an old mansion block, lead to a breathtaking viewing spot. Architect Steven Forman chose a stainless steel handrail above carpeted stone stairs to connect all three levels. Vertical "light troughs" run the length of the stairs.

6 Stolid stairs washed in midnight blue are lit all the time by low lighting in grid panels by Luxo, throwing a shaft of pyramidal light. Luxo believe that it is vital that nightlights stay on a low dimmer for staircase safety.

5

7

Heating

When the French celebrity designer Philippe Starck brandishes his firedogs and pokers designed for New York's fashionable hotel, the Century Paramount, and puts them into mass production, it is time to sit up and notice that the humble, and sometimes obsolete, hearth is getting the designer treatment.

After centuries of fulfilling general household and cooking needs, the fireplace is now banned in smokeless zones, or glows artificially with fake logs and pine spray that simply reinforce the illusion that the fire is really gas-fed. Central heating has brought about the changes in our attitude to what was formerly the focal point of the home—the fireplace. Nowadays, heat is beamed into our homes in three ways: directly as rays from the sun or the blaze from the fire; convected with warm-air currents circulated by a fan heater; and conducted as in direct contact, like the heat from an electric blanket.

The Romans, who were first with many

Previous page In architect John Young's penthouse the underfloor heating system is supplemented by wall-mounted, industrial heating elements from the Tranter Corporation. These take the form of stainless steel coils, ranged in tiers like rows of Samurai shields.
2 A semi-cylindrical, rendered brick fireplace provides the focal point in a large galleried room by Gwathmey Siegel. The central hearth, flanked by storage recesses for logs, is screened with wire-mesh safety curtains.
3 Commissioned by architect Charles Jencks, designer Michael Graves and sculptor Celia Scott conceived this fireplace on a monumental scale. Constructed of MDF, the fluted posts and lintel, and column above, have been marbelized to convey solidity and enhance classical references in the design.

1 Believing modernists were ill-served by standard domestic fittings, Mark Marcinik set up design company Next to M. Their fire surround is constructed of oak, plywood and galvanized steel, and incorporates a bar and firewood storage.

4

4 Sculptural column radiators, such as this black, strip-paneled model in architect Michael Russum's apartment, accent the distinctive lines of the surrounding architecture, rather than fading anonymously into the background.

5

5 From the Platonic Fireplace Company, a gas-fired and geometrically inspired fireplace comprising a fire surround of marbelized spheres, tetrahedrons, cones, cylinders and cubes, and a chrome-finished steel "Plato" grate housing high-heat ceramic "Geologs."

6 Designed by Arbonia, the sinuous X-stream radiator turns a functional device into a piece of domestic sculpture. It stands 75 inches tall and is available in more than 1500 stove-enameled colors, or plated in brass, nickel, chrome or gold.

6

architectural innovations, had underfloor heating installed in the city of Bath in England in AD60, where they piped hot spa water in underground pipes throughout the interiors of their buildings. Today's underfloor hot-water systems do not rely on spas; the water is heated by gas-, oil-, coal- or wood-burning boilers, or solar panels and heat pumps.

Baseboard and underfloor heating have been popular in the United States for many years and they are now catching on in Germany. These concealed systems are the most unobtrusive method of heating in the architectural interior. Baseboard radiators emit heat all around the room and are nearly invisible, thus imposing no restrictions on the placement of radiator panels, entrances or furniture.

One stage further, without even baseboards, which most late-modernists eschew, there are underfloor heating

1

3 "Acostyle" from Runtal is assembled from four blocks of slatted panels, available in various sizes and heated by either hot water or electric filaments.
4 Aluminum flooring is an ideal heat conductor for this gas-fired "Radia-Vector" by Zehnder, in Jan Kaplicky's apartment conversion in a 19th-century city house.
5 "Griglia," a 30-bar grid radiator from Runtal, which runs on one-fifth of the hot water required to heat a conventional radiator, can also be used to partition a room.

6 The "Ideal Elan 2," a wall-mounted, gas-fired radiator panel from Stelrad, can be unobtrusively inserted into a run of kitchen cabinets.

1 Usually concealed in the walls, the plumbing is revealed in this copper piping towel holder from Butler and Radice.
2 A towel rail, ladder radiators and classic radiator by Arbonia, all chromed and the latter available to order, curved or angled, floor- or wall-mounted.

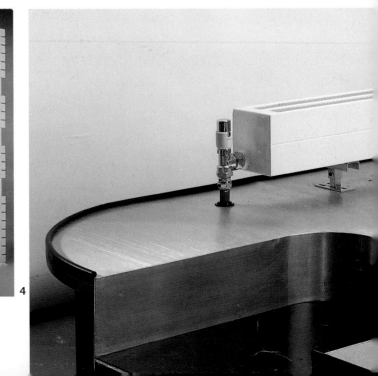

7 Classic, con-certina-style, Clyde combustion radiators run on the gas boiler system and are bolted together on site to the required length. Architect David Chipperfield, who favors the industrial appearance of these chunky units, has placed them near the windows of this small studio house to maximize convection.

7

10 The "Sculptur" curved towel rail from Zehnder can be supplied with an optional electric immersion heater to make it independent of the central heating system and operative all year around. Never install the system on open circuits or underfloor systems.

10

8 Floor-mounted, the short, squat Runtal "Reflex" radiator is the ideal size and shape for installing beneath windows in order to make best use of convection currents.

9 Stelrad Ideal's "Accord" central heating, gas-fired panel radiators, by Caradon, are available in a wide range of sizes and are notable for their plainly tailored simplicity.

8

11

13

systems that warm the entire surface area of the floor. Every other heating system depends on convectional currents to disperse the heat around the room, rising as hot air always does. In high-ceilinged rooms this can cause prob-lems, and could result in cold corners and chilly surfaces.

Underfloor heating systems run at surprisingly low temperatures, less than blood heat, which allows you to use a wide range of flooring finishes, even wood, without any risk of damage or warping. These finishes can be laid on the original concrete base, on a screeded floor or on sleepers.

Low-temperature, radiant heat, rather than the much higher, hot-air tempera-ture type, can come from radiators hidden behind the narrowest and slimmest of baseboards, or from slen-der panels that are a mere 5 inches

12

11 Made to be recessed in small, low room spaces, the Runtal "Convettore" functions at pre-set temperatures. When sited beneath a plate-glass window, the stainless steel radiator body appears to double up as a baseboard.

12 The "King" radiator from Runtal was designed by Paul Priestman to look like a tall, cylindrical torch. It is manufactured in naturally anodized aluminum.

13 The "JeT X" (model HX) by Runtal, is a wall-mounted, strip-paneled radiator.

9

1 Runtal's wall-mounted tubular "Acovex" radiators run off the hot water systems in bathrooms or kitchens.

2 Wall-mounted column radiators from Runtal's "Scaldasalviette" range are available in various dimensions to suit most room sizes.

3 A modern interior which makes a virtue of contemporary fittings, rather than trying to hide them. The radiator panel, loudspeaker, window shade, Eileen Gray chrome table and vase and flowers are assembled to create a pleasing still life out of everyday modern elements.

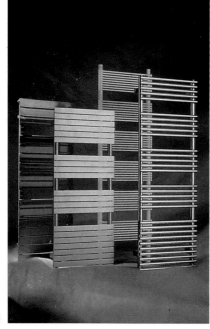

4 Radiant crystal, pioneered by microwave ovenware and used for cooktops for years, has made its way into this innovatory wall-mounted heater panel, the "Omeglass," from Runtal.

5 Chrome "Classic," white panel and red and yellow "Crea-Therm" radiators by Arbonia prove that radiators need not be utility objects. English distributors Bisque claim the range is "heating art."

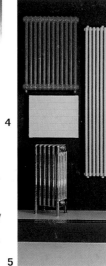

high and positioned above any existing baseboards.

If you intend to use direct heat dependent on a fireplace, then you need to pay careful attention to detail to ensure that the most energy is conserved. Glass-fronted fires and enclosed stoves are considerably more efficient than open-fronted fires. Some of the most energy-conserving offer 80 percent efficiency, which allows them to take over as the primary source of heat rather than acting as a supplement to a radiator system. A chimney damper will narrow the flue and control the air flow that causes hot air to rush up the chimney to the outside.

Modern fireplaces have a grate with a hood, looking much like a kitchen exhaust ventilator above the oven, or else the free-standing fire has a modern flue lining over the wider old flue to

6 An electric fan heater designed to be built into the kickspace under kitchen cabinets and save valuable floor space. Controls are located on the counter, and there is a cool air setting for summer.

7 The "Chorus" radiator by Marimex, with six slats on a shallow radiator panel, has a distinctive yet unobtrusive presence in this light-filled corner.

8 Industrial radiator ducts, originally concealed under steel fascia, are stripped to reveal their slinky coils in architect Ben Kelly's factory conversion.

connect with the hood. Channels around the fire casing heat the air drawn toward the fire and recycle it to warm the room, producing nearly twice the heat of an ordinary flame-effect fire for the same input of gas. A fireplace is not just a pretty face or, indeed, the visual focal point of a room. If our planet is to survive, we need to address the basic problems of heating and room insulation effectively, since both of them have a dramatic effect on overall energy consumption.

Before the advent of scientific combustion theories, houses were buffered against the cold with tapestries, wall-hangings, porches, paneling and window shutters. These types of decoration have no place in the modern interior. In their place, the strictures— and structures—for engineering must reside with the heating specialist and the homeowner. For example, in Britain the domestic market accounts for

9

9 Marimex's "Novella Bains" laddered towel rail in bright scarlet adds a jolt of bold color to a white bathroom.
10 Because this free-standing Zehnder radiator runs on low-temperature oil- or gas-fired systems, it can safely double up as a partition wall.

10

11

11 These colorful and robust multi-columned "Classic" radiators from Zehnder run economically on low-temperature heating systems, and come in more than 100 listed sizes to fit almost any space.

1 Abundant space and light in a villa by architect Jo Crepain provide the perfect background for the uncompromising functionalism of a classic, cast-iron, wood-burning stove.

2 A prototype for a cast-iron, wood-burning stove by Benn Gurleyik has ridged and stippled sides to increase the surface area and so maximize the convection of heat.

3 "Gyrofocus" by Atelier Dominique, ingeniously suspended from the flue, highlights the sculptural potential in fireplace design, for too long anchored to the hearth. The ensemble is finished in a high-heat-resistant, matte-black coating.

4 Made by Piazzetta, the "Romeo" wood-burning stove features a glazed pottery casing that convects heat from a cast-iron firebox.

5 Most wood-burning stoves are given a pseudo-antique casing, but the "Seneca" from Vermont Castings has been designed for contemporary interiors. It also burns clean to meet the stringent requirements of the American Environmental Protection Agency.

almost 50 percent of the energy used in the country. Consumer awareness can affect regulations as well as manufacturers' products, and awareness of energy-saving, though yawningly dull when presented in therms, can make the difference between running an efficient, economic home and a casual but expensive one.

Thus far, only the fireplace surround, that consummate piece of ornate framing to the glow within, has been neglected in the design treatment. On the whole, products made today are arrested in a time warp with Adam

6 Solid-fuel-burning stoves are architects' favorites for homes equipped with a coal or wood bin, since their industrial shape and functional form make them a focal point. Since heat rises, freeing the flue of a wood-burning stove to act like a tubular radiator on the floor above will save energy. David Wild protects surrounding surfaces by inserting a marble fire surround and hearth.

carved surrounds clustered with cheaply molded and glued-on cornucopias, or perhaps Louis Quinze marble veneers. Fireplaces are period pieces, and the clean lines and fresh designs of the modern fireplace few and far between. Perhaps it is a reflection of the fact that in the last 20 years flues have not been built into modern homes. Now there is a realization that every home needs an open flue, since it provides natural ventilation that keeps the air fresh at the same time as it removes water vapor in the air. One of the main causes of dampness in temperate climates is condensation, which occurs not only because walls are poorly insulated, but also because damp air without a natural escape route condenses on all cold surfaces.

One important contemporary detail to have emerged in the last ten years as a functional heating system and stolid focal point is the kitchen range.

6

9

7

8

Central-heating cookers or ranges, which have been regarded as standard equipment in French, Swiss and German farmhouses for a century, have been updated to heat back boilers that hold water for baths, and pump it around a system of radiators extensive enough for the requirements of a four-bedroom home. You no longer need a farmhouse, and a coal bin or a woodshed, to support one of these ranges, since modern ones can happily run on oil, gas or electricity.

Solid fuel, for years in the doldrums, has received better press, especially

7 The hexagonal-shaped "Brooklyn" from Thermocet runs on natural or propane gas to give a coal-fire effect when viewed through the angled safety-glass front.

8 Thermocet's handsome "Elite Focus" free-standing stove combines a pressed steel canopy and hearth unit with an "Elite 7000" Prima convector, with flame effect. It runs on natural or propane gas to give a 4.8kW output.

9 Sited on a ceramic tiled hearth, the stainless steel coal-burning stove becomes the focal point of David Wild's interior.

HEATING

1 A prismatic wall fitting in fireproof glass, the "Visiofocus 900" by Atelier Dominique features a completely visible hearth that slots into a space 36 inches high and 39 inches wide.

2 "Leina," a stylish set of stainless steel firetongs designed by Pep Bonet for Alessi, brings state-of-the-art accessorizing to the formerly much-neglected hearth.

since the larger ash cans need emptying only once a week. Also, smokeless fuels and modern fireplaces get fires burning quicker, and the industry has poured money into designs that take advantage of these innovations to ensure that once more fireplaces are burning brightly as focal points in modern rooms.

One of the great advantages of central heating is that it freed the home from electric heaters, wood-burning stoves and gas fires, and all the consequent cords and clutter needed to fuel and tend the system. Remarkably realistic gas-log and gas-coal fires have made many of the accessories for the fire obsolete, yet designers still tackle the task of welding weird shapes for grates, fender stools, log holders and fire doors for those contemporary homes where coal is still king.

As architects try to reconcile themselves to the battery of equipment that central heating requires, perversely they still choose the unimaginative corrugated radiators. These giant industrial cylinders are the old war-horses of an ancient regime, yet they seem infinitely preferred for their unrelenting presence than the newer, slimmer, pared-down versions in plain white. Thermostatic controls on every radiator make heat output adjustable and, in larger houses, the radiator circuits for each floor are separated so that the thermostat and timer controls operate independently. The flat-faced designs that avoid the clumsy joints with pipe

3 Marble fire surrounds usually follow traditional patterns, but this one breaks the mold. And the unusual effect is enhanced by the halved ziggurats in glass and travertine on the mantel.

4 The "Dovre 2000" fireplace system incorporates folding glass doors which can be closed to allow wood or solid fuel to burn safely and economically overnight.

5 The inglenook fireplace dates back to Tudor times and incorporated a seat or bench beside or within the chimney breast. This contemporary version by architect Frank Fitzgibbons provides ample seating (and reading material) on a zig-zagging platform.

8 Elgin and Hall's reproduction of a Louis XV fluted pedestal, negra marble fire surround – the "Louis Petite"– is proof that period pieces can be dramatic in a modern setting. Originally conceived for Louis' state rooms, this is one of the most enduring of all fire surround designs.

9 "Tito Lucifer" fire-dogs are a striking feature of the fireplaces designed by Philippe Starck for the Royalton Hotel, New York. Their classic horn shape became Starck's *leitmotif* throughout the Royalton project. They have been put into production by OWO.

10 Starck's designs for the Royalton are a fine example of how traditional methods of heating can be successfully integrated into a modern interior.

9

8

6 In an interior combining curves and right angles, the unusual corner viewing window to the firebox has been cleverly accentuated by a semi-circular sweep of marble below the hearth.

7 The traditional combination of built-in hearth and flue, decorative mantelpiece of wood, brick, stone or marble, and overmantel mirror above, is given a stylish modern twist by Lighthouse Interiors. Flanking light-box columns augment the blaze in the hearth and refract light into the room – an effect accentuated by the glass shelf above.

7

connections at their bottom edge, the Swiss Zehnder ladder towel radiators and the adventurous models with curvaceous pipes in the shape of a giant X are some of the flamboyant newcomers to the radiator scene.

Many architects still cling to the belief that radiators are best placed beneath windows, since the cold night air is counteracted by the warm air rising from the radiators. Just as fireplaces are best positioned centrally, so, too, should radiators be placed around the internal walls. Their form and color can then be used to decorative effect. After all, period-piece restorers have traditionally been hard put to cut out of their scheme the essential central-heating radiator, and instead camouflage it behind ridiculous trellis frames. So why not draw attention to the hearth and heart of the modern building? 10

1 Frank Fitzgibbons makes an architectural feature out of a necessity with a scarlet exterior chimney flue dramatically visible through the glazing above the fireplace.

2 The Hursley fireplace from Dimplex incorporates an electric, real flame effect "Optiflame" heater, compatible with six other designs from their range.

3 An elegant *pare feu* (firescreen) from Avant Scene's "Terrazzo" range. It co-ordinates with the tongs and poker illustrated in picture **7**.

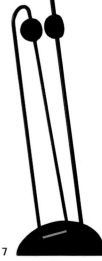

4 The Platonic Fireplace Company's gas-fired "Socrates" incorporates ceramic "Geologs" and variable flame controls.

5 Fires that draw well depend as much upon the shape of the design as the convection of the flue behind. Philip Hearsey's handsome stone-surround fireplace incorporates a spacious hearth and an appropriately generous storage recess for logs.

6 Designer Philip Hearsey, working with blacksmith Peter Smith, often uses salvaged metal – specifically chosen for its "inimitable" naturally worn and weathered surface texture – to create the individual firebacks, hoods, tools and fire-baskets in his "Radnor" range.

7 "Pince" and "Soufflet" (tongs and poker), are from Avant Scene's "Terrazzo" range, which was created in a "new spirit to present the objects and furniture of young designers and sculptors."

Lighting

Technological innovation has moved the concept of lighting a long way from the point where lights were no more than openings between the mullions of a window. The first electric lights were modeled on, or converted from, gas lamps or candle holders. Even today, many light fixtures still show their origin in the chandelier or candlestick. By the 1970s an alternative had reached the mass market—batteries of spotlights marshaled on tracks across the ceiling. However, the heat and size of tungsten bulbs proved to be a drawback for designers.

Today, electricity is seen by many as the most potent force in design and architecture. The invention of low-voltage lights, first called "sealed reflector lamps," in 1972, brought about a revolution in lighting design because this new system miniaturized the source, while giving it tighter optical control. The new generation of low-voltage tungsten or metal-halide lights are capable of bathing a wall in light, highlighting any area, and washing objects in warm

Previous page Crystal horn-shaped lights, "Lucefair," designed by Philippe Starck for the Royalton Hotel, New York, are available for the domestic market from Flos.
1 Stephan Copeland's gooseneck "Tango" table lamp in aluminum, houses a single 50W 12V quartz-halogen bulb.
2 De Pas, D'Urbino and Lomazzi's ceiling lamp, "Nessie," in lacquered or anodized metal for Stilnovo houses five dichroic bulbs.
3 Alberto Fraser designed "Nastro" for Stilnovo. Multicolored computer straps support the halogen head, and a friendly "mouse" is the transformer and switch.

4 Battened onto the scaffolded, galleried floor in Sir Richard Rogers' home are two enormous theatrical lights, with flaps and reflectors to harness the beams. No single light source is better than another—it depends on the functions and positioning of the lamps.

1

2

3

4

5 In this apartment designed by Munkenbeck & Marshall, a pool of opaque light is beamed down from the ceiling. This low-level lighting is reinforced with a ring of low-voltage downlights, their transformers hidden in the ceiling, and their small, intense beams diffused by the more general, centrally positioned light.

5

6 A modern classic fixture from Woka Lamps' Art Collection series. "Spectrum" is made in a contemporary material – acrylic glass – and was designed by Mathias Pfeffer.

6   7

7 Oil lamp and candlestick imagery for lamps prevailed until the 1920s, when Mario Fortuny first housed a 500W bulb in a photographer's cast-iron studio fixture. It is still made today by Ecart International.

8 "Titania" from Luceplan suspends a halogen bulb from steel cables. It is screened by an elliptical shade that changes color according to rib-like filters. Designers are Alberto Meda and Paolo Rizzato.

8

LIGHTING

1 Dean Wang installed a line of uplights in the floor to wash the wall in light where it was most needed. The lights are sealed with shatter-proof glass.

2 A lighting layout for concealed or recessed fixtures has to be planned by an architect or electrician ahead of decoration.

3 Most concealed and recessed fixtures are inflexibly positioned in the ceiling or floor. So iGuzzini's development of an adjustable downlight whose beam can swivel is an innovative approach. The "Pixel" model, which is available in two sizes, uses different types of lamp.

3

4 & 5 "I hate ceiling lights," says architect John Pawson, who always uses floor lights fitted with tungsten-halogen sources for an intense white beam from small fixtures. The transformer that converts the mains voltage is concealed under the oak floorboards.

5

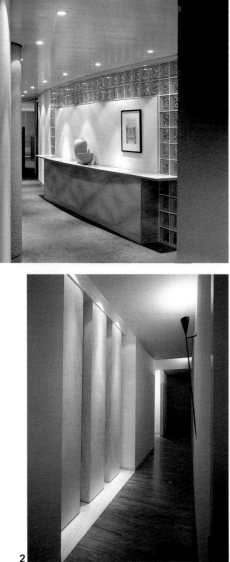

1

2

4

6 "Myriad" low-voltage downlights from Concord now include a dichroic version accepting "True-Aim" sealed-beam lamps.

6

7

7 "Equinox," Concord's versatile range of cone downlights, includes the recently developed elliptical metal-halide 100W lamp.

8 Ceilingward glances will spot the unobtrusive ring frame harnessing the white light of tungsten halogen in Concord's "Chorus."

golden or silvery light, depending on the reflector being used.

Contemporary lighting systems can also help to structurally enhance an interior. For example, an architect can isolate **8** solid walls of storage shelving by bathing the wall above and below the system with light from the new miniaturized fluorescent tubes. Slimmed down by Philips for use in supermarkets, these tubes are capable of creating an icy white light that, concealed behind battens, floods the wall with brightness and thus helps to reduce the visual impact of the massed volume of a library of shelves.

Lighting design is a question of balance between the quality of light and of shadows. Too much light is too obvious —diffusion, not glare, is the object. So it is hardly surprising that the dramatic spotlit effects in schemes by architects such as Philippe Starck use the same overhead system as theater designers – banked spotlights. From compact fluorescents to metal halides, from incandescent to low-voltage halogen, phosphor and high-pressure discharge lamps, spotlight fixtures are strung up

9 Lighting can brighten or soften, dramatize or minimize. In a darker room, reflective light is reduced, so there are usually more light sources to compensate.

9

10 Fixtures are less important than the quality of light they shed, as these unobtrusive wall and ceiling lights from the architectural team of Stanton Williams for the Issey Miyake shop highlight.

11 Ideas borrowed from commercial fixtures have validity at home, just as theatrical lenses and beams are now making their way into domestic fixtures. Overhead background lighting will wash a wall with light. **10**

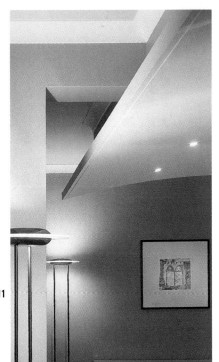

11

1 The miniaturization of light sources has encouraged the design of playful fixtures in which to house them – unlike the earnest track systems of 20 years ago. This record store is highlighted by neo-baroque spots suspended from tentacled arms over the ceiling.

4 Concord's lighting concept, "Infinite," by Woodgate and Lawrence extends the frontiers of conventional track systems. Components screw together, doing away with visible wiring from the transformer.

5 With "Infinite" (see picture **4**), because spotlights can be attached above and below the track or, using the extension power rods, at a distance from the track, unusual features are easy to highlight.

2 Like its namesake, the "Shuttle" spotlight for iGuzzini by Bruno Gecchelin sheds sections and casings as required. With this system, there are different shields and reflectors that fit onto a cylinder that houses 22 varieties of lamp. With different accessories, the beam becomes a thread, a blade or a sea of light.

3 Projector lights by Erco, from the "Emanon" range, which was developed with Roy Fleetwood. They are high-performance units that are characterized by multiple light, color and projection effects, which all reflect the growing domestic interest in theatrical lighting.

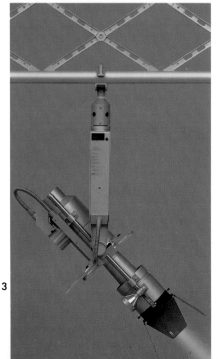

alongside each other, with shields, reflectors and colored glass disks to change angle and widen or color the beam of light. Fresnel lenses, named after the French physicist Fresnel, soften the edges of shafts of light on these technical lighting systems. (They were originally designed for showrooms and exhibitions, but made the crossover into the home.)

The range and complexity of contemporary lighting is daunting to the non-professional – wonderful effects can be achieved, but often not without specialist advice, as well as an electrician's help. For example, you can create a ceiling studded with prismatic light by building in a selection of downlights – recessed tungsten downlights and eyeball spotlights. Not unexpectedly, this technical talk serves to take the medium further away from the amateur,

6 A variety of spot-lights is available for Concord's "Infinite," including a 20W capsule (smaller unit) and a 50W capsule (larger unit). The track and spotlights are available in either black or white.

8

7 Positioned above steel storage units, powerful spotlights beam light into architect John Young's apartment. On the desk, the low-voltage task light is made by Artemide and is entitled "Berenice."

6

9

8 & 9 Two views of the uncompromisingly stylish "Tijuca" from the talented designer Ingo Maurer, who says: "My idea was to create a light that flies like a bird. A light that dances, glides, tilts, balances, rotates." Its main innovative feature is the freely sliding ring connecting the lighting elements to the cables. The ring conducts the current and makes it possible to turn the lighting element through 360° and to move it up or down through 140°.

but it is worth seeking out expert advice or literature because good lighting is the most unobtrusive and effective detail you can bring into your home. However, partly as a result of its technical mysteries, lighting is the most undervalued commodity in the contemporary interior. No one visiting the latest apartment makeover in a gloomy New York brownstone would realize how dingy and dark and Dickensian that space would seem to be without contemporary lighting.

What an advance for the domestic interior designer to have such flexibility at home. Instead of the clumsy incandescent bulb, ubiquitously shaded in paper or silk, there are downlights and uplights to build into the scheme, and an extensive selection of original table lamps for specific tasks. Beamed up – or down – these newly poised and angled lights supply general background and task lighting.

10 Whenever a person moves within an 8-feet radius of the infrared detector built into the "Sensa" light, it switches itself on. Photocells gauge the level of natural light and automatically adjust light output by 25 to 100 percent in direct response to ambient daylight. A world first for Thorn.

10

11 The aptly named "Expanded Line Kit" from the brilliant design duo of Perry King and Santiago Miranda for Arteluce. Different halogen heads –"Lucy," "Alma," "Tor" and "Ra"– fit low-voltage ceiling roses. The inventive shapes and prismatic reflectors in this range are matched by detailed accent color designed to catch the light.

11

109

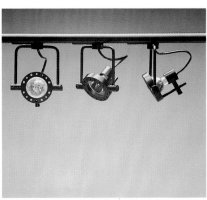

1 Wall-mounted spots are the modern equivalent of the old picture light, which casts a localized beam onto a single image. Architect Peter Wilson has chosen a task light shaped like a downlight to illuminate modern furniture.

Low-voltage systems brought light, quite literally, to the architect's fingertips, since low-voltage light (as its name implies) operates on an electrical supply of 12 volts or less. The German lighting designer Ingo Maurer took advantage of this by hanging a collection of birdlike, low-voltage lights on electrical wires strung across the room like a trapeze. "Adjustable or hanging elements create a jungle of light that dances, glides, tilts, balances and rotates and, above all, provides a clear and precise light by which to work, read or dream," he says about his "YaYa HoHo" system, one of the most popular lights of the 1980s.

Technological advances have affected that most traditional, and popular, of fixtures, the table lamp. The new generation of table lamps is made from

2 Tightly controlled beams of low-energy light in Candela's "Micron" range vary from a gentle 20W floodlight to a penetrating 75W spotlight, housed in a system.

3 The adaptable "Shuttle" spotlight by Bruno Gecchelin for iGuzzini (see picture **2**, page 108), shown with a different configuration of casings and reflector accessories.

4 "Futura" from Garcia Garay, designed by J. A. Garcia Garay, is a family of lamps which features two aluminum shades that move through a full 360° to open or shut, as well as to vary the angle of the light.

5 All in a row – the wall lights from Tebong are shielded by reflector shades on trifid-like angular arms.

6 & 7 Four new spot-lights, three of them using dichroic bulbs and a monophase track, are iGuzzini's latest minispots, two of which are pictured here. "Disc," designed by Pasquale Ajello (above left), and "Wing," designed by Bruno Gecchelin (above right), both use low-energy 50W 12V bulbs and the spots can be either fitted to a "Limelight" ceiling track or wall-mounted on curved rods. All fixtures have a joint that enables power to be delivered through a 360° vertical and horizontal swing.

Shape Memory Alloy, more commonly used in orthodontics and auto bumpers, since the alloy has a memory that responds to heat. For example, a horse-shoe shape cut from the metal and crumpled into a corkscrew, when warmed will return to its original shape. So a lotus petal of a light will, when warmed up as the light burns within a tightly closed bud, gradually unfurl. Other than the visual senses are challenged too; Kreon's inventive lights diffuse scent as the light warms, working on the principle that with dichroic low-voltage systems, the source passes heat backward rather than in the path of light, thus scenting the room.

As lighting technology has become increasingly flexible and responsive, the ability of lights to accentuate is being pushed to new limits by designers. Two

8 "Poe" from Giugiaro Design, made by Lucitalia, is a low-voltage system for ceilings and walls. Lamps are fully adjustable on support arms and electrical circuits allow full rotation.

9 "Contacto" by Belux is a contact plug system for halogen lamps, in which 125 combinations can be created out of 18 elements. The Jurgen Medeback design can be wall-mounted or set on lighting tracks.

10 "Duo" is a low-voltage lamp designed by Erwin Egli, systemized by Diefo Bally for Belux. Two individual lamp elements, with a 100V transformer fitted to a ceiling strip, form a single unit designed to be suspended over a table. Both lamp elements move up and down on a system of chrome-plated counterweights, and opal and blue glass contribute strongly to its elegant presentation.

11 & 12 Spotlights positioned on beams, rather than attached to the more usual lighting tracks, help to demonstrate the flexibility of a system of spotlighting that here has low-voltage transformers built into neat, cylindrical fixtures.

1 The quality of light emitted, the controlled direction of the halogen beam and the splendid formality of this lamp, the "P-1170" by Estiluz, meet the description "classical."

2 "L'Escala" by Estudi Blanc for Metalarte is a metalic floor lamp with an adjustable diffuser and a dimmer control switch on the wiring.

4 The "Bi-Arp" lamp, by Enrico Bona for Skipper Pollux, has a base and stem in transparent plexiglass and a sanded Pyrex glass reflector.

3 "Mantide" by Mauro Canfori for Oluce inclines gracefully on a slender stem, which supports a widened bowl that pools the halogen beam.

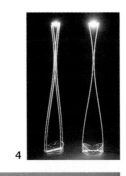

5 The overhanging, pendulous floor light that enshrines the lamp source in a large, shaded fixture makes a useful task light in this room by John Pawson, who tries to avoid ceiling lights in his interiors.

6 "Maja" by Sergi Devesa for Metalarte uses indirect halogen light on top of a swiveling support, which is metalicized graphite gray and chrome-plated.

Spaniards, Bigas and Sant (see page 28), have produced an aluminum molding which lights a lamp wherever one is clipped in, and is ideal for stairs or to illuminate pictures. And furniture makers outline features with built-in lights and create backlit panels in storage systems; for example, a beveled glass edge on a shelf will have a fine line of light running along it. The latest trend is to use metal-halide discharge lamps, which are brighter yet cooler than dichroic low-voltage bulbs.

As designers explore shape, the result is less a light show of dazzling theatricality than a collection of new lights assembled with the express notion that "light can evoke fantasy and fable, create effects and get involved in shadow play," as the organizers of Euroluce, the lighting industry's international lighting fair, claim.

8 "Victory" by De Pas, D'Urbino and Lomazzi is a floor or extendable wall lamp in lacquered metal with a porcelain diffuser to soften the 300W halogen bulb. On a lacquered metal structure, it is made by Stilnovo.

9 Coveted design award Compasso d'Oro has been won on several occasions by designer Rodolpho Bonetto, whose "Eviter" floor light uses a diffuser of pressed, satin-etched glass, made by Luci.

7 "Sinclina" is an inclined lamp by Estudi Blanc for Metalarte. Its height can be adjusted by lowering the light on its anodized silver or black column.

10 Unusually, "Penombra" by Antoni Flores for Gargot uses low-energy fluorescent tubes and a reflector within its slender aluminum body. It is available in either a matte-anodized or a matte-gold finish, and stands on a cast-aluminum base.

16 This free-standing lamp, "Aeto," is by Fabio Lombardo for Flos. It is nearly 6.5 feet tall and uses a single 450W halogen bulb.

12 Halogen bulbs on free-standing uplights will throw a strong wash of light up to the ceiling. Uplights such as this, used by architect David Wild, need to be set above eye level to avoid glare from the bulbs.

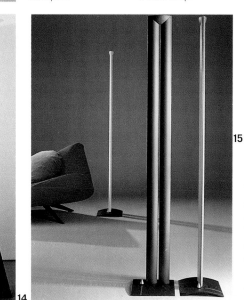

13 Free-standing lights can be moved to where the light is most needed. Depending on the shade and reflectors, they can be either up- or downlights, like the "Berenice" by Luceplan.

14 "Stele" by Jurgen Medeback for Belux offers indirect lighting on a pair of slender columns that are so attenuated they make the piece more sculptural than a mere lamp.

11 A diffused-lighting halogen lamp, "Sake," by Paolo and Marco Piva for Stilnovo, is available as a floor or wall lamp in anthracite, metalic blue or green. It has a lacquered, aluminum-molded body and a sand-blasted diffuser.

15 Like Santiago Calatrava's architecture, the "Montjuic" for Artemide appears to defy the laws of gravity. The painted-fiber, diagonal support for the tubular halogen lamp neatly conceals the cord.

1 Post-modernist architect Michael Graves designed a series of lamps for Baldinger Architectural Lighting. His "Urbino" lantern, made of brass and white opal acrylic, is an imposing 35 inches high.

3 The "Firenze" wall sconce from Michael Graves, manufactured by Baldinger Architectural Lighting is made of brass and white opal acrylic.

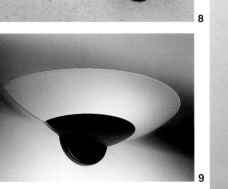

2 Soft polyurethane is used by Fabian for "Gum" 705D07 wall lamp, available with interchangeable color spots.

8 The "Aramis" by Gourdon and Brux for Luxo has a satinated glass diffuser. It takes a 300W halogen or 70W metal halide bulb (shown here) with column to hold the ignitor and capacitor.

9 "Estiluz" A1133 halogen wall light by Leonardo Marelli. It uses a 220W halogen bar behind a satin glass shade held in a disk that can be black pearlized or gold finished.

4 "Eco" by Giugiaro Design for Luci has a swiveling cone-shaped reflector in stove-enameled metal. It is available in many colors and holds a single 250W linear-halogen bulb.

5 & 6 Best of Brass stock a wide range of switches that gives a conventional frame to a plain, unadorned switch plate. And from Clipsal, electrical, shave, TV and telephone outlets in impact-resistant polycarbonate.

7 "Bisbi" by Achille Castiglioni is a wall light with a ceramic outlet and a die-cast aluminum rotating reflector, from Flos. A twist of the ring changes it from uplight to wall-washer.

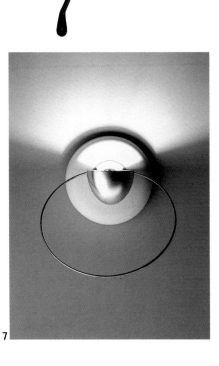

10 "Vulcanos" by Sergi Devesa for Metalarte is a wall bracket that can be fitted to the ceiling. It has a swiveling metal arm and a matte, tempered glass diffuser to shield the low-energy, 15W halogen light bulb.

13 Breaking out of the Murano glass mold to create enlightened fixtures, Barovier and Toso took the design of Giusto Toso and created a range of floor, wall and ceiling lights called "Flu."

13

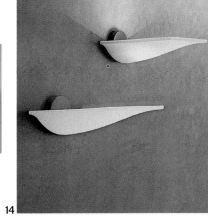

14

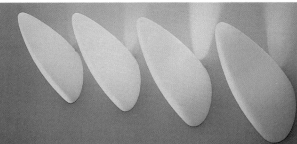

15

14 A wall-mounted light, the "Evipar" by designer Rodolgo Bonetto, houses a 500W linear halogen bulb in a stove-enameled support. It is available in a range of different colors, with a diffuser in acid-etched, pressed glass, and is produced by Lucitalia.

15 Stilnovo's "Victory" by de Pas, D'Urbino and Lomazzi is of lacquered metal with a porcelain diffuser. The floor-standing version of this light is shown on page 112 (picture **8**).

16

17 The "Malibu" follows maestro Ettore Sottsass' enthusiasm for place-naming his designs. His wall light for Stilnovo is in white or anodized aluminum with a lacquered metal body and a glass diffuser that houses a single 60W bulb.

18 "Pleak" designed by Nemo and made by Tebong gracefully supports on a ledge this 200W pencil-slim linear halogen lamp on its epoxyated steel book frame.

16 The horn-shaped light became Philippe Starck's *leitmotif* in the New York Royalton. Each of the 30-40 doors in that hotel's lobby supports above it a crystal light fixture like the "Lucefair," subsequently put into production by Flos.

17

11

18

11 Architects Studio Epton had to work with lights bought by their clients. By flooding the room with natural light, these simple spots were sufficient.

12 "Trybeca" by Bernhard Dessecker shields two halogen bulbs. The wall light can move up or down and swivel on its adjustable fixture.

12

19

19 A hinged flap like a torch flips the light head back or swivels it on this "Land" wall light, designed by architect Robert Pamio for Leucos. It can also be ceiling-mounted, and is equipped with two movements that rotate the structure on its axis through 360°, and also allows just the head to rotate on a hinge through 90°. This freedom of movement gives either directional control of the beam or a more generalized light effect.

20 Ingo Maurer extends his concept of light in motion with the bird-like "Eclipse-elipse," which hovers on the wall on touch-sensitive cords and controls that do away with traditional wiring and switches. The light holds a 50W bulb with a swiveling mirror to reflect and direct light.

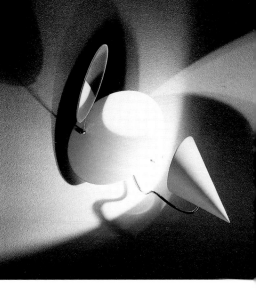

20

115

1 "Torino" ceiling fixtures from the Michael Graves collection by Baldinger Architectural Lighting in brass with white opal octagonal glass.

2 Woka's 1032 "Mini" by Walter Schmögner in brass with metalic green details holds eight 12V halogen spots on spider-like supports.

3 A customized design by Michael Graves for a pendant fixture. It re-creates the American Ranch-type spoked wheel concept and has three candelabraed torch lights.

1

2

3

4 The "Verona" lamp from the Michael Graves collection, by Baldinger, is a recessed ceiling fixture with trim in antique brass holding the white opal, conical-shaped glass shield.

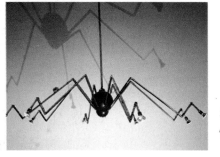

4

7 "Bergamo" chandelier from the Michael Graves collection for Baldinger, shown in antique brass. Other finishes and customized heights available.

5 World-famous modernist architect Cini Boeri, working with Murano glass, brings craftsmanship to a functional form with "Feltro."

5

8

6 "Lucia" is designed by architect Cini Boeri, who manages to blend craft skills, age-old Murano glass and good functional design.

6

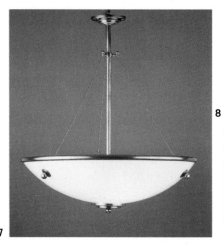

7

8 "Spilla" designed by Luciano Pasgani for Arteluce is a ceiling light with a 200W halogen bulb, backlit by a pressed and etched-glass diffuser.

9 When the "Atena," by Ezio Didone for Arteluce, is seen from below, a star-burst of light appears in the conical glass diffuser, which is held either by a matte-gray enameled reflector or by a sanded glass disk colored opalescent pink, blue, white or green.

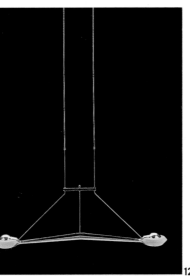

10 "Nebula" by Jordi Vilardell for Gargot houses a 500W halogen lamp in a matte, metalic-gray disk.

11 Thomas Edison's incandescent light is here invoked by Valerio Sacchetti for Sirrah in a lamp holder entitled "Edison 45."

13 & 14 Pendants that are adjustable make useful counter or dining-table illuminations. The "Gavina" (see in detail below right) by Josep Llusca for Blauet is extendable, with a chrome-plated stick to adjust the height of two crystal lampshades shielding either 50W or 75W halogen lamps.

12 Lovegrove and Brown designed the "Bab-ilis" metal ceiling light for Metalarte. Its pressed-glass diffuser shields a 100W bulb.

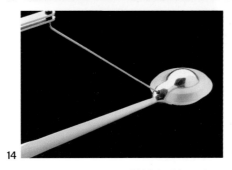

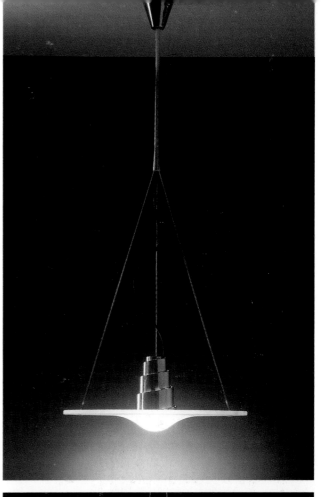

15 Michael Graves' selfconscious emulation of floral forms reverts to Art Nouveau, but the geometry of this pendulous pendant is postmodernist rather than organic.

16 "Futura," designed by J. A. Garcia Garay, is equipped with two aluminum shades that open and shut, and revolve 360° around the 500W bulb.

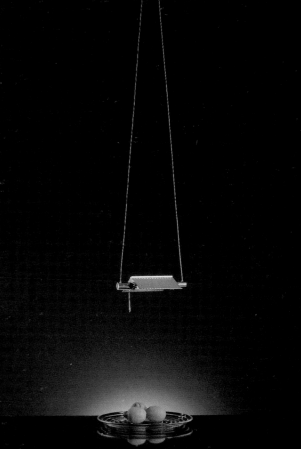

1 & 2 Murano glass from Venice has been collected for centuries, and Foscarini pride themselves on focusing on functionality as well as esthetics with their range of lights, "Colora," designed by Vecchiato and Ricci.

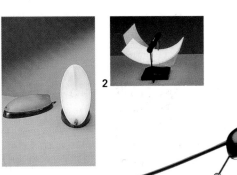

1

2

3 "Calder" is a halogen lamp designed by Enric Ranch for Metalarte as a desk light with dimmer switch. It stands nearly 16 inches high, with a reach of 36 inches.

3

4 "Vaticana," designed by Josep Llusca for Metalarte, is a metalic portable table lamp. It has a dimmer switch incorporated into its base and a Pergacel winged shade set into the graphite-gray cone.

4

10 The "Pap" floor lamp is a faithful copy of the original, designed in 1923 by Gyula Pap. Plate glass is connected by a nickel-plated tubular unit to a black-lacquered iron baseplate.

5 If it were necessary to define an elementary solution for task lighting, it would probably be similar to this small table light, "Bluebird," by Jorge Pensi for Belux.

7 A sober, matte-black design from Samuel Ribet called "Heron," for Stilnovo, houses a 50W 12V halogen bulb in lacquered metal. The lighting arm is adjustable.

5

6 A thin, rod-like support holds a dichroic halogen bulb and reflector in Shiro Kuramata's original lamp called "Hydrogen Dream." The light was designed in 1988.

6

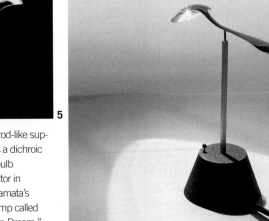

7

8 From designer Sergi Devesa for Metalarte comes "Zen." This brushed-aluminum table light stands 6.5 inches high and will accommodate a single bulb up to a maximum output of 25W.

9 Like a "Metronome" in name and characteristics, J. Garcia Garay's table lamp moves side to side for use as a reading lamp, while from inside the sand-blasted crystal shade, a gentle light permeates the room.

9

11 F. Fabbian and F. lli created a series of metal-and-glass lights, designed by G.P. Derai, called "Master," "Major," "Big" and, shown here, "Senior." There is also a scaled-down "Junior."

10

11

12 & 13 In a conversion of a 19th-century terrace house, Jan Kaplicky of Future Systems placed banks of switches in the aluminum sheets that line the false floor, beneath which pipes and cables run.

17 Woka Lamps' chain-styled bureau light, designed by Udo Maurer, certainly has a presence, and perhaps even an air of menace.

13

14 Philippe Starck's unusual adjustable table lamp, "ARA" for Flos, is turned on and off by grasping the horn-shaped shade. The lamp is chrome-plated cast aluminum.

17

18 Designed by Ferdinand Porsche and Christian Schwamkrug for PAF, "Jazz" folds flat like a handset. When in operation, its two-stage, telescopic arm allows a variety of lighting positions. A dimmer switch is incorporated.

12   14

15 Woka "159" is from a collection designed by Josef Hoffmann and Adolf Loos. This classic series of lamps draws on the past for its inspiration, this one being originally designed in 1925.

16 Mario Barbaglia and Marco Colombo designed the poised "Dove" for PAF. It is an adjustable halogen lamp, with tubular supports in polished black. The base and lighting arm are in matte-black, white, yellow, red or blue.

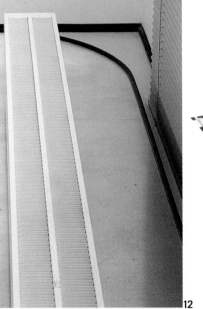

15   16

18

LIGHTING

1 A table lamp leaning forward to cast light upon the page at the required angle is Asahara Sigeaki's "Tokio" for Stilnovo – a 500W 12V halogen light with an adjustable inclination of lacquered metal, and the mekralon reflector holding a built-in transformer.

2 "Lola" by C. Bermudo for Marset stands 22 inches high on a crescent-shaped base.

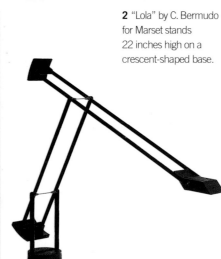

3 "Tizio" by Richard Sapper for Artemide marked in the 1970s the first of the new generation of low-voltage lights. Set on a swiveling piece of scaffolding, the light has become a design icon on contemporary surfaces.

4 "Tolomeo," by Michele de Lucchi and Giancarlo Fassina, stands in Gary Cunningham's conversion of an electricity sub-station conversion. The lamp shows the tension wires that allow the arms to move at a touch.

8 Lampshade makers traditionally use parchment paper, a material seldom seen in modern lighting where glass or metal diffuse the beam. But for Woka's Art Collection, Jörg Wurmitzer has revived "pergament" paper as a reflector for three halogen spots on a brass-and-wood fixture.

5 "Zoom" lives up to its name by elongating its probe-like head, or zigzagging up on its rods out of the way. Patrick Magnin for Arteluce uses either one or two 50W halogen bulbs with rotating reflectors.

6 Inventive creator of "One From the Heart," Ingo Maurer, describes this light as an adjustable bedside lamp, its romantic form made of metal, glass and plastic. It stands 37 inches high.

7 "Hasard" by Ingo Maurer is intentionally industrial with a raw, hand-made base and shade. The light turns, bends, swivels, and stretches to a height of nearly 18 inches and has a 50W halogen bulb.

Storage

2

Previous page
Banks of beech drawers and cupboards, equipped with simple metal D-pulls, provide bedroom storage in a house by David Chipperfield.

1 Frosted glass supports for clear Crown glass shelves with their beveled green edges on aluminum tubes are Andreas Weber's storage solution in an 18th-century apartment.

1

Storage, that boring hold-all, hide-all for so many things that each and every one of us needs to give long-term house room to, is one of the most fickle aspects of modern living. Essentials that had to be stored a century ago would reveal a different lifestyle, different preoccupations – even different uses of leisure time – from those with which we are familiar with today. The products – and their proportions – have changed for a start. The music room no longer houses a piano and wind-up gramophone with its pile of fragile, 78 rpm records. Instead there are the compact disk player and speakers. Even the study or home office, which replaces the library, is now dominated by the computer, monitor, printer and fax and telephone back-up, all housed in their own lightweight, mobile storage systems. How to accommodate the changing technology at the same time as living companionably with your possessions easily at hand is the crux of modern storage.

A decade ago, storage walls of shelves

2 A wall-mounted ziggurat by Duravit offers 18 drawers of varying size for the accumulated trivia of everyday life while freeing valuable floor space in a small room for other use.

3 Made of pear, amaranth and rosewood, Driade's "Eloise" by Antonia Astori is beautifully crafted.

4 Interlubke recognize the need for open shelving in "Duo-tone." Linked with the matching "Cockpit" bureau, it provides easy access to everything from music to tax returns.

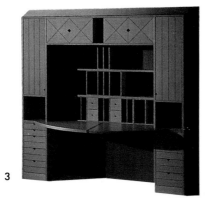

3

4

5 Architect John Pawson demonstrates his belief that space is the most luxurious thing a minimalist can provide. Enormous storage blocks, capable of holding a vast amount of material out of sight, rid the room of unnecessary objects and clutter.

and closet stacked on top of each other seemed to be the answer. They were even known as working walls. Today, the lack of floor space that results from expensively engineered systems of stacking shelves makes these types of system obsolete. Extendable trolleys, lightweight wall runners capable of supporting long spans of shelves, work units with vertebral cord systems to hide the tangle of wires behind every work-efficient electronic system, and sculptural wardrobe accessories such as coatstands and the valet to hold shoes, slacks and ties, all free-standing, represent modern attempts to balance esthetics with practicality.

Not everything these days is designed to be small. Weary of the black-box gadgetry that houses electronic equipment from hi-fi to computers, the new designs for sound systems shape them like giant cellos or tubas. Free-standing, they don't require shelving systems to support them.

For most people, the greatest number of items to be stored is in the bedroom, which is usually dominated by fixtures with sliding doors and/or walk-in

5

6

6 Giant wheels give a fantastic impression of some futuristic, sci-fi airlock system, mounted on four huge sliding units, designed by architect John Young. Inside the steel-paneled closets are easy-access corridors giving onto space sufficient to house acres of domestic clutter.

7

7 Tebong gives an intriguing interpretation to the umbrellas housed in this stand, inverted so that its spokes replicate the shapes of the furled umbrellas within.

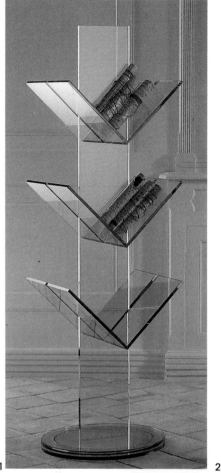

1 Using a base of ball bearings held between two disks of glass, the Tonelli "Cactus" is a free-standing angular bookshelf. A single sheet of clear glass provides support for the V-shaped shelves.

2 Like the "Cactus," Tonelli's "Albero" provides six angular shelves, holding books at 45°. Also resting on a ball-bearing base, the structure of sheet glass creates a zigzag pattern – a geometric extension of "Cactus."

3 Marcello Morandini's imaginative manipulation of geometry, in his free-standing "Corner" shelving for Rosenthal Furniture, is made of five differently sized components to provide a flexible storage unit.

4 The black uniformity with colored edgings of "Corner" (see **3**) makes it both similar and complementary to "Mobile," also by Marcello Morandini for Rosenthal.

5 Pruning back the bulk and paring down describe architect Eva Jiricna's free-hanging shelving design. Thick sheet glass rests on small stoppers attached to thin steel wires hanging from a girder-like support bolted securely to the wall. Maximum storage space is provided without blocking any sight lines.

10 The all-glass, wall-mounted library from Marais, the "MB 1500," is made of five half-moon-shaped glass shelves within a transparent frame.
11 This system of fixed shelving was designed by Munkenbeck & Marshall. The custom-built storage is tall and deep enough for more than just books. Frosted glass wrapped around cylindrical wall fittings provides stable, but non-adjustable, shelving.

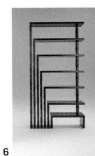

6

7

8

6, 7, 8 Archille Castiglioni's "Joy" table for Zanotta extends from two horizontal platforms into seven, pivoting from a central column, like a flight of stairs, or acts as a multi-level storage unit.
9 Before the 1980s, glass could not be cut into the exacting shapes demanded by modern storage systems. Then thc laser cutter arrived, allowing safety glass to be cut into the shapes seen here, in "Scenario" by Tonelli.

closets. In the contemporary apartment, some rooms can be so small that it becomes simpler by far to hang clothes on the types of open rails favored by shop and store fitters, thereby converting a single bedroom to a storage system. Unconventional storage solutions come from designers who use fitters' furniture, from fashion store swing rails to garage mechanics' tool-box trolleys. Extendable arms used with hospital beds have been redeployed as domestic nightstands so that the television, telephone or books can be readily brought to hand. In a child's room, the bed is often elevated above the closet space, with a ladder ascent and an enclosing safety rail.

"Honey, I Shrunk the Kids" is the title of a popular movie of the late 1980s, and while the advantages of making people Lilliputian are obvious, the reality is that more and more people are occupying smaller and smaller living spaces. In every case, the answer to storage is to draw up a list of your priorities. There is no one answer because everybody's list will differ. Modern systems usually give you somewhere to store the single fold-up bed when it is not required by sliding it into a recess. Such features as corner

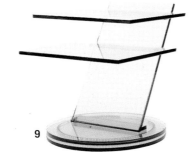

9

12

12 From Fucina, part of the Skipper group, comes the "Cidonio" bookshelf in scogliera gray marble, designed by Afra and Tobia Scarpa.

11

STORAGE

1 Landing-pad feet connect the new Enea "Naos" aluminum storage unit, designed by Gabriel Teixidó, to its shelves, which can be fixed to the ceiling, wall or floor.

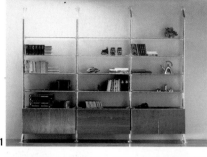

2 & 3 Designed for Driade's modular "Oikos" system by Antonia Astori, "Cubo" (above left) consists of modules, each containing six boxes. In the same system is the slimline "Favo" for the small room (above right).

4 The three-tiered bridge of the versatile "Naos" system is by Teixidó.

5 Tecta's "S 69" system consists of five curvaceous black and blue panels connected by three colored boxes and a drawer.

6 These metal storage frames, as roundly folded as fabric yet firm in their support, were designed by architect Eva Jiricna.

carousels or lazy susan racks, stacking shoe racks, containers for storing clothes, and suitcases, in the hard-to-get-at upper parts, are revealed behind space-saving sliding doors. Built-in lighting is also usually a feature.

Fashionable hanging systems are revealed in the bedroom with the new sculptural furniture designed to hold clothing draped over it. Lord Snowdon's design now in production, entitled "Weekend Wardrobe," looks like a wooden ladder, the top rung supporting a slanted mirror, and each of the other rungs holding slacks and ties. Two broad, leather straps are provided to support shallow pouches large enough for several shirts and, at the base, shoes. De Pas, d'Urbino and Lomazzi designed for the Italian company Zanotta a teepee of clustered sticks, each one notched to hold an article of clothing; a

7

9

8

7 This central storage facility by architect Franklin D. Israel usefully combines an artwork display area on one side and adjustable shelving for records or a hi-fi system on the other.

8 The blue central column of Interlubke's ziggurat consists of two cupboards and four drawers, flanked on the left by two glass cabinets and, on the right, by five open shelves for easy access to often used objects, such as the stereo.

telescopic tensile-steel arc from Spanish Disform adjusts to bow beneath ceiling and floor, with adjustable knobs sliding up and down the bowed rods to hold whatever is required; even the low-cost retail furnishing group from Sweden, Ikea, sells in its worldwide outlets sculptural male and female wire outlines, life-sized, for you to cover up with clothing.

These sculptural forms are a mobile, though less-substantial, alternative to furniture lined up against the walls, which tends to become part of the fabric of the house. Bedrooms in modern houses are rarely larger than approximately 12 feet by 10 feet, which means that floor space is limited to just one wall dedicated to built-in closets or cupboards, or else the individual pieces that literally come out of the closet. A free-standing chest of drawers takes up 12

10

11

9 Architect Eva Jiricna designed these thick glass shelves on metal cylinders to provide spacious wall-to-wall storage. The television is supported on a pivoting metal bracket.
10 Wire mesh, spiky feet and a small flag give this bookcase by J. Borris a medieval look.
11 The five shelves and the frame of the Marais "Mec 500" system simply rest casually unsupported against the wall.
12 Enea's wall-to-wall design has open shelves that are fixed to extruded aluminum clamps by non-skid polyethylene disks. These clamps are attached to side channels within the metal stanchions so that shelves can be fixed at any height.

127

1

1 A home library of books can be housed in this capacious shelving unit from Interlubke. It contains 32 storage boxes and six drawers on the central column of five.

2 Interlubke's long closet system provides a "working wall" for clothes storage. This modular system with hinged doors is both smart and practical, shown here in a combination of cupboards and drawers in both natural wood and white lacquer.

8 Architect David Wild has gained valuable additional storage areas in his own house by using normally inaccessible staircase space, with paneled wood closets and shelves reachable from the stairs above by stretching out over the railing.

2

3

3, 4 & 5 Interlubke's highly versatile freestanding TV/VCR bar, "Duo-center," designed by Siegried Bensinger, rotates through 360° on its central pole. Its design makes it suitable for private living space, but it could be successfully used in an office as well. Other views of the "Duo-center" reveal perforated mesh back panels to ventilate the TV compartment, and a drawer beneath the VCR shelf for storing tapes.

5

6

6 Marshall Erdman's frameless "Techline" closet system is predrilled to receive a variety of hinges, glides or shelf supports. Its laminated case is surrounded by PVC, eased to a soft radius.

7 Built around a doorway, Arc Linea's "Odeon" by designer Carlo Bartoli, permits easy access from both sides of the wall. It is available in black- or white-lacquered Italian walnut.

4

7

8

less overall space but requires more free space in front of it so that you can pull out the drawers. The façade of each built-in bedroom depends on closet doors, and such a line-up determines the style of the room – hence the contemporary fashion for paint finishes on cheap wood veneers.

Storage needs vary within each household. A professional designer will ask his or her client a range of questions in order to determine the best storage configuration. For example, a kitchen planner will ask the following: How many meals do you prepare a day? What sort of food do you like? How much cooking equipment do you use? How many sets of dishes do you own? Do you eat in a separate dining room with its own storage facilities? The professional person living alone who owns a microwave and small freezer box probably needs very

9 The closets in this house, designed by architects Gwathmey Siegel cleverly follow the contours of this unusual room to form a barrier between the living area and the glass-encased hollow shaft onto the floor above. Logs for the fire are stored in the single-piece concrete box at the end of the unit.
10 This unit is a custom-built design by David Chipperfield. Eight cherrywood drawers of increasing size run the length of the unit. Recessed in the unit, a TV is on a sliding drawer. Two high closets provide additional storage for material not often needed.

little space for canned or dried goods and just a window box for herbs. The large family kitchen with a gas-fired range and a walk-in pantry clearly needs storage space for heavyweight cast-iron cooking pots, a dishwasher, dishes, and space for basic foodstuffs bought in bulk. Glasses, utensils and china all need storage space, sensibly hidden behind cabinet doors or on open display.

Ease of access, with the heavier objects on a lower level and objects in constant use in front, encourages professional cooks to hang their utensils and other equipment on open hooks above the work-tops or counters. Versatile, ventilated pantry cabinets and smaller cabinets with wire baskets for vegetables, bread or pastries are also available.

Storage in the main living area is more exacting, less specific. Here, friends are entertained, television is watched, the VCR is housed and music is listened to.

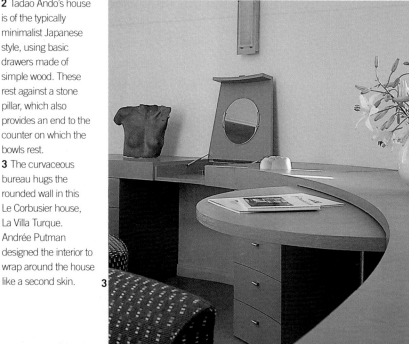

1 This configuration of the Arc Linea "Odeon" by designer Carlo Bartoli creates a doorway out of closed closets. The variety of drawers, cupboards and boxes means that normally wasted space can be brought into play. For other "Odeon" variations see pages 128 and 133.

2 Tadao Ando's house is of the typically minimalist Japanese style, using basic drawers made of simple wood. These rest against a stone pillar, which also provides an end to the counter on which the bowls rest.

3 The curvaceous bureau hugs the rounded wall in this Le Corbusier house, La Villa Turque. Andrée Putman designed the interior to wrap around the house like a second skin.

4 Driade's "Oikos" system takes on a new dimension by using metal in its "Dilemma" storage system. The reflective qualities of the material give the room a feeling of greater space and depth.

130

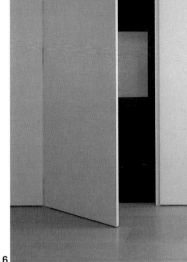

5 Two wooden cabinets without pulls are positioned under the Gaggenau oven on this storage unit, which is made entirely of pine, by David Chipperfield. Spartan designs such as this make suitable storage for any room in the house.

6 Architect John Pawson displays here the monastic principles that underlie his designs.

7 Thin panels have been arranged into a gently sinuous storage unit in architect Franklin D. Israel's design. Without doors or hidden shelving, three glass shelves jut out from the far end of the wall, and below these is a simple square fireplace with a flat polished hearth in front of it.

8 Driade's system by Antonia Astori is an unusual departure in this "Abaco" configuration. The combination of glass, laminate and tubular metal is a colorful accompaniment to the "Oikos" system.

9 Interlubke's solution to retrieving items from high-level storage is a rail built just below the topmost shelf of this seven-layer wooden unit. A simple metal ladder can then easily be attached between the rail and the floor, providing easy access to the higher shelves, without the need for a bulky step ladder or for resting an ordinary ladder on the shelving itself.

1 Roll-up doors slide back into the cabinet to reveal the contents of these multi-purpose "Perseo" storage units by Estudi Blanc.

5 Piero Fornasetti, who died in 1988, left behind a legacy of brilliant design work and architectural perspectives, a tradition carried on by his son, Barnaba, in pieces such as his classic screens and this commode.

3 Modular units looking like clones need distinctive coloring and detailing, such as these inverted triangular and dot metallic pulls, to make their simple form, adaptable to any space, stand out. "Cubiform" is designed by Estudi Blanc.

4 Built on the beanstalk principle, this storage system by Pepe Bonet for Bd Ediciones de Diseno offers a visionary approach to the problem of limited floor space.

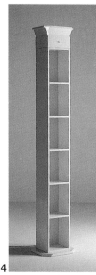

2 Artespana focus on the VCR storage problem with "Maya," a trapezoid shelving system looking like truncated pyramids, designed by P.G. Bellas.

6 Designer Jeannot Cerutti's totemistic unit, "Libabel," for Sawaya & Moroni has tensile wires to hold the contents in place.

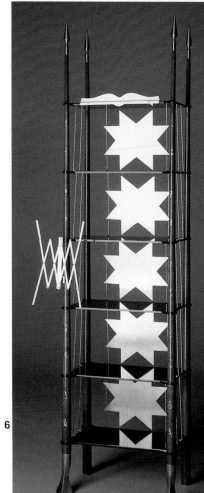

This space also has to double as a library and a display area for objects. Wall space must be freed for shelves at the right height both for viewing and for access. Specific siting next to power outlets as well as cable lengths determine the positioning of electronic equipment, surrounded by clear floor space for furniture so that the entertainment they offer can be enjoyed.

Worse, wall space will be at a premium – every radiator panel, window, large-scale piece of furniture limits your storage options. Purpose-built storage systems are sometimes free-standing and ideally suited to deal with this problem by creating a room divider. A line-up of shelves on adjustable tracks against the wall is another solution, one that also provides extra insulation and soundproofing – no insulation material is as thick as a covering of paperbacks.

7 Arc Linea's "Odeon" is an impressive wall shelving system, constructed from Italian walnut, with a high-gloss, black- or white-lacquered finish. It is designed by Carlo Bartoli and it combines in one unit both open and closed display space, depending on what is required.

8 From Rosenthal comes "Life Service" by Jochen Flack – a mobile sideboard that brings cutlery, plates, glasses to the table. Its flap extensions provide instant counters and pivoting drawers give easy access.

9 This combination filing cabinet and bureau employs cleverly angled geometry in a thoughtful storage solution. Still in prototype, it is by architect Klaus Block, whose interesting work, exhibited by avante-garde furniture movement Berliner Zimmer, has attracted attention at many furniture fairs. Berliner Zimmer claim to kick out against the "upright worthiness" of much of German design.

10 "Kuubi," by Pirkko Stenros for Muurame, is a modular series which had items added to it each year, so that over the 1980s it grew from a simple collection to an all-purpose storage system for any room in the home.

11, 12, 13, 14 & 15 Cult movie of the 1980s, "Batman," featured crafted cabinetry by Jamie Tresserra Clapes. With high standards of craftsmanship, and only 25 pieces made of each design, his small collection of furniture is highly prized. These different views show his hand-made walnut "Samuro" unit, which, like its Japanese namesake, is guardian of all the family's possessions.

16 The inverted triangular sides of the free-standing "Laurenziana" unit, which is designed by Colantoni, Contini and Stella, provide an improbable balancing act for a series of clear glass shelves.

STORAGE

1 This "Taka" coatstand in black enameled metal with a black marquina marble base is from Atrium.

2 An anorexic coat rack, "N.A.U., from Inno, runs like a seamstress' thread up the wall to end in a convenient, four-fingered hook.

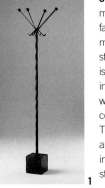

3 The ubiquitous metal clothes rail, so favored by garment manufacturers for storage and delivery, is here interpreted in a very individual way by the design company Tebong. The result is a stylish and sturdy yet inexpensive little free-standing wardrobe.

4 Designed by Salvadó and Solé, this haloed hatstand is called "Percha." The user will find that, like its name, this little detail is the easiest and tidiest way to accommodate a winter overcoat, a scarf and a hat on one single clamp attached to the wall.

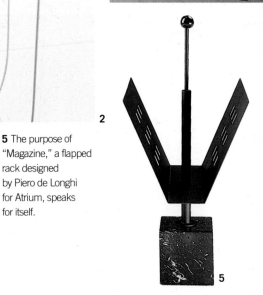

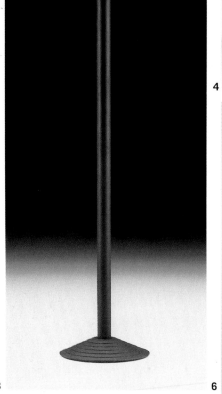

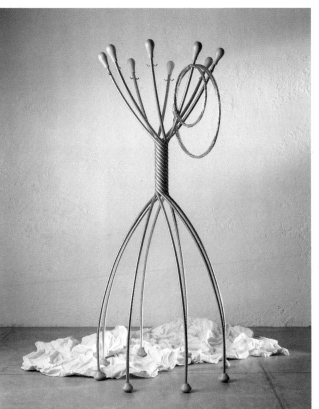

5 The purpose of "Magazine," a flapped rack designed by Piero de Longhi for Atrium, speaks for itself.

6 This interestingly frazzled silhouette called "Parrucca" for Disform, by the trio De Pas, D'Urbino and Lomazzi, offers you many angles on which to hang your hat and coat.

7 Fashionable hang-ups are revealed by Carl F. Petersen's utensil rod. Butcher's hooks are supposed to be a useful storage adjunct, until you try to find them that is. No such problems here!

8 The aptly named "Octopus" wraps around its slender stem to branch out into an imposing steel structure, by Zero Disengo.

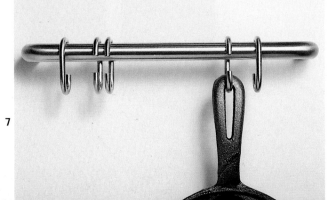

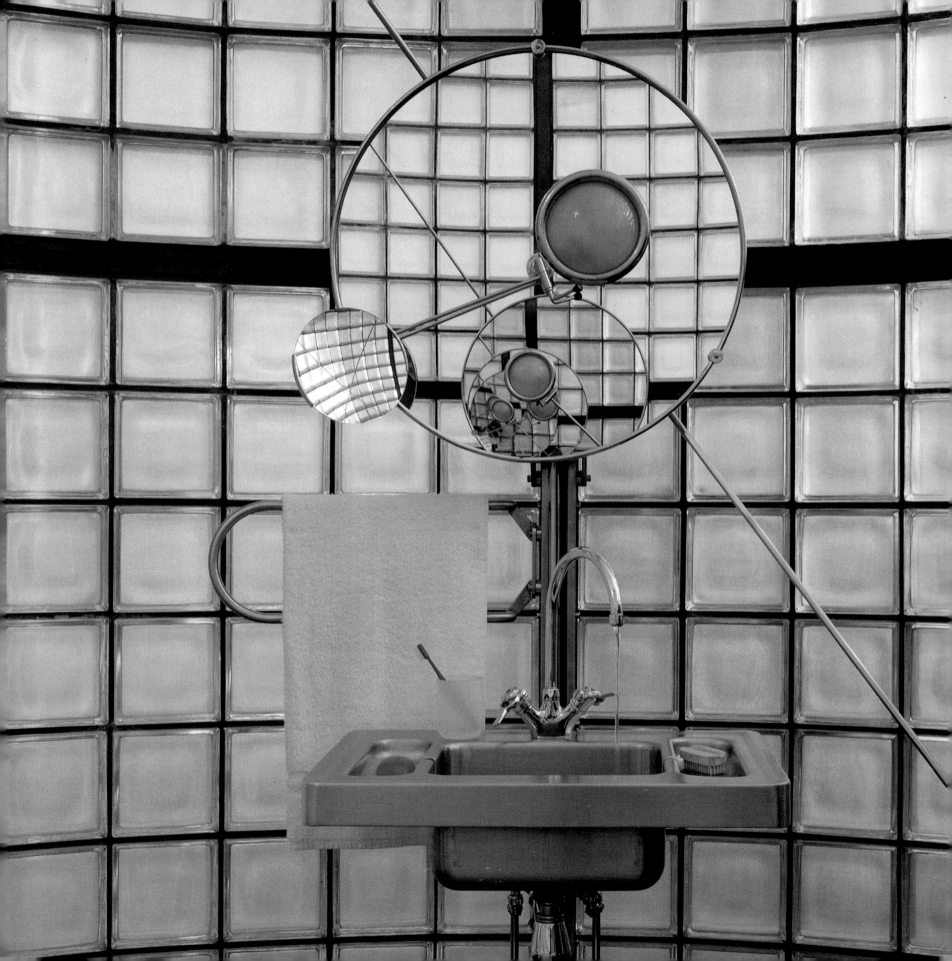

Bathrooms

Previous page
Architect John Young installed S-shaped tubular chrome bars to warm towels and compliment a stainless steel sink and an Eileen Gray mirror.
1 From the former team of Pawson and Silvestrin comes this minimalist design. A chink of light filtered through a triangular wall highlights the travertine sink and its curved faucet. A slabbed Santanyi stone floor and matte-white walls reinforce a monastic approach to bathing.
2 A power substation, converted by architect Gary Cunningham, has many surfaces in the raw, reflecting the building's utilitarian heritage.

The best contemporary bathrooms are those that cloak fitness for purpose in a Spartan simplicity, thus conforming with Western cultural traditions based on ideas of segregation and minimum contact. In the 1990s, despite what appears to be people's preoccupation with health and body consciousness, few have turned over one of the larger rooms in the home to a health spa with whirlpool bathtub or sauna. Health-conscious exercise devotees have, however, pioneered some new uses for the bathroom, turning it into a mini-gym by installing such items as an exercise rail against a mirrored wall, as well as the new compact rowing or treadmill walking machines that are designed to be folded flat against the wall when not in use.

It is a sobering reflection that there have been so few innovations since the Romans introduced hot, piped water into soak tubs, still visible today in the old spa towns. In America in 1931, Buckminster Fuller introduced his astonishing Dymaxion bathroom, a mobile

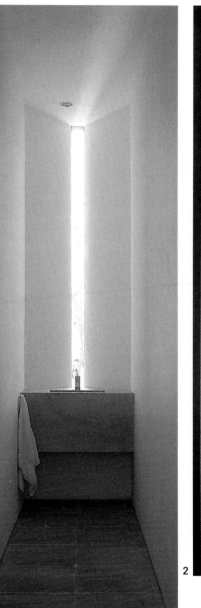

3 A post-modernist Gothic spirit can be discerned in this oval-shaped sink, entitled "Point," produced by Dornbracht, which is housed in a hexagonal top and supported on a triangular lectern base.

6 The open plumbing on a stainless steel sink, set against a midnight-blue bath panel, emphasizes the high-tech approach of the architects of this bathroom. They designed contrasts and repeats in the many reflective surfaces used in the scheme.

4 Stone is the favorite hard surface for bathrooms, since it is waterproof and easy to clean. A trio of accessories from Dornbracht on a slab of granite echo that material's same hard-edged and geometric form.

5 This bathroom in a riverside apartment was designed by architect John Young. The girdle of tubular stainless steel carries both the plumbing and heating pipes. This same circular form is replicated in the shower rail above, while the bath is a cedarwood Japanese tub, sealed for safety reasons when not in use. Pilkington's double-glazed roof panels keep this penthouse room light and warm.

7 "The best hotels are always unpretentious, abstractly comfortable, never challenging," says Andrée Putman, whose hotel-designed bathroom products are now available for the domestic market from Societe André.

room cast as a single sculptural unit of pressed steel and inserted into his Dymaxion prefab house. But his patented idea for the American Radiator Company never really caught on, possibly since bathroom detailing is too cumbersome to transport easily.

Fitted as it is to the wall with pipework inlets and outlets, the contemporary bathroom is the most inflexible room in the home to plan. Since it is also the most dedicatedly equipped room, with fixtures that have only a single function, it is the most difficult space to utilize for another purpose.

Furthermore, planning regulations concerning the plumbing of waste pipes and water sources vary from country to country. For example, in the United States it is permissible to have a bathroom leading directly off a bedroom, while in Italy there has to be a lobby space between the two rooms.

All these factors make bathroom planning no easy task. While sales networks provide kitchen buyers with a complete service, from design to installation and redecoration, bathroom suppliers tend to provide only a basic service of plumbing and installation. Unlike kitchen design, bathroom design is

1 This California bathroom, designed by architect Arata Isozaki, secluded and meditative within white walls, is finely fitted with banks of storage units, like kitchen cabinets. The window visible here is in fact one of three set high in the south wall, leaving plenty of unbroken wall space lower down.

2 Mass-produced modular units provide ample storage behind the doors that hide the plumbing, and also support the sink. Marble-effect "Clipstone" vinyl flooring from Amtico replicates real stone.

3 In this bathroom, by architects Gwathmey Siegel, modular units make use of a narrow space. Oval sinks, symmetrically placed either side of the tub, incorporate modern comfort into a classical theme.

4

5

4 & 5 A recessed bathtub sunk into a raised platformed area will give the illusion of an increase in the height of a room, especially a small one. This is particularly the case in a bathroom such as this, which is also fitted with mirrored walls. The designer, architect Michael Carapettan,

has concealed the controls for the hydromassage tubs beneath the sculptured form of the 5-mm thick molded fiberglass metacrylic material.

6

6 Designer Finn Skoedt at Studio Rapsel produced "Euclide," this sculptural column sink made of chrome-plated metal.

8

9

7 Milldue's vanity units and counters in walnut, laminate or polyester veneers have matching tops in granite. Their "Clio" collection supports an oval sink on an overhanging counter, freeing valuable floor space.

7

8 The cabinet, which incorporates an illuminated mirror, is in the "Giamo" range from Duravit. It liberates the room from line-ups of built-in furniture, and its curved lines echo the shapes of the fixtures, also by Duravit.

9 Travertine flooring on the curved stairs leading to this bathroom is channeled to allow water to drain away. Design is by architect Peter Wilson in collaboration with architect Chassay Wright.

1 Bathtubs with showers double up on space but need a watertight enclosure when used with a pressure pump. Factory-assembled doors from Daryl include this hinged bath screen, style "950," shown here with white-finish frames and safety glass.

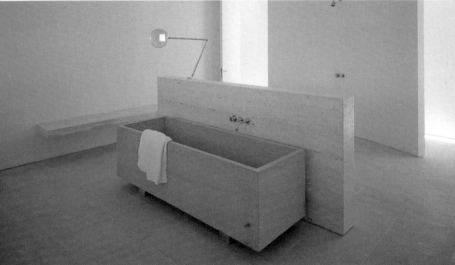

3 Steps leading to a raised, travertine-tiled area around this tub create the impression of a sunken bath. Architects Gwathmey Siegel offer a leafy view of water, with a louvered shade for privacy. The boxed-in feeling that bathtubs often create is lifted by the tiling, mirrors and glass – and this attractive view.

2 In this Majorcan house, designed by the former architectural partnership of Claudio Silvestrin and John Pawson, the austere, yet soaking-sized bathtub is separated from the sink by a travertine wall hand-carved from local Santanyi stone.

largely a matter of choosing fixtures from builders' suppliers and then piecing together the accessories that will complete the look and co-ordinate with the bathtub, shower and so on. Manufacturers of sanitary fixtures and accessories still do not provide overall concept planning for the bathroom.

In the United States, French designers Andrée Putman and Philippe Starck have marketed for the home owner their original designs for hotel bathrooms, found installed in Putman's Morgan's Hotel and Starck's Royalton. This was in response to the lack of

4 A paneled bathtub is lit by a grid of glass blocks, which allow the light that falls at the head to be doubled and returned by the mirrored surfaces. White-on-white detailing gives this city bathroom, designed by architects Gwathmey Siegel, the fresh feeling of a health spa.

5 Although the wall-mounted telephone in this Trump Tower bathroom in New York, designed by architects Gwathmey Siegel, makes it a contender for a set in Tom Wolfe's "*Bonfire of the Vanities,*" the Wall Street effect is somewhat moderated by the use of wood, glass and clay tiles. This imparts an atmosphere of quiet spaciousness to a small room in a city where space is at a premium.

good-looking sink hardware with the necessary backup of matching accessories in the same chrome or lacquer detailing. This is the first significant step toward the design of the complete bathroom.

Architects are much preoccupied with the troubling issue of the incompatibility of hardware with plumbing fixtures, cabinets and accessories, all of which that must be contained within the usually small area of a typical bathroom. Research into the amount of space the average adult needs in the bathroom – the room with most equipment and the least space – shows that the bare minimum clear floor area in front of the bathtub for comfortable drying measures 43 by 28 inches.

Those interested in saving space invariably suggest a shower cubicle or stall to cut down on bathing space. In Japan, however, bathers wash and soap themselves in a space no wider than a narrow corridor, rinse clean and then soak in deep hot tubs that take up little more floor area than the standard shower stall. The standard Western bathtub measuring 66 inches in length

6 Laufen with Porsche Design reduce conventional bathroom ceramic ware to an oval and triangle, fusing that geometry into a complete, ergonomically designed furnishing system.

1

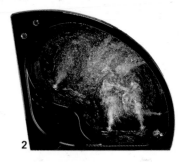

2

1 A high-sided bathtub shaped from a marble block by architect John Pawson features marble grain that runs on the diagonal one way on the bathtub panels, and contrasts with the angle created by the diagonal grain along the floor.

2 The "Unica" corner tub in molded acrylic by Gruppo Novellini offers whirlpool hydrojets.
3 Architect Jan Kaplicky omitted the panels of this Ideal Standard "Michelangelo" bathtub, and set it on the conventional skeletal frame. The toilet and sink are from the same series, all designed by John Beauchamp.

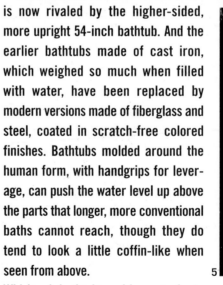

3

is now rivaled by the higher-sided, more upright 54-inch bathtub. And the earlier bathtubs made of cast iron, which weighed so much when filled with water, have been replaced by modern versions made of fiberglass and steel, coated in scratch-free colored finishes. Bathtubs molded around the human form, with handgrips for leverage, can push the water level up above the parts that longer, more conventional baths cannot reach, though they do tend to look a little coffin-like when seen from above.

Whirlpool bathtubs, with controls to vary the intensity of the jet of water, are a much-lauded, recent domestic introduction. As well, electric pumps that vary the amount of the water flow make it possible to achieve aerated water in the shower. Pumps can also

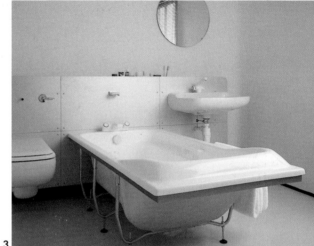

5

4 Eva Jiricna combines customized steel fixtures with manufactured white ceramic ware and a sloping reflective bath panel that effectively reduces the visual volume of this large item.

5 This sinuously designed bathtub, "Sinuosa" by Gruppo Novellini, has three hydrojet massage nozzles, adjustable in intensity and direction, activated by a motor pump.

4

6 Designer Philippe
Starck was com-
missioned to tackle
the old-fashioned
Royalton Hotel
in New York, formerly
a sleazy, turn-of-the-
century establishment
that had dime-slot
waterbeds. Here, in
the hotel's Edwardian
bathrooms, he
brilliantly combines
bathtub and shower
by creating a
semi-circular wall,
with a protective
circular shower rail.

7 Architects John
Pawson's and Claudio
Silvestrin's use of a
roll-top tub against a
minimalist background
of a monolithic shower
wall exaggerates the
scale from the floor up.
This is accentuated
by the use of giant
slabs on the floor
and smaller ones on
the panel.

3 Showers are often the last item to be chosen, and so have to respond to the style already set. This shower tray from Cesana's "Boglass" series has a built-in corner seat, and glass panels shaped to follow the tray contours with either pivoting or bi-fold doors.

take water directly from the main supply and heat it using a small electric or gas heater near the shower. Water temperature is varied by increasing or decreasing pressure — the higher the flow, the cooler the water.

The shower market is divided into electric, mixer and power showers and bath/shower mixers. The cheapest to install are simple electric showers, but power showers are the most popular multifunctional models, with heads for spray patterns and a pump to drive the system under pressure.

Basic sinks can be fixed on a pedestal or wall-hung, usually mounted at a height of 32 inches from floor to rim. The appropriately named "vanity" sets a pair of sinks side by side in the manner of the modern deluxe hotel. This is not as bland a mix as it might sound, since this can be the way to line up fixtures and bring additional water points into the bathroom without taking up as much space as, for example, two discrete pedestal versions. The shapes of sinks are oval, rectangular, square or circular. At Starck's imaginative Café Costes in

1 For a high-tech apartment, architect Eva Jiricna specified a circular shower, with the heating elements and controls enclosed within this space capsule.

2 With this model, Cesana's "Logic," for the first time the plumbing is marshaled in a pillar alongside the activating mixer valve. In addition, the pillar is also equipped with eight different massage functions.

4 Along with traditional shower bases and stalls, manufacturers have introduced new, space-utilizing, corner-mounted models, such as the Cesana Sene 700 "Compass."

5 This triangular shower, style "635 Pentagon," by Daryl, fits seamlessly into a 36 x 36-inch corner. Its pivot-hung door has 8-mm-thick glazing, amply robust to repel the steam generated by the new generation of power showers.

6 Bathroom fixtures from Laufen relate to each other in harmonious shapes. The toilet, which has a detachable seat for easy cleaning, is condensation-proofed along the cistern. This is an important consideration when placing fixtures in the same room as a shower cubicle.

7 Fitted like a conventionally hinged door that opens outward, the glazed panels either side of this Daryl shower, style "961," open up the entire length of the rectangular stall to give easy and safe access. Glass can be clear, as here, or etched with a grid pattern.

8 A generously sized, chrome-plated shower nozzle is illuminated from above by a circular glass panel set into the bathroom ceiling. The shower head pumps aerated water onto the bather in this fully tiled installation by architect Arata Isozaki.

Paris, triangular glass sinks are washed by a jet of water from a curvaceous tube above the angled glass, triggered by a convenient floor pedal. "Warm furnishing" is the marketing catchphrase for the obvious solution to the problem of cold surfaces, exemplified by heated towel bars and underfloor heating that blows warm air out into the room through grills, and the large steel radiators with warm water transmitting heat with rigorous, functional simplicity.

Since bathrooms seldom have vast areas of unshielded windows, natural light often has to be supplemented with artificial illumination. The accurate placing is important – overhead light

9 The Daryl "933" triple-panel sliding door fits any size of shower tray. Ideal in tight spaces, the doors can move left or right behind each other, sliding on a slimline, self-cleaning, grooved track system.

1 Architect John Pawson's inspiration is clear in this bathroom. A slab of marble, angled to fill a shallow channel with water from an overhead spout, takes both its form and function from the old dairies before the time of refrigeration, when channeled marble sinks were vital to the preservation of milk products. Industrial forms are an important influence on Pawson, along with the design traditions of Japan.

1

2

4 Duravit, more than 170 years old, specialize in ceramics. Their interchangeable pedestal sinks, in the form of a steel cylinder, an urn, a chimney flue and a bronzed fruitwood slab, serve to hide the plumbing.

  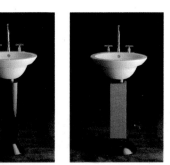

4

5 Duravit's "Dellarco" white ceramic double sink is state of the art for shared living. Within a small counter area there are two sinks – ideal for working city couples who are short on both space and time.

5

2 The "Pump" sink by Agape is made of steel and has tubular supports on either side designed to hold towels – a useful device in a small bathroom.

3 This circular pedestal sink, by architect John Pawson, is scooped out of a block of marble. Its simplicity and purity of line is accentuated by the faucet – a chrome tube that would normally qualify as plumbing and be hidden from sight by the pedestal.

and mirrors can create unflattering shadows. Most bathroom lights are low voltage, perhaps arranged on a strip panel above the mirror, or bulkhead lights covered in nonreflective glass, such as those found on board ships. The most successful bathrooms are those that overcome their solemn and frequently unprepossessing functionality with a simplicity of sculptural form and an unostentatious background. Such rooms feature the comfort of hot running water, a fast-jetting shower, capacious sinks, warm towels and clean, elegant finishes.

6 Architect Philippe Starck designed his "Lola Hertzburg" stainless steel and chrome sink for Rapsel to be self-sufficient, like the sci-fi character whose name inspired the design. The usual add-on fixtures, such as mirrors, towel bars or soap trays, are built into the frame.

6

7 The "Rapsody" sink, designed by Berger and Stahl for Rapsel, sets an oval, stainless steel bowl in a glass rectangle. This example is finished with a stylish Vola chrome-plated faucet – the contemporary architects' favorite choice for baths and sinks.

7

147

1 Dornbracht faucets line up to show their variety of waterproofed and rust-proofed finishes.

2 This selection of mixers in chrome is from Vola, a preferred supplier for many architects working worldwide.

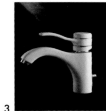

3 The Rubinetterie "Time 95" model is a single-handle mixer faucet with a stream-lined design.

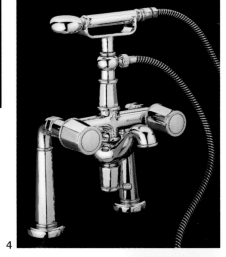

4 Rubinetterie's "Chantal 27" is a brass and chrome design based on the Edwardian style, with faucets and shower nozzle. Faucets evolved from this basic cross-bar type to mixers with a central control button to trigger a warm water flow from a central spout.

5 The award-winning furniture designer Kevin Walz, whose first faucet design, "Univers," updates Art Deco, uses chrome and brass trimmings in a hexagonal mixer system.

6 A new design for a Rubinetterie faucet, "Ondatris 78" is engineered for function.

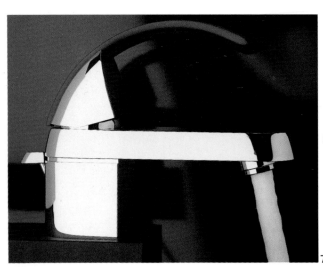

7 The Dornbracht mixer has an elongated, curved control handle.

8 Gruppo Metals produce "Giro tondo" faucets, designed by Davide Mercatali, featuring pop-art imagery in the orbs clustered on the hot and cold water controls set on either side of the spout. Continuing the theme, a single satellite orb is located perched on top of the central mixer spout.

9 Børma produces a full range of bathroom ac-cessories to coordinate with their mixer faucets, such as this white-lacquered "Lux" faucet. This design is also avail-able in both chrome and brass finishes.

11, 12 & 13 These three faucets from the innovative company Gruppo Metals show how to make a basic bathroom item more amusing and certainly more colorful. Designers are (left) Edgardo Angelini; (middle) Davide Mercatali; and (right) Roberto Boni.

14 An assertive approach in F. A. Porsche's "Eclisse," designed for M. & Z. Rubinetteria.

15 A very different approach to bathroom faucets is seen here in the spiraling forms of Schmidt-Lackner's design "Roca."

16 "Elemta" from Toni is a simple yet stylish solution to designing single faucets in chrome.

10 Art and design combine in this bathroom, designed by architectural company Munkenbeck & Marshall. Artist Danny Lane's custom-built sink shows sculptural form and implicit functionality.

17 Rubinetterie's "Toscane Ponsi" faucet is tactile as well as formal. Its form recalls past elegance, while its function is ultra modern.

18 Called "Domani," Italian for tomorrow, this Sieger design regulates the water flow according to the pressure applied to it via a single control.

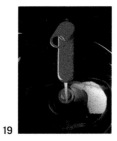

19 Dornbracht reverses the traditional geometry of a faucet, making it taller when the thrust of the design is more diagonal in nature.

1 "Ego," a narcissistic metal-framed dressing table and valet by Renzo de Liberali for StudioLine, features a swivel-drawer storage drum and Carrara marble counter.

2 A concrete bathtub, embedded with copper heating coils and functional accessories, preserves the design integrity of an old disused powerhouse converted by architect Gary Cunningham.

6 Carl F. Petersen's smoothly rounded chrome glass holder and soap ring is both unobtrusive and stylish.

7

8

9

1

3 Framed in black and incorporating a scooped bowl light, this Barovier & Toso mirror is a fine example of traditional glass-making techniques working in perfect harmony with modern design.

2

3

4 "Pan," by Turi and Gagliardi for Rapsel, features concentric disks of sanded or painted crystal and a rectangular mirror, supported by a wall-mounted, nickel-plated brass column.

5 Restructured by Andrée Putman, the bathroom at Le Corbusier's Villa Turque incorporates a shaving mirror, with extendable arm and built-in light and magnifying glass, by architect Eileen Gray.

4

5

7 Kartell's "Delphi" mirrors, by Mattheo Thun, nonchalantly incline against the wall on rubber grip feet.

8 This chrome-and-plastic soap dish is by Jorge Pensi, from a range of accessories commissioned by Inno to be "rough but in a classical way." Revealing a fine attention to detail, the dish incorporates a channeled and hollowed, clear acrylic insert, which allows water to drain and collect below the soap.

9 This simple circular towel holder is by Agape.

Kitchens

H istoric houses open to the public offer the interested observer some glimpses into the life and customs of a bygone age. As well, they remind us of just how much of that age is now obsolete. The kitchens of these grand, old houses stand as a testimony to changing social custom, the absence of home help, the habit of informal dining, and the development of labor-saving gadgetry that has done so much to fashion our present lifestyles.

Llanhydrock in north Cornwall, England provides a record of the splendor of a late-Victorian kitchen. Barely a century has passed and yet the tools and equipment are now mostly obsolete. Copper jelly molds hang alongside game hooks; the meat safe stands beside the butler's sink; the marbled dairy room with butter churns offers icy water in place of refrigeration; the separate laundry, pantry and larder, as well as the dining room beyond the green baize doors, define vividly the way in which today's kitchen space has to take on so many

1 A nautical-influenced "porthole" inserted into a kitchen cabinet by Eva Jiricna echoes the viewing window featured on many laundry appliances.
Previous page Inspired by the patina on steel trucks in Japan, architect John Young specified this unusual finish for stainless steel kitchen cabinets.

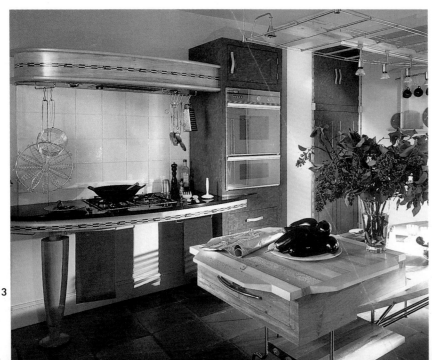

2 The matte-black good looks of Roberto Pezzetta's appliances in Zanussi's "Wizard" collection attract deserved attention. The mechanisms are housed in melamine rosin, enameled steel and glass.
3 Architect Johnny Grey specializes in awkward kitchens. "Like a tailor-made suit, the kitchen should fit the house and client," he explains. Craftsmen make everything, even down to cast-iron forged pulls.

3

4

4 Isolated in the lofty living room in architect Sir Richard Rogers' London home is this free-standing, stainless steel kitchen island. It is a multifunctional installation, and features a double sink unit and a four-plate gas cooktop. As well, there is a centrally located waste disposal.

6

5

5 Black laminate cabinets by Alno are paired with an update of the traditional butcher's block – a serious cook's tool for chopping and slicing.

6 Strato is a kitchen company dedicated to the research of "the concept of open space." Wood, stone and metal are combined on modular kitchen cabinets. Illuminated by a violet drawer front, this rectangular island has an extension of five metal tubes in the middle of the room, and against the wall a cabinet that houses sinks and appliances.

7 Built in a fairly tight corner, this kitchen by Gwathmey Siegel appears spacious due to clever architectural intervention – reflective tiles bounce back the light from the narrow-paneled, glass-fronted wall that flanks the window with its Venetian shade.

7

1 First appearances deceive with this "Woodline Structure" kitchen from Bulthaup, made entirely from lacquered wood. This complete kitchen features their designed fittings – from the free-standing beech preparation island with drawers to the wire-mesh ceiling fitting.

different and varied roles as circumstances change.

In the 1960s, for example, every kitchen boasted endless casseroles, storage for freeze-dried foodstuffs, and the artificial air of a laboratory inspired by the technology of space exploration.

A change of emphasis in the 1970s produced the idea of the kitchen playing the key role in defining the "quality of life". The kitchen table was central to entertainment, as well as to tasks like homework, and there was a certain homespun air that went with the potted herbs and the use of such "honest" building materials as brick, stone and wood.

Then, in the 1980s, *nouvelle cuisine* launched the cook's kitchen – not only a set of ideas but also a collection of equipment that could shred, extract, pulverize, stir-fry and steam in the most efficient and purposeful of fashions. This gleaming stainless steel room, with

4 This irregularly shaped table, which is curved on one side and has a sharp corner on another, has a tubular-steel support that rests on an aquamarine base. Sensitive spring-touch mechanisms mean that the cabinet doors have no profile in this kitchen of angular contrasts. The good-looking designer stainless steel kitchenware is from Alessi.

its array of architect-designed Alessi cookware, made the kitchen the most expensively outfitted space within the contemporary home.

Behind surfaces of steel, enameled sheet metal and industrial glass teamed with hardwood, cost-effective appliances took the drudgery out of washing, cooking and cooling. The cook's kitchen was one in which every inch of space was taken up by containers, shelves and drawers, with floor and wall cabinets containing all manner of space- and time-saving accessories. Storage carousels, hooks, bins, compartments,

2 Unusual finishes on doorfronts with combinations of counters are a specialty of Miele. Their "Program 560" has laminated fronts in four pastel shades, shown here in platinum gray, to team with beech counters, and any one of 130 pulls on offer.

3 Woodstock's custom-built "Tracz" kitchen combines maple and colored sycamore veneered cabinets with a Welsh granite counter. Spotlights illuminate the essentially duotone colored room. The octagonal table in the foreground is a space-saving way of accommodating eight diners in a small kitchen area. And beneath the gray floor tiles lies a ducted central heating system.

7 A classic modern design, originally pioneered by Poggenpohl, is this white laminate kitchen by Strato. Stainless steel counters bring this timeless look right up to date. Strato produce modular cabinets that can adapt to different rooms and different needs.

wine racks, ice crushers...there was something for every enthusiast. In contrast, the busy professional's kitchen exhibited the new minimalism, with a single, rounded, stainless steel sink, streamlined mixer faucet, two-burner gas cooktop, and a microwave on top of a freezer for convenience food, all set against a background of a slate counter and anonymous cabinets.

But in today's kitchen this impressive battery of specialized equipment is being refined and relaxed. The current kitchen unbends a little, is much less laboratory-like, and is definitely more

8 Polished metallic lacquer flows over soft curves in this Siematic kitchen, the "SL 808," while segmented marble flooring fans beneath the circular swoop of the counter.

5 Not just a pretty face – beneath the red lacquer of Miele's "Program 600" lies a sturdy structure. The high-gloss contemporary finish on a classical frame conceals a stolid particle board carcass.

6 There are 45 door front and pull options, nine front styles, and pulls in maple, beech, cherry, chrome and black, within the extensive "Profile 2000" program from Poggenpohl.

1 Splitting the functions of cook and bottle-washer and dividing the kitchen territorially is the idea behind Scovolini's briarwood kitchen. The rectangular cabinet, divided by a matte-black exhaust hood, houses a built-in oven and cooktop.

5 Poggenpohl's 2400 "GH" kitchen uses high-gloss laminates to bring the esthetic quality of their "LH" range to the middle market. Sheer fronts without pulls feature a polished, horizontal aluminum trim.

3 Effeti's classic "Misura", designed in 1974 by Barsacchi and Vegni, has been brought right up to date with a new proposal from Giancarlo Vegni to utilize all those awkward little corners that are so common in most kitchens.

4 John Young's kitchen gives no signs of cozy domesticity. Stainless steel cabinets with a machined texture and two spring-loaded tables, which can flatten against the wall, allow ample seating for as many as eight people.

2 Even the conventional oven fits gracefully within the curves of this Effeti kitchen, banked in black cabinets that almost appear to float.

people-friendly. Dining amid towering banks of cabinets and aluminum surfaces is not pleasing. Hence the addition of a much-loved piece of old furniture—a kitchen table, perhaps, now scoured to the color of pale straw, a corner cabinet with carved pediments, or a grandfather clock ticking in a companionable sort of way.

What is more, the reintroduction of these pieces of furniture reflects the new mobility. You can, for example, move them when your circumstances change —a new job, a new apartment, a new relationship. They are not fixed to the wall by installation experts, so you don't have to walk away from all of your kitchen forever.

Every client comes to a kitchen showroom with a basic floor plan. Behind the scenes, however, cooperation between the manufacturers of built-in kitchens

6 This kitchen has a workbench with a curved end to prevent painful hard knocks. As well, it provides an informal dining bar.

6

7

7 Blocks of color in blues and red stacked in this kitchen, "Logos," from F.lli Ferretti di Ferrotto, are grouped under a counter. The catwalk breakfast bar emphasizes the detailing and the workmanship.

and the appliance makers has led to the packaging of kitchens which focus more on designs that will suit the lifestyles and habits of the client.

It is inevitable that in the room where the preparation, cooking and presentation of food is one of the main concerns, together with the washing of plates and the laundering of clothes, appliances are critical to the scheme. The kitchen is by far the most automated room in the home, yet contemporary kitchens tend to confirm that the hearth, or the image of the hearth, is still a cultural icon in today's society. Why else would appliances be disguised behind reassuring wooden fronts that cloak the functional innovations of industrial research?

Technological advances mean that as the energy output of appliances increases, their size reduces. The traditional 23.5-inch square built-in appliance is now available in 18- or 16-inch sizes without any reduction in workload. In a decade, these appliances have reduced consumption of electricity by 50 percent, of water by 70 percent, and of detergent by 40 percent, and the materials that some are made of make them ecologically disposable. Only the refrigerator continues to grow in size, now acquiring double doors since it is also used as a combination pantry and larder, with a cooled section for wines.

Though not actually colored green, the thinking behind appliance performance is definitely "green," lurking behind a matte-black mask. "White" goods are

8

9

10

8 Kitchens that curve sinuously around corners are a sensible way of providing more storage space without creating the problem of inaccessible far-reaching corners. The new Siematic "9009" kitchen uses polyester in soft curves, aggressively colored in tomato red or also available in black, ivory or gray.

9 This sharply right-angled kitchen by Sera Noce is in stark contrast with the curved glass-block wall. The kitchen has wooden counters and splashback with sleek black-lacquered cabinets, and behind the cooktop a slab of marble provides an effective hard surface.

10 Floor-to-ceiling solid blocks of glossy cabinets are matched by lower, counter-height cabinets for appliances. The counter is steel, which, with the glass storage shelves, creates a theatrical space.

11 Blocks of kitchen cabinetry are placed diagonally in this room in an unusual forked-stick design pattern using the new Poggenpohl "Time" range, available in chrome, black, maple, beech or cherrywood.

11

undergoing a major technological transformation – instead of hiding behind wooden façades, they are drawing attention to themselves as free-standing objects in their own right.

Ovens, combining steam cooking and special steam pressure cooking with roasting and broiling, are housed in boxes of insulating material that will not adversely affect the furniture on which they sit. So now there is far greater flexibility over where to site them. And the free-standing cooking range, released from the confines of furniture frames, brings the cooker to the focal point of today's kitchen.

The result of this process is the negation of the built-in kitchen. That line-up of perfectly flush-fitting modular cabinets, structurally engineered and then scumbled, rag-rolled and decorated with machine-produced fretwork, is an

1 To celebrate the Le Corbusier centenary in 1986, his Villa Turque, built in 1916, was renovated, and interior designer Andrée Putman was commissioned to revive the interiors in the first building ever constructed around a reinforced concrete frame. Putman's company, Ecart, created specific furniture for each space. In the kitchen, one single, free-standing island in stainless steel is covered with three slabs of black maple.
2 A maple top to an island in this chrome-and-laminate Allmilmo "Atlanta" kitchen coordinates well with the wood-block flooring.

3 Proof that high-density particle board is strong enough to support stone is provided in this stacking drawer system from Techline, whose aim, according to Chairman Marshall Erdman, is to "combine quality materials and simple, classic design with the highest technology."

4 Corian(R) cleverly combines naturally occurring minerals and acrylic to produce counter surfaces that can then be edged and shaped to fit seamlessly around sinks. Alno offers Corianware in "Sierra dark" (bottom), "Cameo white" (middle) and "Sierra light" (top).

6 John Pawson's solid slab of gray marble runs the entire length of this kitchen cabinet. In keeping with his minimal interiors, every surface is featureless, without extrusions, curves or fussiness of any sort.

5 Granite is a hard-wearing counter. Alno, which offers "Sardo rosso" (bottom), "Tiffany black" (middle) and "Nador light" (top), describes the stone as hygroscopic – moisture evaporates without leaving watermarks.

7 Marble and stone are popular, if expensive, counters. Architectural duo Gwathmey Siegel, who use combinations of warm-toned woods in their interiors, replicate that look with a single slab of stone to house the sink.

8 Three solid blocks of marble create a workbench in this kitchen, supported in the middle by a wooden panel. David Chipperfield's architectural pre-occupation with joints is vividly illustrated here in this solid marble counter, which, despite its obvious weight, gives the impression of somehow floating above what are in themselves substantial side pieces. Delicate grooves, where the counter meets supporting stones, simply enhance the light and airy effect.

embarrassing reminder of the new opulence and conspicuous consumption. The ideal kitchen these days is fitted out with ecologically conserving appliances, and with them comes a new sense of identity. With everybody in a rush, and with more and more women going to work outside of the home, that traditional picture of the status-symbol kitchen has become something of an anachronism.

There is now more experimentation with styles of eating, too, than was previously the case. People are more adventurous with their cuisine, happily eating Japanese, Vietnamese, Thai, Malaysian, Californian. And they are

1 Salima's "Monoblocci" storage island consists of two base cabinets housed in a laminated wood frame with a counter for the sink, cooktop, and plate racks, which can be concealed with a shade when not in use. The kitchen is designed to be compact and self-contained, to suit the smallest apartment.

2 Cooks need to have their utensils easily to hand. Hanging the *batterie de cuisine* on butcher's hooks from a stainless steel rack is Andrée Putman's solution. This stylish interior is a makeover of Le Corbusier's own kitchen in the Villa Turque, which was built in 1916 and refurbished in 1988.

5 Open shelving is not always convenient in a kitchen that does double duty as a dining area as well. Poggenpohl's solution is to conceal fixed shelving behind a sliding panel for a quick cover-up.

6 This modern version of a dresser, by architect Michael Carapettan, is designed to house tableware in a small space. It is balanced by recessed counters with a white-tiled splash-back and granite counter offering a practical working area.

3 The contemporary pantry in Poggenpohl's "Form 2000 CS Vorratsschrank" range has two deep, sliding drawers and a rotary storage cabinet that puts provisions within easy reach. Shelf heights are adjustable.

4 Organic waste goes into a green compartment within Alno's plastic triple waste bin, which is fed by a chute from the sink when the cabinet door is closed. Different-colored bins are used to separate waste products that can be recycled from those that cannot.

7 By displaying this handsome collection of cookware on hooks set against black mesh panels, Eva Jiricna has created a contemporary still-life rather than conventional storage.

8 A pair of smoothly contoured columns slide out on runners to reveal food storage in this space-efficient kitchen from Strato, who borrow from grain silo imagery to house provisions.

9 Cooks always accumulate utensils, yet space is finite. This "Esprit" range from Boffi offers a system of horizontal bars to hang shelves at convenient heights for all manner of gadgets.

10 The Museum of Modern Art in New York has exhibited Boffi kitchens, so their design credentials are excellent. But it is for their innovation that they are honored: the first colored polyester-finish door, 1954; the first wood and laminate door, 1960; the first door without a pull, 1974; and now, with "Dogu," the first kitchen with vertical wooden slats 6 inches wide.

11 Boffi's polyester finish "Xila" range first came into production in 1974, and was the first kitchen with doors that opened with pressure from the top edge of the door, rather than an indented pull grip.

12 Maple pulls with sculpted grips are in fact one of 45 choices available in Poggenpohl's "Form 2000 WP" range.

13 Wasted space is converted into heavy-duty service. All the kitchen base cabinets stand on raised platforms like baseboards, and Siematic exploit this space for additional storage that can be opened with a kick.

KITCHENS

1 This industrial-style cooking range in white with chrome pulls is ranked beside free-standing cabinets and appliances in an imaginative rejection of the fitted kitchen. Sergio Puente unites disparate elements with a soaring, tiled splashback with decorative frieze frame.

2 This handsome Neff "1071 N3" stainless steel oven is pulled forward from the line-up of kitchen cabinets into the room with a work cabinet that sets the cooktop immediately above the oven.

3 From defrosting to pastry settings – all are easy on this "AKG 334" single oven from Philips Whirlpool.

4 With a stainless steel frame, Ariston's "Gilda" is the first free-standing steam cooker. It has a steam condenser inside, alongside conventional and fan-assisted heat, and a broiler.

8 The Siemens dishwasher, positioned beneath a wall-mounted Siemens oven in this Poggenpohl kitchen, can be matched in color fronts to virtually any kitchen's decorative theme.

also reinterpreting traditional dishes in relation to modern knowledge of nutritional requirements.

With the advent of new functions, the old, claustrophobic kitchen is revealing itself as being too static, too purpose-built. Now it seems that in these flexible spaces, which often do double duty as dining areas, it is no longer a matter of displaying wealth, but rather showing your preference for a quality of life that revolves around shared food, enjoyed in a room where the hand of the architect is not too intrusive.

5 Unlike most advanced ovens, Smeg's "S20XMFR Multi-function" oven has a classic, analog clock rather than a digital face, under-stating its high-tech performance.

6 The "Wizard" collection from Zanussi, designed by Roberto Pezzetta, won international acclaim. This oven is styled in matte black and features a horizontal metallic silver pull that blends into the design with six other decorative gray bars, which double as viewports on the black exterior.

7 Offset against a dramatic cobalt blue ground, these white F. lli Ferretti di Ferretto kitchen cabinets house, in a marble counter, gas burners and a horizontally opening Gaggenau oven.

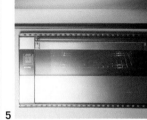

8

9

10

9 Ariston's "Four Seasons" fridge-freezer is a versatile food-storage system. Its central drawers allow either refrigerator or freezer capacity to be increased. It is also available in white.

11

10 The kitchen in a converted electricity plant by architect Gary Cunningham is enclosed by a computer-engineered steel-frame structure. Plywood panels were then erected and simply screwed onto cabinets, rather than carefully mitered.

12

11 Kitchen appliances and fittings are slimmed down in the new Bosch "Concept" series, designed for small-space living. This goes with the growing trend of child-free singles or couples needing less space.

12 John Outram is to British architecture what Steven Spielberg is to the American movie industry – a fantasist who overlays a workable plot with an allegorical and elaborate ornamentation. This kitchen by Outram assembles a battery of appliances – a Miele dishwasher, two Neff ovens plus four gas and four electric burners on the counter, which is dominated by an extravagantly scaled ventilator hood.

163

1 Boffi produces stainless steel counters to support deep sinks and cooktops for the professional chef or serious home cook. These steel wells hold Zanussi equipment and fit any Boffi-made kitchen. The aptly named "Gourmet" range is shown here.

3 In this kitchen by architect David Chipperfield, a square, almost free-standing block for cooking is balanced by a linear one against the wall for dish- and food-washing. The container frames are concrete, the doors walnut, and four powerful burners under an elevated stainless steel rack to cool skillets are framed in matte black.

2 The "AKG 085" gas cooktop from Philips Whirlpool has a thin, black skeletal cover and four burners of varying sizes. It can be installed in any type of surface of 1-inch depth.

4 Dacor feature five ceramic glass burners, heated by electric elements, star-shaped and in coils, that illuminate the smoky, black-glass, heat-conductive top. The controls are boldly illuminated, and the burners outlined in white, in this stylish cooktop.

6 This matte-black, four-burner cooktop from Zanussi's "Wizard" collection, designed by Roberto Pezzetta, has brightly illuminated controls.

7 The Vetroceramic cooktop from Zanussi uses electric elements and ceramic glass for efficient heat control, with markers from the controls to heat zones.

5 This white Corian counter features removable stainless steel rods slotted into 3-mm deep grooves. These rods absorb heat and so allow hot skillets to be placed on the counter without any fear of damaging it.

9 Four dual-circuit ceramic heating zones are assembled in an unusual format within the stainless steel cooktop, "1094 85NK", by Neff. They co-ordinate with the built-in Circotherm Plus oven with hood in Neff's "Stainless Steel" collection.

10 The imaginative "Piano Ectura Circolare" by Salima features five burners in a semi-circular design, which ensures that skillets do not overlap. An added bonus of the design is the free space it creates for either storage or food preparation.

8 In any household the kitchen poses more daily ventilation problems than the bathroom. Bulthaup co-ordinate a stainless steel, four-burner cooktop with an overhead stainless steel exhaust fan, which can also be used to circulate the air. The exhaust fan also features built-in spot-lights above the burners, and a hanging bar for utensils.

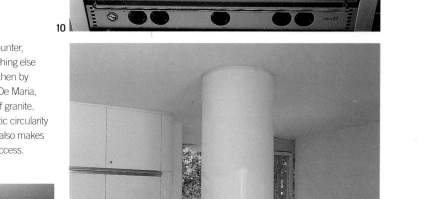

12 The counter, like everything else in this kitchen by architect De Maria, is made of granite. Its dramatic circularity of design also makes for easy access.

11 The Italian company Smeg's stainless steel "S93AX" cooktop is of ample proportions – it is 3 feet long. It is equipped with a fish broiler and ultra-rapid burner to meet the culinary demands of almost any function.

3 This small "Venus" sink from Avonite can be base-mounted or top recess flush-mounted, making it ideal for custom positioning in any Avonite counter. Avonite is a man-made, modified polyester sheet material in granite- and marble-effect finishes.

4 Villeroy & Boch move away from the traditional ceramic sink to produce a range in a new hard-wearing synthetic material. Although it looks like ceramic, this material has a greater elasticity, which means that there is less chance of breaking pottery and glass. It is also extremely hygienic and easy to clean. This sink with matching draining board is called "Mira," and the color "Brazil."

2 Low, horizontal planes feature in this spacious kitchen by architects Cecilia and Ottorino Berselli. Custom-cut marble in a long run features a window bay recess and a circular sink, as well as an additional long, shallow, rectangular sink for soaking fish or vegetables.

5 An undermounted bowl in stainless steel from the sink specialists Franke is set into a stylish marble counter.

1 Ciatti a Tavola's innovative wall-mounted sink makes obsolete the standard base cabinet that supports the conventional sink. Below the shaped marble cabinet, the plumbing for water and gas and the electrical circuitry is hidden. A tubular-steel rail runs the entire length of the counter. In this kitchen, storage cabinets and counters also double up as dining tables.

6 The acrylic material known as Colorcor, shows up different banded colors beneath its durable surface when incised. It has been employed here by architect Eva Jiricna for this grooved drainage board surrounding the deep, rectangular sink set into the counter.

7 Made from Siligranit, a composite material composed of granite rock and an acrylic mix, this "Blancostone" sink from Blanco resists scratching, heating, cooling, acids and alkalis. The sink's design offers two bowls, drainage area, china basket, chopping board and waste disposal.

8 Franke's "Compact" sink is designed as a work center and was developed after research into the demands of the modern cook. A removable chopping board closes off the sink when it is not in use.

9 The Avonite "Athens" sink is a pair of bowls that can be base-mounted or top-recessed flush into any Avonite top, like this one in clean, porcelain white. Avonite can be fused to steel sinks without seams.

12 An unusually deep bowl, paired like the traditional butler's sinks, is shaped in a contemporary fashion by F. lli Ferretti di Ferretto in white with a grooved draining board.

10 & 11 Siematic's sink separates food from cleaning with a shower for washing vegetables in an adjoining bowl. Undersink space is organized with a system of pull-out baskets and bins.

KITCHENS

1 This versatile "Ladyline" mixer faucet from Barking Grohe features many removable, labor-saving attachments, including a pull-out spray, a shower head and a constantly rinsed skillet scrubber and bottle brush. An add-on water filter is also available.

2 & 3 Unlike most manufacturers, who make either bowls or faucets, Franke combines both functions, thus creating a more integrated product. Two examples are the Franke undermounted bowl (far left and left) for fitting in solid counters, such as Corian or granite.

4 Pegler's sleek "CD" monoblock mixer is available in chrome, gray, white, beige, mocha red and yellow.

4

5

5 A bird's-eye view of the "Uranus" sink, made in easy-care, hygienic synthetic material by Villeroy & Boch. The "Europlus" single-lever chrome mixer faucet is by Friedrich Grohe.

6 Architect Charles Rutherfoord customized this Vola faucet, adding industrial on and off knobs. Customizing many types of kitchen accessories is possible, but you will invalidate the manufacturer's guarantee.

7 Blanco's "Borma Lux" mixer faucet on a "Blancoprimo" stainless steel sink. Smooth to operate, the faucet is available in chrome, white, brass, savanna, beige, platina, brasil and black.

8 This Tantofex "Tantadisc" sink mixer faucet with swivel spout is chromium plated, but is also available in gold-plate, white, brown, red, yellow and beige. Hard, ceramic disks provide a permanent, water-tight seal.

6

7

Directory

Walls & Ceilings

Abet Laminati SpA
Viale Industria 21
12042 Bra
Cunio
Italy
Tel: (172) 429 353
Fax: (172) 423 619

US outlet:
Abet Inc
100 Hollister Road
Teterboro
NJ 07608
Tel: (1201) 440 5440
Fax: (1201) 440 6373

Abet Laminati is one of the world's leading manufacturers of high-pressure laminates. With a daily production capacity exceeding 120,000 square meters of laminate, its products are distributed worldwide. The company's success is based on continual technological innovation and close collaboration with the design community. This led, in 1987, to the company being awarded the Compasso d'Oro for the introduction of Diafos, the world's first translucent laminate. In 1990, Abet Laminati was awarded the European Community Design Prize.

Walls & Ceilings: pp. 22/**3**, 23/**6**

Bigas and Sant
See *Luxo Italiana SpA*

Blockleys Brick Ltd
Sommerfield Road
Trench Lock
Telford TS1 4RY
Shropshire
England
Tel: (0952) 251 933
Fax: (0952) 641 900

Walls & Ceilings: pp. 30/**1-4**, 31/**8-10**

Jaime Tresserra Clapes
See *J. Tressera Design SL*

Dimensione Fuoco SAS
Via V. Veneto 58
30027 S. Dona'di Piave
Venice
Italy
Tel: (41) 50444
Fax: (41) 330592

US outlet:
Danny Allesandro
307 East 60th Street
New York
NY 10022
Tel: (212) 421 1928
Fax: (212) 759 3819

Architects Afra and Tobia Scarpa designed glass screens for Dimensione Fuoco, who revitalized the ancient craft of stained-glass windows, using lead-framed colored glass with a gilded metal frame.

Walls & Ceilings: p. 26/**3 & 4**

Chr. Fabers Fabriker A/S
DK-5856 Ryslinge
Denmark
Tel: (62) 671200
Fax: (62) 672114

US outlet:
Faber Industries Ltd
5127 Park Drive
Fredericksburg
VA 22408
Tel: (703) 898 7574
Fax: (703) 898 5681

Founded almost 100 years ago, Faber is an international company selling in 47 countries. Danish precision engineers design ranges of Venetian, vertical and roller shades in a wide range of colors which run with the smoothness of butter for internal or external use.

Walls & Ceilings: p. 26/**5**
Windows: pp. 74/**3**, 75/**9**

Fendi
See *Nouve Ceramiche Ricchetti Srl*

Fornasetti Srl
Immaginazione
Via Brera 16
20121 Milano
Italy
Tel: (2) 8646 2271
Fax: (2) 7060 1130

US outlets:
Barneys
106 7th Avenue
New York
NY 10011
Tel: (212) 886 1653

Blumenthal
280 Park Avenue South
New York
NY 10010
Tel: (718) 361 1234
Fax: (718) 361 2257

Design West Inc
1855 Griffin Road
Suite A
Dania
FL 33004
Tel: (305) 925 8225

Fifty/50
793 Broadway
New York
NY 10003
Tel: (212) 777 3208

280 Lafayette
280 Lafayette Street
New York
NY 10012
Tel: (212) 941 5825
Fax: (212) 274 1612

Modern Living
8125 Melrose Avenue
Los Angeles
CA 90046
Tel: (213) 655 3898
Fax: (213) 655 1677

Niedermaier
2828 North Paulina
Chicago
IL 60657
Tel: (312) 528 8123

Fornasetti Srl continues the production of furniture and objects created by trompe l'oeil cabinet maker Piero Fornasetti since the 1950s. His son Barnaba has made additional items, sometimes drawing his inspiration from the same source. The company is essentially craft based, and its hand-made products are available in limited editions.

Walls & Ceilings: p. 27/**9**
Storage: p. 132/**5**

Foscarini Murano SpA
F. ta Manin 1
30141 Murano
Venice
Italy
Tel: (41) 739344
Fax: (41) 739835

Foscarini sees glass as a means to reach an objective – a philosophy far from the Murano tradition which has tended to focus production on esthetic considerations rather than on functionality. However, Foscarini still capitalizes – in a modern key – on the inimitable know-how which Murano has bequeathed to the working of glass, and the company's products follow the modernist dictum which advocates the union of function and esthetics. Widening its original activity in the contract market toward large-scale production for furnishing, Foscarini has transferred into a larger market its experience in pursuing new and original solutions to problems.

Glass Design's Domino System
See *Tecno SpA*

Hunter Fan Company
2500 Frisco Avenue
Box 14775
Memphis
TN 38114
Tel: (901) 743 1360
Fax: (901) 745 9376

Innovations Inc
969 Third Avenue
New York
NY 10022
Wallcoverings

Luxo Italiana SpA
Via delle More
24030 Presezzo
Bergamo
Italy
Tel: (35) 611562
Fax: (35) 610196

US outlet:
Luxo Lamp Corporation
36 Midland Avenue
Port Chester
New York
NY 10573
Tel: (914) 937 4433
Fax: (914) 937 5002

Luxo Italiana is an offshoot of the Norwegian Luxo Group and was established in 1966 to produce one type of economic lamp intended for mass outlets. Production extended to include a line of technical lamps, but since 1984 Luxo Italiana has been producing its own lines of "interior design" lamps commissioned from international designers which have won awards at some of the most prestigious trade fairs in the lighting sector.

Walls & Ceilings: p. 28/**5**
Stairs: p. 90/**6**
Lighting: p. 114/**8**

DIRECTORY

Michael Manwaring & Dixi Wells
1045 Sansome Street
Suite 304
San Francisco
CA 94111

Paint

A.V. Mazzega
Fondamenta Vivarini 3
Murano
Venice
Italy
Tel: (41) 736677
Fax: (41) 739939

A.V. Mazzega produce glass blocks and screens for partitions and dividers. The company's aim is to preserve the ancient skills of Murano glassblowing, giving birth to unique forms which are able to catch light and color.

Walls & Ceilings: p. 24/**4**

Mito Srl
Via Lamia
S.S. 18 – Km. 41,500
84015 Nocera Superiore (SA)
Italy
Tel: (81) 5142364
Fax: (81) 5141919

US outlet:
Gercomi Corporation
Albert & Corrado Mion
4474 NW 74 Avenue
Miami
FL 33166
Tel: (305) 477 7080
Fax: (305) 477 5986

Mito Murano glass tiles, hand-made in Venice from a process that is over 1000 years old, produces three-dimensional glass tiles designed by the artist Lucio Fontana. Cast in a mold and hand-shaped, the tiles range in size from 2 x 2 inches to 23 x 23 inches in a variety of shapes. The glass is thick and strong enough for interior and exterior installations, as partitions, doors or windows in private homes or bars, hotels and restaurants. Mito also produces doors and partitions in precious wood, as well as exclusive light fixtures and mirrors.

Walls & Ceilings: pp. 18/**1**, 25/**8-10**, 26/**2**

Norton Blumenthal Inc
979 Third Avenue
New York
NY 10021

Wallcoverings

Nouve Ceramiche Ricchetti Srl
Via Radici in Piano 428
41049 Sassuolo (MO)
Italy
Tel: (536) 5740 1076
Fax: (536) 805401

Fendi tiles are produced by Nuove Ceramiche Ricchetti, which, together with Klingenberg GmbH in Germany, make up the ceramic division of the Swedish United Group, a worldwide leader in the production of floor and wallcovering materials. Ricchetti manufactures ceramic tiles in three production units—at Sassuolo, Fiorano and Mordano. Established in 1925, Ricchetti's aim has always been to present architectural products inspired by established fashion themes which enable the individual to create personalized surroundings.

Walls & Ceilings: p. 28/**1**

Orac Decor
Orac N.V.
Oudenburgsesteenweg 90
8400 Oostende
Belgium
Tel: (59) 80 3252
Fax: (59) 80 2810

US outlet:
Outwater Plastics
4 Passaic Street
Wood Ridge
NJ 07075
Tel: (201) 340 1040
Fax: (201) 916 1640

The Orac range includes cornice, panel and chair rail moldings, as well as door surrounds, sconces for wall lighting and ceiling medalions in a range of classical, traditional and contemporary styles.

Walls & Ceilings: pp. 28/**3**, 29/**10**

Pilkington Glass (Architectural)
Alexandra Works
Borough Road
St Helens WA10 3TT
England
Tel: (0744) 692998
Fax: (0744) 451326

US outlet:
Pilkington Sales (North America) Ltd
10 Gateway Boulevard
Suite 510
Don Mills
Ontario
Canada M3C 3A1

The name Pilkington is synonymous with glass innovation and panel structural systems in buildings. Their Wall Planar Structural Glazing System has flexible silicone-sealed joints between panels to provide a complete glass envelope without using frames or mullions so it can be used for vertical, sloping and horizontal applications.

Walls & Ceilings: pp. 24/**5**, 25/**12**

Riflessitaliani (UK) Ltd
451 Kingston Road
Ewell
Surrey KT19 0DB
England
Tel: (081) 786 7026
Fax: (081) 786 7027

Riflessitaliani (UK) Limited are distributors of specialist hand-made wallcoverings. The collection includes the high profile Karta Pergemena Collection of antique-finished parchment papers dusted with gold and silver; Tonga, a unique wallcovering and upholstery fabric with the appear-ance of suede and the texture of leather; and Heavy Metal, a totally new concept which creates a satin sheen of oxidized and iridescent effects, including warm golds, pewter, aluminum, steel and bronze. Other exclusive ranges are Intarsio, Maya, Metropolis, Roma, Venexia, and Verona.

Walls & Ceilings: p. 32/**4-9**

Gianfranco Salvi
See *Riflessitaliani*

G. Schrattenecker Holzwaren GmbH
Magetsham 19
A-4923 Lohnsburg
Austria
Tel: (7754) 3100-0
Fax: (7754) 3342

The company was founded in 1952 as a cabinet maker's workshop with only one employee. By 1991 it was employing 300, producing Tilo moldings, wooden ceilings, panels and parquet flooring with fine modern technical machines which guarantee top quality.

Walls & Ceilings: p. 28/**2 & 7**

Svedbergs
1 Dalstorp AB
51095 Dalstorp
Sweden
Tel: (321) 60460
Fax: (321) 60777

Market leader in Scandinavia, Svedberg bathrooms offer the complete package, including tubs, showers, sinks, lavatories, and specialist fittings like whirlpool baths and vanity units, as well as ceiling tiles with built-in stereo loudspeaker and halogen lights.

Walls & Ceilings: p. 28/**6**

Tecno SpA
Via Bigli 22
20121 Milan
Italy
Tel: (2) 760 20341
Fax: (2) 784 484

Tecno SpA produced Glass Design's Domino System as a one-off for a client. Founded in the early 1950s by Osvaldo and Eugenio Borsani, Tecno was originally a joinery company but now works in many furniture materials, including wood, metal, laminates and glass. The company has five factories outside Milan in northern Italy, together with other facilities in Spain and South America. All its products are design by prominent architects or designers: "Nomos" by Sir Norman Foster (system furniture), "Ianus" by Luca Scacchetti (executive furniture), "Qualis" by Emilio Ambasz (seating) and "Barcelona" by Ricardo Bofill (interiors of Barcelona Airport) to name but a few.

Tilo
See *G. Schrattenecker Holzwaren GmbH*

J. Tressera Design SL
Freixa 42
08021 Barcelona
Spain
Tel: (3) 2004922
Fax: (3) 2004734

Tressera designs were used in the set fittings for the movie "Batman." They regularly win international awards for their design and quality of cabinetry. The materials used are, essentially, walnut veneer, finished with various light- and dark-toned varnishes blended with inlaid marquetry which bring out the quality of the furniture.

Walls & Ceilings: p. 27/**13**
Storage: p. 133/**11-15**

Zanotta SpA
Via Vittorio Veneto 57
20054 Nova Milanese
Italy
Tel: (2) 362 40453
Fax: (2) 362 451038

US outlet:
ICF
305 East 63rd Street
New York
NY 10021
Tel: (212) 750 0900
Fax: (212) 593 1152

Zanotta is one of Italy's respected manufacturers of furniture designed by the great names in Italian architecture. Achille Castiglioni is one of the stars in their collection. His movable screens and pivoting stairs present mobile functional alternatives to more conventional and cumbersome fixtures.

Walls & Ceilings: p. 27/**12**
Storage: p. 125/**6-8**

Floors

Ability Floors
66-93 Broadway
Bronx
NY 10471

Amtico Co. Ltd
Kingfield Road
Coventry CV6 5PL
England
Tel: (0203) 665615
Fax: (0203) 667280

Inspired by nature, Amtico floors mirror the traditional beauty of wood, marble and stone. Design flexibility is the key to the Amtico collection: with its extensive range of shades, patterns and textures, virtually any design is attainable. The CAD facilities combined with advanced cutting technology can make a dream floor become a reality.

Floors: pp. 35/**6**, 37/**9**, 45/**17**
Bathrooms: p. 138/**2**

Art et Industrie
594 Broadway
New York
NY 10012

Rugs

Azu-Vi SA
Avenida de Italia 58
PO Box 26
12540 Villarreal
Castellon
Spain
Tel: (64) 520600
Fax: (64) 530218

US outlets:
Azuvi Inc
1070 Kraemer Place
Anaheim
CA 92806

Azuvi Inc
8030 Philips Highway
Suite 5
Jacksonville
FL 32256

Azu-Vi produce single-fired glazed tiles decorated with exclusive designs in a wide chromatic range.

Floors: p. 34/**2**

Matteo Baldini
See *C.I.S. Baldini G. & C. SnC*

Bosanquet Ives Ltd
3 Court Lodge
48 Sloane Square
London SW1W 8AT
England
Tel: (071) 730 6241
Fax: (071) 730 5341

Bosanquet Ives are specialist carpet suppliers to the trade. They concentrate on custom-made body and border Brussels weave and velvet-pile Wilton and a wide range of natural floor coverings.

Floors: p. 50/**5**

Elizabeth Browning Jackson
140 Watts Street
New York
NY 10013

Rugs

Capel Rugs Inc
831 North Main Street
Troy
NC 27371
Tel: (919) 576 6211
Fax: (919) 576 0718

Founded in 1917, Capel is one of the largest and oldest braided rug manufacturers in the world. In 1964 Capel added hand-knotted, hand-hooked, flat-woven, dhurries, kilims, machine-made orientals and machine-made needlepoint rugs to the total collection.

Ceramica Bardelli SpA
Via Pascoli 4/6
20010 Vittuone
Milan
Italy
Tel: (2) 901 11030
Fax: (2) 902 60766

US outlet:
Hastings Pavement Co Inc
30 Commercial Street
Freeport
NY 11520
Tel: (516) 879 3500

Since 1960, Bardelli have manu-factured ceramic tiles in Italy. Three fundamental principles characterize their present production line: even colors, a wide range of sizes and modern graphic design.

Floors: p. 40/**8**

Ceramica Sant'Agostino SpA
Via Statale 247
44047 S. Agostino (FE)
Italy
Tel: (532) 844111
Fax: (532) 846113

US outlets:
Arley Wholesale
North-South Road
Scranton
PA 18501
Tel: (717) 344 9874
Fax: (717) 344 6436

Fuda Tile
313 Broad Avenue
Ridgefield
NJ 07657
Tel: (201) 797 8980
Fax: (201) 797 0781

Genesee Ceramic Tile Distr.
24701 Telegraph Road
Southfield
MI 48034
Tel: (313) 354 3550
Fax: (313) 742 6670

Hastings Pavement Co Inc
30 Commercial Street
Freeport
NY 11520
Tel: (516) 379 3500
Fax: (516) 379 3187

Italian Ceramic Tile Center
7521 North Milwakee
Niles
IL 60648
Tel: (708) 647 0194
Fax: (708) 647 9441

Metco Tile
291 Arsenal Street
Watertown
MA 02172
Tel: (617) 926 1100
Fax: (617) 926 9714

Moreira Tile
1297 Kaumualii Street
Honolulu
Hawaii 96817
Tel: (808) 845 6461
Fax: (808) 845 7461

Nemo Tile
177-02 Jamaica Avenue
Jamaica
NY 11520
Tel: (718) 291 5969
Fax: (718) 291 5992

Richmond Ceramic Tiles
31 Northbridge Street
Staten Island
NY 10309
Tel: (718) 317 8453
Fax: (718) 317 5580

Tamiami Tile Supply Corp
7500 Northwest 41st
Miami
FL 33166
Tel: (305) 592 2600
Fax: (305) 592 1919

The Tile Shop
1803 West Country Road "C"
Roseville
MN 55113
Tel: (612) 881 2595
Fax: (612) 631 9645

Since 1964 Ceramica Sant'Agostino has made floor tiles, diversifying in the 1970s to double-fired wall tiles. Their production capacity exceeds 21,500 square yards a day: 9,500 square yards of enameled, decorated hardbake and 12,000 square yards of white paste single-fired tiles strengthened with their hard stratos glaze, rich in aluminum and quartz. Continuous research both in classic and contemporary design are making Ceramica Sant'Agostino one of the leading companies in the ceramic field.

Floors: p. 41/**2**

C.I.S. di Baldini G. & C. SnC
Via Acquale 3
Zona Industriale
Massa 54100
Italy
Tel: (585) 832310
Fax: (585) 832038

US outlet:
Mauro Gennareti Italianissimo Inc
1000 Clintmore Road
Bocaraton
FL 33487
Tel: (407) 241 0662
Fax: (407) 241 0664

C.I.S di Baldini commissions architects and designers such as Adolfo Natalini, Michele de Lucchi, Matteo Thun, Andrea Branzi, Alessandro Mendini and Luca Scacchetti to create marble interiors using select marbles for floor and wallcoverings.

Floors: p. 40/**3-5**

Corres Mexican Tiles
Circuito Novelistas 3
Cuidad Satelite
Naucalpan Edo De Mexico
Mexico
Tel: (525) 572 3070

Established in 1851, Corres are the largest company manufacturing hand-made tiles in Mexico. They control, with a skilled workforce using traditional methods, the entire production and distribution, from the quarrying of the finest clay to the delivery of the finished product.

Floors: p. 41/**13**

Crucial Trading Ltd
77 Westbourne Park Road
London W2 5QH
England
Tel: (071) 221 9000
Fax: (071) 727 3634

US outlet:
GCC International
PO Box 121
Closter
NJ 07624-0121
Tel: (201) 567 1574
Fax: (201) 567 2251

Crucial Trading offer one of Europe's largest and most versatile collection of natural floor coverings, with over 90 designs in sisal, coir, seagrass, rush and sisal and wool mixes.

Floors: p. 50/**6, 7, 10 & 11**

Ege Axminster A/S
230 Grejsdalsvej
7100 Vejle
Denmark
Tel: (75) 833300
Fax: (75) 720696

US outlet:
ABC Rug World
888 Broadway
New York
NY 10003

Ege Art-Line carpets, made in Denmark using the traditional Axminster broad-loom weaving process, replicate the work of contemporary Scandinavian artists such as Josef Albers and Asger Jorn and famous paintings by 20th-century artists, including Paul Klee, Rene Magritte, Salvador Dali and Wassily Kandinsky.

Floors: p. 46/**1 & 3**

Forbo Nairn Ltd
PO Box 1
Kirkcaldy
Fife KY1 2SB
Scotland
Tel: (0592) 261 111
Fax: (0592) 205 461

Forbo Nairn Ltd is a manufacturer of high-quality linoleum, contract vinyls and cushioned vinyl. The company, founded under the name Nairn, is based in Kirkcaldy, Scotland, and has been in existence for over 100 years. Since 1985 it has been a part of Forbo SA, Switzerland, and has a number of sister companies located throughout the world.

Floors: pp. 44/**3-5 & 9**, 45/**12**

Formia Golvgruppen AB
Fredsgatan 18
S-703 62 Orebro
Sweden
Tel: (19) 117 525
Fax: (19) 170 750

US contact:
RIAB (UK) Ltd
Evergreen Industrial Buildings
Broadway Lane
South Cerney, Cirencester
Gloucestershire GL7 5UH
England
Tel: (0285) 862277
Fax: (0285) 862233

RIAB Interiors, manufactured in Sweden by Forbia AB from recycled auto tires, solves a worldwide environmental problem with the production of a superb sound-deadening rubber floor. Available in unlimited colors, it is suitable for stairs or any flooring area.

Floors: p. 45/**16**

Gerland SA
50 Cours de la Republique
Villeurland
69625 Cedex
France
Tel: (78) 03 64 01
Fax: (78) 03 64 39

Gerland manufacture vinyl, rubber, olympic sport and specialist flooring.

Floors: pp. 44/**6-8**, 45/**13-15**

Hartco
900 South Gray Street
Ste. 1902 Knoxville
TN 37902
Tel: (615) 544 0767
Fax: (615) 544 2071

Hartco is a leading manufacturer of high-quality pre-finished wood flooring to suit virtually all commercial and residential applications. The Hartco brand of floors, moldings, and exclusive floor care and maintenance products is made by the Tibbals Flooring Company headquartered in Oneida, Tennessee. Founded in 1946, Tibbals was purchased by Premark International, Inc. in 1988. Hartco distributors are located throughout the United States and abroad.

Floors: p. 37/**8**

Junckers
Wheaton Court Commercial
Centre
Wheaton Road
Witham
Essex CM8 3UJ
England
Tel: (0376) 517 512
Fax: (0376) 514 401

US outlet:
Junckers Hardwood Inc
Suite P
Building No.1
187 West Orangethorpe Avenue
Placentia, CA
Tel: (714) 579 3188
Fax: (714) 524 1902

Junckers is a leading producer of solid hardwood floorings in beech, ash, elm and oak in a wide range of colors, grades and thicknesses for multi-purpose or specialist sports purposes.

Floors: p. 36/**4 & 5**

Kentucky Wood Floors Inc
4200 Reservoir Avenue
Louisville
KY 40213
Tel: (502) 451 6024
Fax: (502) 451 6027

Kentucky Wood Floors provide the discriminating specifier of interior furnishings with a wide range of hardwood flooring from ash to zebrawood which includes "Custom Classics," "Custom Borders," "Plank" and "Parquet," both prefinished and unfinished. Through its subsidiary, Kentucky Millwork, a comprehensive selection of architectural millwork and casework, such as windows, doors, entry frames, moldings, stairs and handrails, and mantels, form part of its product range.

Floors: p.36/**2**

Kirkstone Quarries Ltd
Skelwith Bridge
Nr. Ambleside
Cumbria LA22 9NN
England
Tel: (05394) 33296
Fax: (05394) 34006

US outlets:
Domestic Marble and Stone Corp
41 East 42nd Street
New York
NY 10017
Tel: (212) 557 1980
Fax: (212) 370 0218

Walker and Zanger
10600 Shadowood, Suite 301
Houston
TX 77043
Tel: (713) 468 7994
Fax: (713) 468 0496

Walker and Zanger (West Coast) Ltd
8901 Bradley Avenue
Sun Valley
CA 91352
Tel: (818) 504 0235
Fax: (818) 504 2226

Walker and Zanger (West Coast) Ltd
2960 Airway Avenue, B-104
Costa Mesa
CA 92626
Tel: (714) 546 3761
Fax: (714) 546 9746

Kirkstone Quarries Ltd, trading for 40 years and with 60 employees, extract, fabricate and market a unique architectural stone. Traditionally supplying roofing, paving and cladding, Kirkstone is now also widely used for many interior surfaces, and the company produce an increasing range of detailed work to specification for British and overseas architects and designers.

Floors: p. 39/**6**

Lonseal Inc
928 East 238 Street
Building A
Carson
CA 90745

Floor coverings

MARBO
See *Rover SpA*

C.H. Masland & Sons
Spring Road
Carlisle
PA 17103

Carpets

Matico Hi-Design Tile
55 Mail Drive
Commack
NY 11725

Ingo Maurer GmbH
Kaiserstrasse 47
8000 Munchen 40
Tel: (89) 381 6060
Fax: (89) 381 60620

US outlet:
I.L. Euro Inc
Ivan Luini
900 Broadway 902
New York
NY 10003
Tel: (212) 477 3188
Fax: (212) 477 4862

Since 1966, when Ingo Maurer's first lamp was instantly recognized as a design breakthrough, he has won increasing acclaim as a designer and manufactuer of lamps and lighting systems. His work combines elegance and simplicity with unique elements of ironic playfulness and imaginative ingenuity.

Modern Age
795 Broadway
New York
NY 10003
Tel: (212) 674 5603

41 East 11th Street
New York
NY 10003
Tel: (212) 353 3450
Fax: (212) 529 2779

A two-location resource center for modern decorative design, Modern Age focuses on every aspect of the interior landscape. It has a continuously changing supply of contemporary decorative accessories from over 25 international manufacturers, as well as the 20th-century classics.

Floors: pp. 46/**5**, 47/**10**

Leah Nelson
110 West Kinzie
Chicago
IL 60610

Rugs

Neotu
25 Rue du Renard
75004 Paris
France
Tel: (1) 42 78 96 97
Fax: (1) 42 78 26 27

US outlet:
Neotu
133 Greene Street
New York
NY 10012
Tel: (212) 982 0210
Fax: (212) 982 0217

Neotu, founded in France in 1965 by Gerard Dalmon and Pierre Staudenmeyer, commissions, manufactures and distributes

contemporary furniture and soft furnishing like rugs, in limited editions. Designers are chosen for an approach that nourishes references from the past as well as lessons from contemporary art to produce an evolution for the future.

Floors: p. 46/**2**
Doors: p. 63/**10**

Elio Palmisano Edizioni Tessili
Via Stra Madonna Cp.142
21047 Saronno
Milan
Italy
Tel: (2) 9670 0654 .
Fax: (2) 9670 0658

From 1960, Elio Palmisano have specialized in hand-made carpets and tapestries, launching designs created by the Italian Futurists Giacomo Balla, Fortunato Depero and Gino Severini. Production on hand-looms of carpets and tapestries designed for them by Oskar Kokoschka, Mark Tobey, Max Ernst and the Italian Abstractists Mario Radice, Mauro Reggiani and Luigi Veronesi increased the art series. Designs now include the work of many young artists and famous designers, such as Nathalie du Pasquier, Ettore Sottsass, George Sowden, Beppe Caturegli, Beatrice Santiccioli, Leslie Ann Keller, Vittore di Sangiacomo, Tarshito and Ugo Marano.

Floors: p. 34/**3**

Paris Ceramics
583 Kings Road
London SW6 2EH
England
Tel: (071) 371 7778
Fax: (071) 371 8395

US outlet:
Paris Ceramics USA Inc
26 Connecticut Avenue
Greenwich 06830
Tel & Fax: (203) 862 9538

Steve Charles of Paris Ceramics sources and commissions his tiles from all over Europe, seeking the best traditional materials and the highest standards of workmanship.

Floors: p. 40/**9**

Porcelanosa
147 Route 17 South
Paramus
NJ 07652
Tel: (201) 261 1991

Tiles

Reed Harris Ltd
Riverside House
Carnwath Road
London SW6 3HS
England
Tel: (071) 736 7511
Fax: (071) 736 2988

Floors: p. 38/**2-4**

Rex Ceramiche Artistiche SpA
Via Viazza, 30
41042 Fiorano Modenese
Modena
Italy
Tel: (59) 536 843854
Fax: (59) 536 844022

US outlets:
Amani Tile International
73 Sherwood Avenue
Farmingdale
NY 11735
Tel: (516) 752 8999
Fax: (516) 752 8991

Hastings Pavement Company Inc
30 Commercial Street
Freeport
NY 11520
Tel: (516) 379 3500

Tamiami Tile Supply Corp
7500 Northwest 41 Street
Miami
FL 33166

Manufacturers of ceramics for over 20 years with a specific market strategy aimed at the highest level of the market, Rex today produces white-body single-fire floor tiles and double-fire wall tiles. Exploiting the most advanced technology and with a marked eye for design, Rex boasts a complete range of products for both the Italian and international markets. Using the talents of a recognized design leader – Nicola Trussardi – Rex offers beautiful collections of wall tiles and single-fired products which are guaranteed abrasion-resistant and resemble natural materials such as marble, stone and briar wood.

Floors: p. 34/**1**

RIAB Floors
See *Formia Golvgruppen AB*

Rover SpA
Strada Della Giara 23
37030 Poiano
Verona
Italy
Tel: (45) 526002/526322
Fax: (45) 526238

Rover SpA produce rosin-bonded conglomerate marble floor tiles and wall slabs.

Rowi Parket International B.V.
PO Box 1033
3430 BA Nieuwegein
The Netherlands
Tel: (3402) 60206
Fax: (3402) 64174

In Holland, Rowi Parket has sold unique hardwood parquet since 1950, exported throughout Europe and to the USA since 1985. Their patented installation system requires no nails or glue. Long and short strips of wood are supplied, varnished and preglued, plus a preglued underlayer to create a total thickness of 7mm. Recent new products include a laminate floor replicating pastel-wood and several marble designs.

Floors: pp. 35/**5**, 37/**10**

Ruckstuhl AG
St. Urbanstrasse 21
Postfach 337
CH-4901 Langenthal
Switzerland
Tel: (63) 282191
Fax: (63) 224870

US outlet:
Ruckstuhl USA Ltd
1480 Ridgeway Street
Union
NJ 07083
Tel: (908) 686 7203
Fax: (908) 686 7232

The Ruckstuhl carpet company in Switzerland, founded in 1881, has never embarked on mass production. To meet the needs of designers, architects and interior decorators, the production of coir, sisal and wool carpets continues to be individual and flexible, while keeping up with technological developments. The company's co-operation over many years with J.L. Larsen of the USA culminated in the takeover of the Larsen Carpet Company; carpets designed by artist Jack Lenor Larsen are now available in Europe.

Floors: p. 50/**8 & 9**

Saraband Designs
Stroud
Gloucester
Glos GL5 5ND
England
Tel: (0453) 872579
Fax: (0453) 872420

Saraband Designs and its associated companies have been importing natural floorcoverings for over 30 years. Available in broadloom sizes, latex-backed and laid like a conventional

carpet, these coverings appeal to both the fashion conscious and the environmentally concerned customer.

Floors: p 50/**1-3**

SICIS International
Via Ravennate 5081
47023 Cesena (FO)
Italy
Tel: (547) 353828
Fax: (547) 353820

US outlets:
Forms and Surfaces Inc
3801 N.E. 2nd Avenue
Miami
FL 33137
Fax: (305) 576 4861

Hastings Pavement Co Inc
30 Commercial Street
Freeport
NY 11520
Fax: (516) 379 3187

Walker & Zanger Ltd
8901 Bradley Avenue
Sun Valley
CA 91352
Fax: (818) 504 2057

Marbled mosaics produced by modern factory methods is the unique skill of SICIS International, who have patented thir method. Specially devised to speed up the ancient craft of hand-laid mosaic floors, the standard pre-assembled, 0.39-inch-thick modules are easily installed.

Floors: p. 40/**6 & 7**

Sisal Collezioni
Via Emilia Pavese 107
29100 Piacenza
Italy
Tel: (523) 41200
Fax: (523) 41894

US outlet:
International Furniture
Ernest Stoecklin
PO Box 206
135 Fort Lee Road
Leonia
NJ 07605
Tel: (201) 585 9420
Fax: (201) 592 6866

Sisal Collezioni, manufacturer of modern carpets, commissions designs from famous names in the world of architecture, fashion and art. The aim of the company is to re-establish the carpet as an esthetic functional element in the furnishing scheme.

Floors: pp. 46/**4**, 47/**9 & 13**

Tarkett AB
Box 3004
S-372 03 Ronneby
Sweden
Tel: (457) 71000
Fax: (457) 70528

US outlets:

Tarkett Ceramic Inc
PO Box 264
800 Lanidex Plaza
Parsippany
NJ 07054
Tel: (201) 428 9000
Fax: (201) 428 8017

Tarkett Hardwood Flooring
PO Box 300
2225 Eddie Williams Road
Johnson City
TN 37605
Tel: (615) 928 3122
Fax: (615) 928 9445

Tarkett is one of the largest flooring companies in the world. The company's aim is to lead flooring technology and design with products that are safe for the environment, and it offers its customers a "total flooring concept" in terms of coordination possibilities. Products include hardwood, sheet vinyl and resilient tiling, carpets and ceramics. Tarkett is the parent company in an international group of companies which market under the brand names of Tarkett, Pegulan, Ricchetti, Klingenberg, Febolit, Durmont and Eybl.

Floors: pp. 36/**3**, 44/**2**, 45/**11**

Tibbals Hartco
See *Hartco*

Toulemonde Bochart
ZI de Villemilan
7 Impasse Branly
91320 Wissous
France
Tel: (69) 20 40 30
Fax: (69) 81 73 12

US outlet:

Toulemonde Bochart US
119 57th Street
Suite 720
New York
NY 10019
Tel: (212) 757 3858
Fax: (212) 757 3911

Founded in the 1940s, Toulemonde Bochart's production falls into two major categories: contemporary rugs in wool or synthetic fibers, mechanical or hand-made, and created by famous designers such as Andrée Putman, Jean Michel Wilmotte, Christian Duc, Pascal Mourgue, Emilio Robba and Hilton McConnico, in more than 150 different designs/colors; and wall-to-wall natural fiber coverings like "Sisalene," created by Jean Michel Wilmotte.

Floors: p. 47/**8**

Christine van der Hurd
See *Modern Age*

Vorwerk & Co Teppichwerke KG
Kuhlmannstrasse 11
Export Department
3250 Hameln
Germany
Tel: (5151) 103-0
Fax: (5151) 103377

US outlet:

Prestige Mills Inc
83 Harbor Road
Port Washington
NY 11050
Tel: (516) 767 1110
Fax: (516) 767 0346

Vorwerk's carpeting collections Dialogues 1 and 2 aim to bring more fun to furnishing. Their star-studded list of artists, like David Hockney and Roy Lichtenstein, join forces with architects like Sir Norman Foster, Jean Nouvel, and Zaha Hadid to produce an imaginative collection of boldly patterned carpets for the domestic and contract trade.

Floors: pp. 34, 35/**7**, 48/**1-5**, 49/**6-9**

V'Soske Joyce Ltd
Oughterard
Co. Galway
Eire
Tel: (91) 82113
Fax: (91) 82301

V'Soske Joyce produce hand-tufted rugs, wall-hangings and carpeting. A major asset is the modern dye house, where the finest grade wools and silks can be dyed to approved customer color tufts.

Floors: p. 47/**11 & 15**

Doors

G & S Allgood Ltd
Carterville House
297 Euston Road
London NW1 3AQ
England
Tel: (071) 387 9951
Fax: (071) 380 1232

US outlet:

Modric Inc
RR3 Box 85
San Augustine
TX 75972
Tel: (409) 275 9651
Fax: (409) 275 9537

Allgood Ltd are architectural hardware suppliers and manufacturers, primarily marketing their own range called Modric which comprises hardware for doors and windows.

Doors: pp. 62/**8**, 64/**1, 5 & 11**

Atlantic Door Service Inc
261 Sunset Park Drive
Herndon
VA 22070

The Atrium Door & Window Corp
PO Box 226957
Dallas
TX 7522-6957
Tel: (214) 634 9663

Baldwin Hardware Corp
841 East Wyomissing Boulevard
Reading
PA 19612
Tel: (215) 777 7811

Pulls

Bd Ediciones de Diseno, SA
C. Mallorca 291
08037 Barcelona
Spain
Tel: (3) 258 6909
Fax: (3) 207 3697

US outlet:

Luminaire
Mr Nasir Kassamali
7300 Southwest 45 Street
Miami
FL 33155
Tel: (305) 264 6308
Fax: (305) 264 2181

Bd Ediciones de Diseno was founded in Barcelona in 1972 by several architects and other professional designers with the intention of producing furniture, objects and accessories for decoration, completely independently, under the direction of architect Xavier Carulla. They make replicas of historic pieces, such as the door pulls designed in 1914 by Gaudi, as well as producing the current designs of international designers and architects. Bd Ediciones collaborates with a variety of supply industries, its technology ranging from simple processes like those required for the Gaudi series to a highly mechanized process for shelving.

Doors: p. 63/**13 & 14**
Storage: p. 132/**4**

Angelo Becchetti BAL
Via Montini 34
25067 Lumezzane S.A.
Brescia
Italy
Tel: (30) 826 131
Fax: (30) 828 029

US outlet:

Simon's Hardware
421 Third Avenue
New York
NY 10016

BAL has produced quality solid-brass hardware for doors and windows since 1882. Their production range, which includes pulls, knobs, hinges, door pulls and knockers and other accessories for interior decoration such as coat hooks, door stops and switch plates, is exported all over the world.

Doors: p. 62/**4**

Best of Brass
See *Handles and Fittings*

Burbank Sash & Door
2518 S. Burbank Boulevard
Burbank
CA 91505

CDI
See *Clodagh Design International*

Clodagh Design International
365 First Avenue
New York
NY 10010
Tel: (212) 673 9202
Fax: (212) 614 9125

Clodagh Design International and its namesake principal, Irish-born Clodagh, have won international recognition for cutting-edge architectural and product design.

Doors: pp. 61/**5**, 64/**10**

Dierre
Strada Statale per Chieri 58
Villanova d'Asti (AT)
Italy
Tel: (141) 946152
Fax: (141) 946649

Dierre specialize in armored doors, producing 70,000 annually, which places it among the top 50 fastest-growing companies in Italy in the 1990s. In this security-conscious age, the group has developed and produced locks, armored fire-proof doors, steel shutters and safes.

Doors: p. 56/**3**

Eurobrass Srl
Via Brescia 104
25076 Odolo (BS)
Italy
Tel: (365) 860761
Fax: (365) 860887

US outlet:

Ashley Norton Inc
PO Box 2
Alamo
CA 94507

Eurobrass, established during the first months of 1985 to produce solid-brass products, has made its presence felt across Europe and the USA, with door pulls designed by architect Giuseppe Raimondi, marketed under the "Design Collection" label.

Doors: p. 63/**16 & 19**

Frascio Giancintro Srl
Via S. Andrea 5
Agnosine
25071 Brescia
Italy
Tel: (365) 866385
Fax: (365) 866102

US outlet:

Italbrass Corporation
Highland Business Park
21 Lime Street
Marblehead
MA 01945
Tel: (617) 639 1992
Fax: (617) 639 2458

Frascio has operated since 1945 as a family business. The balance between machine molding and manual work within the factory gives the pieces a tactile and friendly quality.

Doors: p. 63/**17**

FSB
See *Franz Schneider Brakel GmbH & Co*

Fusital
See *Valli & Colombo*

Handles and Fittings Ltd
Unit 1A Hazelwood Court
Hazelwood Lane
London N13 5EY
England
Tel: (081) 447 9094
Fax: (081) 886 2317

Specializing in architectural ironmongery, Handles and Fittings, formerly known as Best of Brass, produce three ranges of contemporary door furniture which have been extended to encompass bathroom accessories, electrical fittings, doorclosers and locks.

Doors: p. 62/**3**
Lighting: p. 114/**5 & 6**

Philip Hearsey
Monkhall Court
Callow
Hereford HR2 8DA
England
Tel: (0432) 351170
Fax: (0432) 354162

Philip Hearsey's hand-forged design work (executed by Peter Smith) is predominantly concerned with architectural and interior projects for both corporate and private clients, including fire backs, hoods and baskets.

Doors: p. 62/**6**
Windows: p. 72/**3**
Heating: p. 102/**5 & 6**

Hewi
Heinrich Wilki GmbH
Prof. Bierstrasse 1-5
Postfach 1260
D-3548 Arolson
Germany
Tel: (5) 6918 2319
Fax: (5) 6718 2326

US outlet:

Hewi Inc
2851 Old Tree Drive
Lancaster
PA 17603
Tel: (717) 293 1313
Fax: (717) 293 3270

Hewi produce pulls and hand-rails which meet the demand of architects and discerning clients for clean lines and technical consistency. All the sections of the collection are compatible and combine individual design with the precision of a machine-produced product. The galvanized-steel, inner core rail gives the constructions a high stability, and combinations of the pull com-ponents can give a wide variety of pulls which can be adapted to suit many purposes.

Doors: pp. 62/**1**, 64/**2 & 14**
Stairs: p. 81/**7**

Huttig Sash & Door Co
Box 7417
Fredericksburg
VA 22404

Kraft Hardware
305 East 63rd Street
New York
NY 10022

Doors and bathrooms

Lualdi Porte SpA
Via Brigate di Dio
20010 Mesero
Milan
Italy
Tel: (2) 9789 248
Fax: (2) 9728 9463

US outlet:

Italian Interior Imports
47-09 30th Street
Long Island City
NY 11101
Tel: (201) 346 0866

Lualdi Porte began door producing in 1960, the first firm to com-mission external designers and the first to produce polyester lacquered doors. Their doors are distributed worldwide.

Doors: p. 57/**8**

Mandelli & C. SpA
Via Rivabella 90
20045 Besana Brianza
Milan
Italy
Tel: (2) 362 994938
Fax: (2) 362 994958

US outlet:

Meroni Locks of America Inc
2121 W 60th Street
Hialeah
FL 33016
Tel: (305) 557 7050
Fax: (305) 556 2405

Italian Mandelli & C. manufacture door pulls. Fashion plays an important role in its line of brass hardware, and some classic ranges are still made as a consequence of contemporary tastes. An assortment of pulls and door accessories is available in brass, bronze, copper, gold-black and 24-carat gold plate, all with the exclusive "Fluxcoating" system, to assure longer wear. Mandelli hardware is now available in more than 34 countries throughout the world.

Doors: pp. 62/**5**

Mark J. Marcinik
See *Next to M*

Ingo Maurer GmbH
See *Floors* p. 171

Miya Shoji & Interiors Inc
107 West 17th Street
New York
NY 10011

Shoji screens

National Hardwood Lumber Association
PO Box 34518
Memphis
TN 38184-0518
Tel: (901) 377 1818
Fax: (901) 382 6419

Neotu
See *Floors* p. 172

Next to M
272 St Charles
San Francisco
CA 94132
Tel: (415) 992 3227

Next to M grew out of architect Mark J. Marcinik's need for standard modern architectural fixtures because the overwhelm-ing popularity of "period

architectural styles" in the USA today drives the building material and fixture marketplace, leaving modernists to fend for themselves. Next to M designs demonstrate an alternative architectural order to express the new modern vision.

Doors: p. 54/**3**
Heating: p. 92/**1**

Carl F. Petersen
G. Koegevej 65
2500 Valby
Denmark
Tel: 364 41138
Fax: 364 40588

US outlet:

Ironmonger Inc
1822 North Sheffield Avenue
Chicago
IL 60614
Tel: (312) 935 2784
Fax: (312) 348 3579

D-Line, manufactured by Carl F. Petersen in Denmark, is a range of high-quality stainless steel or polished brass hardware which meets practically every interior requirement, including doors, windows and bathrooms.

Doors: p. 64/**12 & 13**
Storage: p. 134/**7**
Bathrooms: p. 150/**6**

Pittsburgh Corning Corp
800 Presque Isle Drive
Pittsburgh
PA 15239
Tel: (412) 327 6100
Fax: (412) 327 5890

Pittsburgh Corning Corporation is the world's largest manufacturer of glass block products. The company's products combine form and function in a truly unique manner for a variety of architectural needs, and it also produces cellular foam glass insulation for several industrial applications.

Doors: p. 60/**2**

RDS la Guarnimec SpA
Via Cavalieri di Malta 6
35038 Torreglia
Padua
Italy
Tel: (49) 5211300
Fax: (49) 5211553

US outlet:

Juralco Inc
15250 East Stafford Street
City of Industry
CA 91744

Since 1945, RDS production has represented the most advanced technology of brass die-casting and hot-press forging of pulls and knobs for doors and windows. High-quality management makes RDS a leader in the world market.

Doors: p. 63/**11 & 12**

Rehabitec & Diseno E.D. SL
Madre Vedruna 18, 2. izqda
50008 Zaragoza
Spain
Tel: (76) 234662
Fax: (76) 237088

Rehabitec was founded in 1987 by Enrique Hualda, an interior archi-tect and designer, and a winner in the Cosmit 2000 design competition held in Milan in 1991. He heads a group of young professionals, who combine design and craftsmanship. Many of his original designs for furniture, doors and counters are produced in his own factory and are sold not only to an established clientele, but to a growing European market.

Doors: p. 55/**7**

Franz Schneider Brakel GmbH & Co
Nieheimerstrasse 38
PO Box 1440
3492 Brakel
Germany
Tel: (5272) 608-0
Fax: (5272) 608300

US outlet:

Ironmonger Inc
1822 North Sheffield Avenue
Chicago
IL 60614
Tel: (312) 935 2784
Fax: (312) 348 3579

The architectural hardware of FSB reflects the "Zeitgeist" of more than 100 years since the FSB company was formed in 1881 by Franz Schneider in a small town in an area called the Weserbergland in Germany. FSB produces architectural hardware made of aluminum, stainless steel, brass and bronze for doors, windows and furniture. To bring new ideas to the market, FSB invited important architects and designers around the world to present their ideas for a new design for the 1990s.

Many participated, among them Arata Isozaki, Dieter Rams, Peter Eisenman, Mario Botta, Alessandro Mendini and Jasper Morrison.

Doors: pp. 62/**7**, 64/**3, 4 & 7-9**

Sellex Innovator SA
Apartado 1366
San Sebastian
Spain
Tel: (43) 291966
Fax: (43) 291278

Sellex was established in 1977 and produces and markets modern design furniture and accessories in collaboration with the most famous Spanish designers. Sellex has been a member of the SIDI Group since it was created in 1984 and was the first company in Spain to organize a national design competition in 1987.

Doors: p. 63/**9**

Simpson Door Company
PO Box 218
McCleary
WA 98557
Tel: (206) 495 3291
Fax: (206) 495 3295

Since 1912 Simpson Door Company has created doors under the Mastermark label. Whether for interior or exterior use, a Simpson Mastermark door reflects a traditional dedication to craftsmanship and a modern-day emphasis on utility and perfor-mance. Internationally renowned designers, skilled artisans and modern production methods stand behind every Mastermark door.

Doors: p. 58/**5**

Tecnolumen Walter Schnepel GmbH
Lotzenerstrasse 2-4
2800 Bremen
Germany
Tel: (421) 444 016-18
Fax: (421) 498 6685

US outlet:

Current
1201 Western Avenue
Seattle
WA 98101

Interlumen
B. Barton
33 Main Street
Tiburon
CA 94920

LIMN
290 Townsend Street
San Francisco
CA 94107

Manifesto Inc
200 West Superior Street
Chicago
IL 60610

Tecnolumen is the producer of hardware accessories, designed in the 1920s and 1930s by famous designers, including the Bauhaus School. Tecnolumen is the sole licensee of these designs and also the producer of contemporary designs by architects.

Doors: p. 64/**15**
Lighting: p. 118/**10**

Treitel Gratz Inc
13-06 Bridge Plaza South
Long Island City
NY 11101
Tel: (718) 361 7774
Fax: (718) 392 8281

Founded in 1926, Treitel Gratz are a custom metal-working company, producing to client specification anything from sculpture to furniture and architectural fittings.

Doors: p. 60/2

Tre-P SpA
Via delle Industrie 2
Birone di Giussano
20034 Milan
Italy
Tel: (2) 861120
Fax: (2) 310292

Tre-P was founded in 1963 at Birone di Giussano, a direct descendent of a famous furniture firm, which had been in existence for three generations, thus continuing in a tradition in which quality is the principal prerogative. The factory is characterized by the most advanced technology.

Tre-Piu SpA
Via Vittorio Veneto 14/16
20060 Cabiate
Como
Italy
Tel: (31) 766000
Fax: (31) 768383

In 1982 Tre-P branched out into the world of design with the creation of a new firm, Tre-Piu. The Tre-Piu company (piu = "more") produces doors designed by designers and architects, and the company's first production was the "Rever" door by Cini Boeri Associates.

Doors: pp. 56/**1**, 57/**10**

Valli & Colombo
Via Concordia 16
20050 Renate
Milan
Italy
Tel: (2) 362 9821
Fax: (2) 362 982235

US outlet:
Valli & Colombo USA Inc
PO Box 245
15000 England Avenue
Duarte
CA 91009
Tel: (818) 359 2569
Fax: (818) 358 0643

Since 1934, Valli & Colombo has been a leading company at international level in the production of pulls and decorative hardware in high-quality brass. Their wide range includes three important collections: "Classic," "Design" and "Casual." Valli & Colombo also produce under the mark Fusital. Fusital is a leader in the design and technology of architectural fixtures. The result of continuing research into shapes and materials, Fusital pulls and co-ordinated accessories have been created by important names in international design, including Mario Bellini and Cesare Boeri.

Doors: pp. 62/**2**, 63/**15 & 16**

Wing Industries Inc
Box 38347
Dallas
TX 75238
Tel: (214) 699 9900
Fax: (214) 470 9304

Wing Industries manufactures and markets interior bi-fold and passage doors. The company uses only the finest Ponderosa pine, tempered glass and contemporary hardware to craft more than 40 different door styles.

Doors: p. 58/**4**

Windows

ABC Windows and Doors
511 W. 33rd Street
New York
NY 10001

Alcantara SpA
Via Mecanate 86
20138 Milan
Italy
Tel: (2) 5201 55400448
Fax: (2) 52030481

Alcantara was founded in 1972 as a joint venture with Enimont and Toray Industries Inc, a leading Japanese company. In the early 1970s 95 percent of the product was used for clothing, but today no more than 30 percent is used in this sector. Interior decoration and transport have become the two other major markets. For the interior designer, the wide choice of color and varying types of Alcantara allow for a truly personal interior with the right solution for every need. Alcantara for interior decoration is available in fire-proof versions.

Windows: p. 76/**12 & 13**

Bali Ultra Blinds
Box 3922
Department C
Schaumburg
IL 60168

Faber Blinds
See *Walls & Ceilings* p. 169

Fonstret EH Podukter AB
Landerigranden 13
S-223 55 Lund
Sweden
Tel: (46) 140370
Fax: (46) 135550

Swedish Fonstret manufacture window shades to a high quality at reasonable prices, and combine a unique design with functional products, such as wooden shades and sun-protective products for inside use.

Windows: p. 74/**6**

Goddard & Gibbs Studios Ltd
41-9 Kingsland Road
London E2 8AD
England
Tel: (071) 739 6563
Fax: (071) 739 1979

Goddard & Gibbs have been designing, making and installing leaded, stained and decorative glass windows since 1868. Today they use traditional techniques aided by modern technology to create decorative glass which floods interiors with colored light. Initially known for their restoration work in historic buildings, their work is now increasingly in demand for enhancing private homes, hotels, shops and even modern office buildings.

Windows: pp. 72/**2**, 73/**4**

S.A. Hesslein & Co
Kreuzburgerstrasse 19
D-8500 Nurnberg 51
Germany
Tel: (9) 1183 32-0
Fax: (9) 1183 3242

US outlet:
Sahco Hesslein-Bergamo USA
37-20 34th Street
Long Island City
NY 11101
Tel: (718) 392 5000
Fax: (718) 784 1214

Founded in 1841 by the Hesslein brothers, the company flourished for most of its first century as an importer of fine silks and brocades. Subsequently it has built a worldwide reputation on the design and manufacture of materials. By the early 1990s the collection consisted of over 450 designs in a wide range of colors.

Windows: p. 76/**11 & 14**

Sahco Hesslein
See *S.A. Hesslein & Co*

Industrie Secco SpA
Via Terraglio 195
31022 Preganziol
PO Box 101
31100 Treviso
Italy
Tel: (422) 389262
Fax: (422) 382643

US outlet:
Optimum Window Manufacturing Corp.
7 Lake Station Road
Warwick
NY 10990
Tel: (914) 469 2240
Fax: (914) 469 2218

Industrie Secco SpA is the leading manufacturer of cold-rolled products for windows, doors and drape walling with distributors worldwide. It produces windows in color-coated steel, bronze and stainless steel.

Windows: pp. 69/**4**, 71/**13**

Levolor Corp
25 Greenpond Road
Rockaway
NJ 07866
Tel: (201) 627-2200
Fax: (201) 627-8138

Since 1915 Levolor Corporation has manufactured high-quality window products. Today's horizontal shades in a myriad of colors and sizes to co-ordinate with contemporary furnishings, fashions and architectural designs are produced with an extensive selection of wood shades, vertical shades and custom shades.

Windows: p. 74/**1 & 2**

LouverDrape
PO Box 7025
Department MH9
Corte Madera
CA 94925

The Louvre Blind Company Ltd
7 Forward Drive
Harrow
Middlesex HA3 8NT
England
Tel: (081) 863 9111
Fax: (081) 863 8760

The Louvre Blind Company have over 20 years' experience of manufacturing and installing high-quality drapes, shades, insect screening and other window treatments. As main distributors of Silent Gliss, Luxaflex, and many other well-known suppliers, they are able to offer shading solutions to suit all domestic and commercial applications.

Windows: p. 75/**10**

Marimekko
Puusepankatu 4
08810 Helsinki
Finland
Tel: (0) 75871
Fax: (0) 7553051

Windows: p. 76/**1**

Metall Kommerz Srl
Via Campi della Rienza 41
39031 S. Giorgio/Brunico (BZ)
Italy
Tel: (474) 30853
Fax: (474) 30747

"Clima" window and door frames from Metall Kommerz combine the functional properties of aluminum externally, with the natural beauty of wood internally.

Windows: pp. 70/**5**, 71/**6 & 12**

Norco Windows Inc
PO Box 140
Department 1006
Hawkins
WI 54530
Tel: (715) 585 6311

Northwest Window Works
3227 164th Street SW
Lynwood
WA 98037

Pella Rolscreen
See *Rolscreen Company*

Rolscreen Company/Pella Windows
Department C28B8
102 Main Street
Pella
IW 50219
Tel: (515) 628 1000
Fax: (515) 628 6070

The Rolscreen Company manufactures Pella windows, doors, sunrooms and skylights, and markets them worldwide.

Windows: p. 71/**9-11**

Shade-o-matic Ltd
335 Eddystone Avenue
Downsview
Ontario
Canada M3N 1H8
Tel: (416) 7421524
Fax: (416) 7424872

Stained Glass Association of America
4050 Broadway, Suite 219
Kansas City
MO 64111
Tel: (816) 561 4404

Sunlight UK Ltd
Unit 7c, Beta Close
Tewkesbury Business Centre
Tewkesbury
Gloucestershire GL20 8SR
England
Tel: (0684) 850933
Fax: (0684) 850895

Established in the UK since the early 1980s, Sunlight Ltd has a reputation for quality vertical shades and also manufactures Venetian and pleated shades to the same standard.

Windows: p. 74/**4**

Timbershade
Tidmarsh & Sons
1 Laycock Street
London N1 1SW
England
Tel: (071) 226 2261
Fax: (071) 226 4115

Timbershade were established in 1828 and produce wooden roller, Venetian and pinoleum shades for windows.

Windows: p. 74/**7**

The Jim Thompson Thai Silk Co
9 Surawong Road
GPO Box 906
Bangkok 10500
Thailand
Tel: (2) 234 4900
Fax: (2) 236 6777

Jim Thompson is the legendary American credited with reviving Thailand's cottage silk industry. The Thai Silk company Ltd was founded in 1951 and is Thailand's largest weaver and exporter of hand-woven silks. The company is fully integrated with complete facilities for mulberry and silk worm production, cocoon reeling and yarn production, dyeing, hand weaving and hand printing. The Jim Thompson furnishing fabrics collection is distributed in 35 countries worldwide.

Windows: p. 76/**6-10**

Valley Sash & Door Company
14829 Oxnard Street
Van Nuys
CA 91411

Zimmer & Rohde GmbH & Co. KG
Postfach 1245
D-6370 Oberursel
Taunus 1
Germany
Tel: (6171) 63202
Fax: (6171) 632244

US outlets:
Zimmer & Rohde
41 East 11th Street
New York
NY 10003
Tel: (212) 475 5060
Fax: (212) 979 0916

Zimmer & Rohde specialize in high-quality jacquards for upholstery, unpatterned fabrics and silks.

Windows: p. 76/**2-5**

Stairs

Albini & Fontanot SpA
Km 7, SS Rep. di S. Marino
47040 Cerasolo Ausa (FO)
Italy
Tel: (541) 759455
Fax: (541) 759545

US outlet:
Import Design
100 Magazine Street
Boston
MASS 02119
Tel: (800) 225 5585
Fax: (618) 442 9633

Albini & Fontanot climbed to
brand leader in stairs many years
ago, and use steel, wood and
polyurethane for their architec-
turally planned stairways.

Stairs: pp. 81/**8 & 9**, 83/**4 & 8**,
84/**2**, 86/**2**

Dimes SpA
Via Provinciale per Modena 49
41016 Novi di Modena
Modena
Italy
Tel: (59) 670155
Fax: (59) 676341

Dimes in Italy, producers of staircases and attic windows for more
than 25 years in quality materials,
manufactures folding, open spiral
and modular staircases.

Stairs: pp. 81/**5, 6 & 10**, 85/**6**,
86/**1**

Hewi
See *Doors* p. 173

Luxo
See *Walls & Ceilings* p. 169

One Off Ltd
62 Chalk Farm Road
London NW1 8AN
England
Tel: (071) 379 7796
Fax: (071) 379 0499

Ron Arad founded the design
company One Off in 1981,
making room installations for
beds, tables and desks from
cow-shed scaffolding called Kee-
Klamp. Always innovative, his
constant experiments with
materials – and fascination with
metalwork – led him to design
highly original stairs.

Heating

Alessi
See *F.A.O. SpA*

Arbonia AG
Industriestrasse 23
CH-9320 Arbon/Frasnacht
Switzerland
Tel: (71) 46 91 61
Fax: (71) 46 81 66

Part of the Arbonia Forster group,
Arbonia make radiators, heating
panels, solar-energy devices, heat
exchanges and storage heaters.
Arbonia radiators are available
in seven different styles, each of
which can be made to a great
variety of different sizes and colors.

Heating: pp. 93/**6**, 94/**2**, 96/**5**

Atelier Dominique Imbert Sarl
Le Fort
34380 Viols le Fort
France
Tel: (67) 55 01 93
Fax: (76) 55 77 77

North American outlet:
Techni Flamme
3238 Autornite Laval
Chomedey, Laval
Quebec H7T 2H6
Canada
Tel: (418) 687 8422
Fax: (418) 687 5969

Focus is the trademark of a
range of contemporary fireplaces
with vents and chimneys, sold
throughout Europe, and in Japan
and Canada, mainly to architects
and interior designers.

Heating: pp. 98/**3**, 100/**1**

Atelier Sedap
3 Rue Sanleque
BP 166
44006 Nantes
France
Tel: (40) 99 85 24
Fax: (40) 35 26 22

Atelier Sedap is a traditional
manufacturer of plaster moldings
and fireplaces which has been
long established in France. Its
reputation for intricate and fine
workmanship has for the past ten
years been translated into the
lighting market in the design and
development of decorative plaster
lighting. All types of lighting
are manufactured, including wall,
pendant, floor and table lights
bringing the benefit of fine detailing
to the modern lighting market.

Heating: p. 101/**7**

Avant-Scene
4 Place de l'Odeon
75006 Paris
France
Tel: (1) 46 33 12 40
Fax: (1) 46 33 92 78

Avant-Scene was founded in 1986
with the intention of offering a
new approach to interiors. The
company produces furniture and
objects designed by young, mostly
French, sculptors and artists.

Heating: p. 102/**3 & 7**

August Brotje GmbH & Co
PO Box 2902
Rastede 1
Germany
Tel: (4402) 80343
Fax: (4402) 80375

Heating: p. 95/**7**

Caradon Heating
PO Box 103
National Avenue
Hull HU5 4JN
England
Tel: (0482) 492251
Fax: (0482) 448858

Caradon Heating is one of
Britain's largest manuacturers
of domestic, commercial and
industrial central-heating boilers
and radiators, setting trends
in boiler design, efficiency and
appearance.

Heating: pp. 94/**6**, 95/**9**

Clyde Combustion
See *August Brotje GmbH & Co*

Country Downs
1302 Camino del Mar
Del Mar
CA 92014

Heating accessories

Dimplex (UK) Limited
Manor House Avenue
Millbrook
Southampton S09 2DP
England
Tel: (0703) 777 117
Fax: (0703) 771 096

US outlet:
M & J Export/Import Corp
PO Box 158
Glens Falls
NY 12801
Tel: (518) 792 0314
Fax: (518) 792 3765

Dimplex is a member of the Glen
Dimplex Group of companies and
the leader in the British electric
heating market. The company
offers a portfolio of over 100
different appliances, including all
the key heating products as well
as portable air conditioners.

Heating: p. 102/**2**

N.V. Dovre SA
Nijverheidstraat 18
2381 Weelde
Belgium
Tel: (14) 65 9191
Fax: (14) 65 9009

US outlet:
Dovre Inc
401 Hankes Avenue
Aurora
IL 60505-1716
Tel: (312) 844 3353
Fax: (312) 844 3238

Dovre International, based
in Belgium, is one of the leading
European manufacturers of cast-
iron fireplace inserts and stoves.
Dovre products were established
in Norway more than 50 years ago
and are now supplied through a
network of subsidiary companies
in Europe and the USA. New
products include the "Premier,"
an elegantly styled non-catalytic
wood stove.

Heating: p. 100/**4**

"Dovre 2000"
See *N.V. Dovre SA*

Elgin & Hall Ltd
Adelphi House
Hunton
Bedale
North Yorkshire DL8 1LY
England
Tel: (0677) 501712
Fax: (0677) 50713

Elgin & Hall's superb workshops
are home to more than 20 artists,
craftsmen, sculptors and designers
producing a sophisticated range
of plasterwork fire surrounds,
pedestals, niches and corbels for
the more discerning buyer.
They specialize in hand-painted
finishes, such as marble and
distressed stone.

Heating: p. 101/**8**

F.A.O. SpA
Via Privata Alessi 6
28023 Crusinallo di Omegna (No)
Italy
Tel: (323) 6511
Fax: (323) 641605

US outlet:
Markuse Corp
10 Wheeling Avenue
Woburn
MASS 01801
Tel: (617) 932 9444
Fax: (617) 933 1930

Alessi, the Italian manufacturer
of stainless steel with style, has
a high company profile worldwide
for its products commissioned
from internationally acclaimed
architects and designers. In the
1980s no designer kitchen
was without an Alessi kettle by
Michael Graves or Richard
Sapper, and now heating and
fireplace accessories may take
over the hearth.

Heating: p. 100/**2**
Kitchens: p. 154/**4**

Lighthouse fireplace with lighting
See *Atelier Sedap*

Marimex SnC
See *Sinimetal*

Next to M
See *Doors* p. 174

OWO
1 Rue Amaury
78490 Montfort Lamaury
France
Tel: (34) 86 76 39
Fax: (34) 86 00 27

US outlets:
Driade
212 East 57th Street
New York
NY 10022
Tel: (212) 888 5375
Fax: (212) 888 5622

Modern Living
8125 Melrose Avenue
Los Angeles
CA 90076
Tel: (213) 655 3898
Fax: (213) 655 1677

Heating: p. 101/**9**

Piazzetta SpA
Via Montello 22
31011 Asolo (TV)
Italy
Tel: (423) 950 350
Fax: (423) 55178

US outlets:
BSW
4680 East 2nd Street
Benicia
CA 94510
Tel: (707) 745 8175
Fax: (707) 745 9708

Waltz Enterprises
280 Earland Drive
Earland Industrial Park
New Holland
PA 17557
Tel: (717) 355 2767
Fax: (717) 355 2421

Since 1961 Piazetta have specialized in ceramic-tiled wood- and gas-
burning stoves and hand-made
marble surrounds for fireplaces.

Heating: p. 98/**4**

Platonic Fireplace Company
26 Ceylon Road
London W14 0PY
England
Tel: (071) 602 3982
Fax: (071) 603 0790

Architect Henry Harrison's "platonic
fires" are the first ever decorative
gas fires designed specifically
for contemporary interiors. Platonic
fires comprise 'geologs' in simple
geometric forms based on the
sphere, the tetrahedron and the
cube. These are set in various
combinations in equally geometric
chrome grates. Architectural fire
surrounds are also available from
stock or to order.

Heating: pp. 93/**5**, 102/**4**

Runtal Italia Srl
See *Runtal-Werk AG*

Runtal-Werk AG
Wil
CH-9500
Switzerland
Tel: (73) 2344 44
Fax: (73) 2371 25

US outlet:
Runtal North America Inc
187 Neck Road
Haverhill
MA 01835
Tel: (508) 373 1666
Fax: (508) 372 7140

Runtal produces over 600,000 radiators annually, manufactured in eight countries and marketed worldwide. Runtal Italia, a licensee of the Swiss company, produce a wide range of models varying in length, depth and breadth in an enormous variety of colors.

Heating: pp. 94/**3 & 5**, 95/**8 & 11-13**, 96/**1, 2 & 4**, 97/**10 & 11**

Sinimetal
157 Avenue Charles Floquet
93158 Le Blanc Mesnil
Cedex
France
Tel: (45) 91 62 00
Fax: (45) 91 62 97

Marimex radiators are produced in France and marketed in Holland, Switzerland, Germany and Great Britain.

Bathrooms: pp. 96/**7**, 97/**9**

Stelrad Ideal
See *Caradon Heating*

ThermoCet Heating Company BV
Zelhemseweg 20-22
PO Box 75
7255 ZH Hengelo GLD
Holland
Tel: (5753) 3900
Fax: (5753) 3954

Thermocet produces inserts and freestanding high-capacity stoves which use wood/coal or gas. All models are efficient, economical, made of high-quality cast-iron and provided with the latest technology. A variety of styles are available to suit traditional and modern interiors.

Heating: p. 99/**7 & 8**

Tranter Corp Inc
Wichita Falls
Texas

Tranter Corp produced the plate coil heating units for John Young's Thamesreach penthouse.

Heating: p. 91

Vermont Castings
Prince Street
Randolph
VT 05060
Tel: (802) 728 3181
Fax: (802) 728 3940

Vermont Castings produce wood stoves that combine the heating efficiency of a stove with the beauty and fire-viewing ambiance of a traditional fireplace. The company is America's largest manufacturer of wood stoves. Its stove line includes the Defiant Encore, Resolute Acclaim and Intrepid II. In 1988 Vermont Castings greatly increased its product offering by acquiring Consolidated Dutchwest, another leading manufacturer of cast-iron wood stoves. Together these companies contribute the industry's largest selection of government-certified, clean-burning wood stoves.

Heating: p. 98/**5**

Zehnder
See *Zehnder-Beutler GmbH*

Zehnder-Beutler GmbH
Postfach 26
7630 Lahr 12
Germany
Tel: (7821) 586-0
Fax: (7821) 52553

US outlet:

Zehnder is a name which has become synonymous with quality in radiator manufacturing. In 1930 Zehnder patented a steel tube radiator setting new standards in heat yield, versatility, pressure resistance and design and rapidly establishing Zehnder as the key European producer with an annual turnover which now runs into nine figures. The extensive range enables designers to choose types, sizes and shapes of radiator that will meet and satisfy the highest esthetic demands.

Heating: pp. 94/**4**, 95/**10**, 97/**10 & 11**

Lighting

Arteluce
See *Flos SpA*

Artemide SpA
Via Bergamo 6
20010 Pregnana Milanese
Milan
Italy
Tel: (2) 9359 0830
Fax: (2) 9359 0254

US outlet:
Artemide Inc
1980 New Highway
Farmingdale
NY 11735
Tel: (516) 694 9292
Fax: (516) 694 9275

Artemide was founded in 1959 in Milan by Ernesto Gismondi, an aeronautical engineer who stressed the importance of developing engineering excellence alongside innovative design. Vico Magistretti's regular range of furniture was among the earliest of a significant range of products from Artemide selected for permanent exhibition in the Museum of Modern Art, New York, including the internationally acclaimed classic Tizio task lamp. The success of the Aton Barra system led to the creation in 1984 of Artemide Litech, a wholly-owned subsidiary formed to research and develop an extensive range of lighting products for the commercial market. The common denominator for all Artemide lighting remains excellence in design and engineering using state-of-the-art technology. In support of its products, Artemide also offers a computer-aided lighting design service.

Lighting: pp. 109/**7**, 113/**15**, 120/**3**

Atmosferica Inc
8500 Melrose Avenue 211
West Hollywood
CA 90069

Heating: pp. 94/**4**, 95/**10**, 97/**10 & 11**

Baldinger Architectural Lighting
Louis Baldinger & Sons Inc
19-02 Steinway Street
Astoria
NY 11105
Tel: (718) 204 5700

Baldinger Architectural Lighting produce a range of ceiling, wall, and table lights designed by Michael Graves.

Lighting: pp. 114/**1**, 116/**1, 4 & 7**

**Barovier & Toso Vetrerie Art.
Riunite Srl**
Fondamenta Vetrai 28
30141 Murano (VE)
Italy
Tel: (41) 739049
Fax: (41) 737385

US outlets:
Bradford & Associates
7317 Cahill Road
Minneapolis
MN 55435

Contract Resources
PO Box 164 338
Miami
FL 33116

Gary & Associates Inc
23239 Calvert Street
Woodlands Hills
CA 91367

Dennis Jones
703 McKinney Avenue
Suite 302
Dallas
TX 75202

Lighting Dynamics
70 West 36 Street
Suite 605
New York
NY 10018

Malcolm Mimms & Associates
214-19th Avenue
North Nashville
Tennessee

Roman Way
15324 Spencerville Court
201 Burtonsville
MD 20866

Speclight Jay Kaplan
219 Highgate Street
Needham
MA 023192

Manufacturers of artistic glass accessories and lighting fixtures in the Murano tradition in co-operation with renowned Italian and international designers, Barovier & Toso have acquired a reputation for unusual and dramatic high-performance lighting outside the conventional high-tech mold.

Lighting: p. 115/**13**
Bathrooms: p. 150/**3**

Belux AG
Bremgarterstrasse 109
CH-5610 Wohlen
Switzerland
Tel: (57) 222091
Fax: (57) 219515

US outlet:
Diva
8818 Beverly Boulevard
Los Angeles
CA 90048
Tel: (213) 274 0650
Fax: (213) 274 7189

Belux has made lights since the 1970s. It began developing and producing lights for offices and workshops, at drawing desks and machines. Quality and durability were always the requirements, met today by lights which integrate the latest technologies in industrial manufacture. In 1982 Belux invented the first suspended light system "Metro," and in 1989 came the new plug-in light system, "Contacto." In 1984 Belux launched a design competition. The jury included, among others, Achille Castiglioni, Robert and Trix Haussmann, Margit Weinberg-Staber. For this competition Benjamin Thut designed the successful pivoting lamp "Lifto," which received several awards.

Lighting: pp. 111/**9 & 10**, 113/**14**, 118/**5**

Best of Brass
See *Handles & Fittings* under *Doors* p. 173

Blauet SA (Grupo Sidi)
Aragon
333 Bajos
08009 Barcelona
Spain
Tel: (3) 207 5311
Fax: (3) 207 3398

Founded in Barcelona in 1983 to produce and distribute lighting designs, Blauet has rapidly gained a distinctive profile and awards for their pendant standard and table lights.

Lighting: p. 117/**13 & 14**

Candela Ltd
51 Abbey Business Centre
Ingate Place
London SW8 3NS
England
Tel: (071) 720 4480
Fax: (071) 498 0026

US outlet:
Primo Lighting
114 Washington Street
South Norwalk
CT 06854
Tel: (203) 866 4321
Fax: (203) 838 1612

Candela Ltd, established 1982, designs, manufactures and markets lighting products with an emphasis on uncompromising minimalist design and practicability. The well-proportioned design elements are reduced to the bare essence of their function. Candela products complement the uncluttered looks of rational architectural styles and the company also do lighting design for projects.

Lighting: p. 110/**2**

Clipsal
See *Gerard Industries Pty Ltd*

Concord Lighting
174 High Holborn
London WC1V 7AA
England
Tel: (071) 497 1400
Fax: (071) 497 1404

Founded in the mid 1950s, Concord was the first company in the world to produce architectural lighting and among the first to develop, manufacture and promote track and spot lighting. It remains in the forefront of design and architectural lighting.

Lighting: pp. 107/**6 & 8**, 108/**4**, 109/**6**

Ecart International
5 Rue des Grands Augustins
75006 Paris
France
Tel: (42) 78 88 35

Ecart, which spells trace backward, develops Andrée Putman's philosophy of making progress while learning from the past. They market worldwide this French designer's tableware, furniture, lights and textiles alongside classics from the Eileen Gray collection, and Fortuny lighting.

Introduction: p. 10/**3**
Windows: p. 70/**4**
Lighting: p. 105/**7**
Storage: pp. 130/**3**, 137/**7**
Bathrooms: p. 150/**5**
Kitchens: pp. 158/**1**, 160/**2**

Erco Lighting Ltd
38 Dover Street
London W1X 3RB
England
Tel: (071) 408 0320
Fax: (071) 409 1530

US outlets:

Edison Price
409 East 60th Street
New York
NY 10022
Tel: (212) 838 5212
Fax: (212) 888 7981

Thomas Industries Inc
Omega Lighting
6430 Flauson Avenue
Los Angeles
CA 90040
Tel: (213) 726 1800
Fax: (213) 728 1319

Erco's objective of selling light, not lights, has been realized both in terms of know-how and of actual products. Working on the perception that light is the fourth dimension of architecture, a range of products has been developed that can be utilized in areas of architecture and illumination. An important element in this process is the need to integrate light, and thus light fixtures, into the architecture.

Lighting: p. 108/**3**

Estiluz SA
Ctra Ogassa s/n
17860 S. Joan de les Abadesses
Spain
Tel: (972) 720125
Fax: (972) 720796

Estiluz, a Spanish company designing and manufacturing halogen light fixtures since 1969 in its own production plant in collaboration with external experts, has penetrated European, American and Canadian markets.

Lighting: pp. 112/**1**, 114/**9**

F. Fabbian & F.lli SnC
Via S. Brigida 50
31020 Castelminio di Resana (TV)
Italy
Tel: (423) 784535-7
Fax: (423) 484395

North American outlet:

Regency Lighting Inc
67 Colville Road
Toronto
Ontario
Canada M6M 2Y2
Tel: (416) 247 9221
Fax: (416) 247 9319

Strong technological knowledge of metal and glass processing, detailed design, safety testing of electrical fixtures and fittings for each country's requirements take Fabbian products worldwide.

Lighting: pp. 114/**2**, 118/**11**

Flos SpA
Via Moretto 58
25121 Brescia
Italy
Tel: (30) 280284
Fax: (30) 290046

US outlet:

Flos Inc
200 McKay Road
Huntington Station
NY 11746
Tel: (516) 549 2745
Fax: (516) 549 4220

Flos began manufacturing lighting fixtures to a high design standard in the 1960s. The company aims not only at the innovative aspects of design, but also to produce models that will stand the test of time: a great number of the first 30 models produced are still in the catalog today, proving that the techniques and forms chosen in the past are still up-to-date and functional. They use materials as different as marble, glass, metals and plastics to meet the latest advances in technology and the safety standards imposed by national and international markets.

Arteluce began producing lamps in the 1930s, during the Art Deco period. Then, the business was mainly contract work for hotels, schools, offices and communities. In 1974, Arteluce was taken over by Flos, who updated production with lighting fixtures and systems which suited both the domestic and contract markets. Now, Arteluce anticipate new trends and aim to create sophisticated environments for their customers. The product image is "young but with style."

Lighting: Flos – pp. 104, 113/**16**, 114/**7**, 115/**16**, 119/**14**
Arteluce – pp. 109/**11**, 116/**8**, 117/**9**, 120/**5**

Foscarini Murano SpA
See *Walls & Ceilings* p. 169

Garcia Garay SA
San Antonio 13
Almacen San Juan 18-20
Sta. Coloma de Gramanet
08923 Barcelona
Spain
Tel: (3) 466 1016
Fax: (3) 386 2372

US outlet:

Illuminating Experiences Inc
233 Cleveland Avenue
Highland Park
NJ 08904
Tel: (908) 745 5858
Fax: (908) 745 9710

Established in Barcelona in the 1980s, the company produces the designs of J. Garcia Garay and other designers, mostly lighting but also some accessory furniture, such as the tables on which to stand his lamps.

Lighting: pp. 110/**4**, 117/**16**, 118/**9**

Gerard Industries Pty Ltd
12 Park Terrace
Bowden 5007
Australia
Tel: (08) 269 0511
Fax: (08) 340 1724

The market leader in electrical accessories throughout Australasia and Asia, Clipsal produce a comprehensive range of stylish, resilient switches and outlets in a large variety of colors, designed to complement color schemes instead of detracting from them.

Lighting: p. 114/**5 & 6**

Gerconi Corp
Alberto & Corrado Mion
4474 NW 74 Avenue
Miami
FL 33166
Tel: (305) 477 7080
Fax: (305) 477 5986

Handles and Fittings
See *Doors* p. 173

iGuzzini Illuminazione Srl
PO Box No. 39-59
S.S. 77 Km 102
62019 Recanati
Italy
Tel: (71) 758
Fax: (71) 987 236

US outlet:

Forluce Inc
4201 Tulane Avenue
New Orleans
LO 70119
Tel: (504) 486 9257
Fax: (504) 484 6890

Lighting: pp. 106/**6**, 108/**2**, 110/**3**, 111/**6 & 7**

Leucos Srl
Via Treviso 77
30037 Scorze
Venice
Italy
Tel: (41) 445777
Fax: (41) 447598

US outlet:

Leucos USA Inc
70 Campus Plaza II
Edison
NJ 08837
Tel: (908) 225 0010
Fax: (908) 225 0250

Leucos use Murano glass, exploiting its qualities of form and brilliance, to produce a wide range of lighting fixtures. The collection includes lighting for walls, ceilings, tables and floors. To complement lighting Leucos also produce glass elements and an exciting range of colored glass tiles which can be assembled into walls, screens and ceilings.

Lighting: p. 115/**19**

Levington Manufacturing Co Inc
59-25 Little Neck Parkway
Little Neck
NY 11362

Light switches

Luceplan SpA
Via Bellinzona 48
20155 Milan
Italy
Tel: (2) 3272249
Fax: (2) 3272440

US outlet:

Artemide Inc
1980 New Highway
Farmingdale
NY 11735
Tel: (516) 694 9292
Fax: (516) 694 9275

Luceplan was founded at the end of 1979 by architects Riccardo Sarfatti, Sandra Severi and Paolo Rizzatto, after more than 15 years of experience in the field of lighting. Their initial intention was to be the first in Italy properly equipped to respond to the needs of the contract sector. In 1981 Luceplan won the XII Compasso d'Oro with the lamp "D7". Luceplan's efforts are directed to realize innovative products which provide a high level of design and, at the same time, are accessible to a wider range of consumers than the designer contract market.

Lighting: pp. 105/**8**, 113/**13**

Luci
See *Lucitalia SpA*

Lucitalia SpA
Via Pelizza da Volpedo 50
20092 Cinisello B.
Milan
Italy
Tel: (2) 612 6651
Fax: (2) 660 0707

US outlet:

Illuminating Experiences Inc
233 Cleveland Avenue
Highland Park
NJ 08904
Tel: (908) 745 5858
Fax: (908) 745 9710

Founded in 1966 by Renato Mammani, Luci Illuminazione D'Interni SnC, later known as Luci, quickly became one of the most original and innovative firms producing lighting equipment. In 1989 Luci, still guided by the Mammani family, changed its name to Lucitalia SpA. Products include lamp fixtures for interiors and lighting fixtures and systems for exterior use in the community. Bonetto Design, Guigiaro Design Toshiyuki Kita, Asahara Sigheaki, Gianfranco Frattini and Ferdinand Alexander Porsche are just some of the best-known designers who have designed for Lucitalia.

Lighting: pp. 111/**8**, 112/**9**, 114/**4**, 115/**14**

Luxo Italiana SpA
See *Walls* p. 169

Marset Iluminacion SA
Alfonso XII 429-431
08912 Barcelona
Spain
Tel: (3) 8732 0462
Fax: (3) 8784 17

Lighting: p. 120/**2**

Ingo Maurer GmbH
See *Floors* p. 172

Metalarte SA
Avda. Barcelona 4
08970 S. Joan Despi
Barcelona
Spain
Tel: (3) 477 0069
Fax: (3) 477 0086

Founded in 1932, Metalarte in Spain has for more than half a century developed, manufactured and marketed lamps by well-known designers, which have taken the name into homes worldwide.

Lighting: pp. 112/**2 & 6**, 113/**7**, 114/**10**, 117/**12**, 118/**3, 4 & 8**, 132/**1 & 3**

Oluce
Via Cavour 52
20096 San Giuliano Milanese
Italy
Tel: (2) 9849 1435
Fax: (2) 9849 0779

Lighting: p. 112/**3**

PAF Srl
Via Edison 118
20019 Settimo Milanese
Italy
Tel: (2) 4891 5671
Fax: (2) 4891 0561

US outlet:

PAF USA Inc
400 Long Beach Boulevard
Stratford
CT 06497
Tel: (203) 378 4000
Fax: (203) 380 0883

Due to rigorous and innovative design and a highly advanced technological level, PAF's image has consolidated worldwide since 1975 when they began making lights. Their aim is to bring design to a wider audience through serviceable, good-looking, reasonably priced lights.

Lighting: pp. 119/**16 & 18**

"Pap" floor lamp
See *Tecnolumen*, under *Doors* p. 174

Sirrah Industria
Via Molino Rosso 8
40026 Imola (BO)
Italy
Tel: (542) 640302
Fax: (542) 640244

Sirrah has collaborated with a series of designers and architects to create contemporary lights and lighting systems for domesticated office use in interiors and gardens since it began production in 1968. Participants include Franco Albini, Kazuhide Takahava, Manlio Brustini Rene Kernna, Valerio Sacchetti and Chanan Gardi.

Lighting: p. 117/**11**

Skipper SpA
Via Serbelloni 1
20122 Milan
Italy
Tel: (2) 7600 5691
Fax: (2) 784613

US outlets:

Current
1001 Western Aveue
Seattle
WA 98102
Tel: (206) 622 2433

Diva
8818 Beverly Boulevard
Los Angeles
CA 90048

Luminaire Inc
7300 West 45th Street
Miami
FL 33155

Mobili d'Oggi
444 Deharo Street
Suite 119
San Francisco
CA 94103

Modern Stone Age
111 Greene Street
New York
NY 10012

Founded in 1973, Skipper aims through careful research of the market to design products which relate form to function. The nine trademarks of the Skipper Group are: Arcani, Comput, Fucina, Green, In-Dy, Horus, Maxmill, Pollux and Relasto.

Lighting: p. 112/**4**
Storage: p. 125/**12**

Stilnovo Srl
Via F. Borromini 12
20020 Lainate
Milan
Italy
Tel: (2) 937 4471
Fax: (2) 937 1074

US outlet:

Hampstead Lighting & Accessories
1150 Alpha Drive, Suite 100
Alpharetta
GA 30201
Tel: (404) 664 0600
Fax: (404) 664 1331

Innovative lighting from Alberto Fraser, Asahara Sigeaki and the Design Trio de Pas, d'Urbino & Lomazzi uses ordinary bulbs, and dichroic as well as halogen sources.

Lighting: pp. 104/**2 & 3**, 112/**8**, 113/**11**, 115/**15 & 17**, 118/**7**, 120/**1**

Tebong
ZI Landean
35133 Fougeres
France
Tel: (33) 99 97 20 77
Fax: (33) 99 97 21 43

Tebong was founded in 1985 as a joint venture of Pascal Bauer and Philippe Daney. It designs,

manufactures and distributes items of furniture, lighting and contemporary objects.

Lighting: pp. 110/**5**, 115/**18**
Storage: pp. 123/**7**, 134/**3**

Thorn Lighting Ltd
Elstree Way
Boreham Wood
Hertfordshire WD6 1HZ
England
Tel: (081) 905 1313
Fax: (081) 905 1287

Thorn Lighting is one of the world's largest fixtures manufacturers. The range includes lighting for commercial, domestic and industrial areas, as well as flood-lighting and street lighting. Recent developments include "Sensa," believed to be the first truly intelligent fluorescent fixture for offices.

Lighting: p. 109/**10**

Woka Lamps Vienna
Singerstrasse 16
Palais Breuner
D-1010 Wien 1
Austria
Tel: (431) 5132912
Fax: (431) 5138505

US outlets:

George Kovacs Inc
24 West 40th Street
12th floor
New York
NY 10018
Tel: (212) 944 9606/900 1212
Fax: (212) 944 5766

Modern Age
David Hurd, Barbara Rathbone
795 Broadway
New York
NY 10003
Tel: (212) 674 5603
Fax: (212) 529 2779

Today Woka is one of the authorized manufacturers of lamps designed by Josef Hoffmann, Adolf Loos and other architects from the turn of the last century in the "Woka Classic Collection." In its futuristic "Art Collection," Woka makes use of today's creativity to produce outstanding lighting designs which meet the demands of art collectors.

Lighting: pp. 105/**6**, 116/**2**, 119/**15 & 17**, 120/**8**

Storage

Arc Linea Arredamenti SpA
Via Pasubio 50
36030 Caldogno
Vicenza
Italy
Tel: (444) 557100
Fax: (444) 588035

US outlet:

IPI Kitchens
150 East 58th Street
New York
NY 10155

Since 1960 Arc Linea in Italy have made furniture for living rooms, kitchens and executive offices, designed by some of Italy's furniture designers, including Carlo Bartoli, Antonio Citterio and Roberto Pamio.

Storage: pp. 128/**7**, 130/**1**, 133/**7**

Atelier International Ltd
IDCNY Center Two
30-20 Thomson Avenue
Long Island City
NY 11101
Tel: (718) 392 0300
Fax: (718) 392 1593

Atelier International Ltd is a leading source for contract and residential furniture designed by some of the most eminent architects and designers of this century. Many of the company's exclusive furniture designs win international design awards and have been selected for the permanent design collection of the Museum of Modern Art in New York.

Atrium
See *Cattelan*

Bd. Ediciones de Diseno SA
See *Doors* p. 173

Klaus Block
See *Martin Nagele*

Cattelan Italia SpA
Via Pilastri 15
36010 Carre
Vicenza
Tel: (45) 314076
Fax: (45) 314289

The Cattelan family has been associated with furniture for several generations but Giorgio Cattelan founded Cattelan Spa in the early 1980s and has been going from strength to strength since. Marble is the principle element used by Cattelan for the

manufacture of furniture but other materials are being introduced such as all-glass furniture, timber and burr woods. The collection consists of tables, chairs and mirrors for the home and waiting and boardroom areas.

Storage: p. 134/**1 & 5**

Colantoni, Contini & Skella
See *Disform*

Jaime Tresserra Clapes
See *J. Tresserra Design SL* under *Walls & Ceilings* p. 170

Diseno y Forma SA
63 Rda. Gral. Mitre
08017 Barcelona
Spain
Tel: (3) 203 9225
Fax: (3) 205 6806

Diseno y Forma is an innovative Spanish furniture-making company which commissions designs from international designers.

Disform
RDA Gral Mitre/63
08017 Barcelona
Spain
Tel: (3) 280 5737
Fax: (3) 280 4443

Established in 1969, Disform has concentrated on producing furniture since 1980. The company's product philosophy is founded on the production of simple folding or easy-assembly pieces, keen prices and, above all, creative presentation.

Storage: p. 134/**4 & 6**

Driade SpA
Via Padana Inferiore 12 (sede)
29012 Fossadello di Caorso
Piacenza
Italy
Tel: (523) 822348
Fax: (523) 822628

US outlet:

Driade New York
212 East 57th Street
New York
NY 10022

Driade SpA is an Italian company whose contribution to contemporary design has been characterized, since its beginning in 1968, by furniture based on modular systems, like the storage system by Antonia Astori, wall-units "Oikos," kitchen cabinets "Driadechef" and office furnishings "Kaos," and individually designed pieces of furniture, grouped as collections and marketed under the names

Driade, Antologia and Aleph. Marketing activities, through agents and distributors, cover most of the worldwide market.

Storage: pp. 123/**3**, 126/**2 & 3**, 130/**4**, 131/**8**

Duravit AG
Werderstrasse 36
Postfach 240
7746 Hornberg
Germany
Tel: (78) 33700
Fax: (78) 33 70289

US outlet:

Santile International Corporation
1201 West Loop North
Suite 170
Houston
TX 77055

Storage: p. 123/**2**
Bathrooms: pp. 139/**8**, 147/**4 & 5**

Enea (Grupo Sidi)
Pol. Industrial s/n
20052 Legorreta (Guipuzcoa)
Spain
Tel: (80) 6275
Fax: (80) 6374

Enea in Spain make adjustable storage systems, wall-to-wall, floor to ceiling, in durable but light-weight aluminum, designed for the domestic setting rather than the contract market.

Storage: pp. 126/**1 & 4**, 127/**12**

Estudi Blanc
See *Metalarte SA* under *Lighting* p. 178

Fornasetti Srl
See *Walls and Ceilings* p. 169

"Fucina" trademark
See *Skipper SpA*, under *Lighting* p. 178

Furniture of the Twentieth Century
227 West 17th Street
New York
NY 10011

Gaggenau Werke GmbH
Postfach 1260
7560 Gaggenau/Barden
Germany
Tel: (497) 2256 5100
Fax: (497) 2256 5105

US outlet:

Gaggenau USA Corp
425 University Avenue
Norwood
MA 02062
Tel: (617) 255 1766
Fax: (617) 769 2212

Built-in kitchen appliances from Gaggenau feature a unique combination of functional efficiency, top-quality material, superior workmanship and sensible design.

Storage p. 131/**5**

Inno
See *Inno-Tuote Oy*

Inno-Tuote Oy
Merikatu 1
SF-00140 Helsinki
Finland
Tel: (0) 0177233
Fax: (0) 0177483

Since 1975 Inno has been manufacturing architectural interior design products, such as furniture, lamps, coatracks, wastepaper baskets and bathroom accessories. The general aim is to be "rough yet classical" since over-refinement in materials and design becomes banal. High touch, rather than high-tech is the aim for a company which creates products with personality.

Storage: p. 134/**2**
Bathrooms: p. 150/**8**

Interlubke Gebr. Lubke GmbH & Co. KG
Ringstrasse 145
Postfach 1660
D-4840 Rheda-Wiedenbruck
Germany
Tel: (05242) 12321
Fax: (05242) 12206

US outlet:

Inter L
236 Dogwood Lane
Hartsdale
NY 10530
Tel: (914) 949 3257
Fax: (914) 949 0956

With the introduction of its 25-inch deep "Cupboard Wall" program 20 years ago, Interlubke upended conventional thinking on how to furnish bedrooms to provide infinitely variable storage systems. They feature standard carcasses which can take hinged, folding or gliding doors coping with every need.

Storage: pp. 123/**4**, 127/**8**, 128/**1-5**, 131/**9**

I.V.M. SpA
Via C. Cattaneo 90
20035 Lissone
Milan
Italy
Tel: (2) 48431-5
Fax: (2) 2456815

IVM, established in 1950, believes in the mass marketing of industrialized products. The present production of home and office furniture and shelving fulfils its philosophy without formalism, in designs that are industrial rather than merely esthetic.

Marais International
16 Avenue Victoria
75001 Paris
France
Tel: (1) 42 33 84 84
Fax: (1) 42 36 06 80

Storage: pp. 125/**10**, 127/**11**

Memphis Srl
Via Olivetti 9
20010 Pregnana Milanese
Milan
Italy
Tel: (2) 9329 2277
Fax: (2) 9329 1454

The influential furnishing design group Memphis was founded in 1981 by Ettore Sottsass. From its beginning, Memphis has overturned and reshaped the assumptions on which the production of so-called modern design is based, and has become the almost mystical symbol of New Design. Memphis pieces appear in the collections of several museums, and are still manufactured to order.

Muurame Oy
SF 15860 Hollola 2
Finland
Tel: (918) 801241
Fax: (918) 805619

US outlet:
Muurame Inc
80 King Spring Road
Windsor Locks
CT 06096
Tel: (203) 623 3902
Fax: (203) 623 0690

Muurame's production consists mainly of storage furniture for both home interiors and public areas, marketed through high standard furniture retailers. The company exports mainly to the USA, Scandinavia and Belgium.

Storage: p. 133/**10**

Martin Nagele
Ausstellungstechnik
Crellestrasse 12
D-1000 Berlin 62
Tel: (30) 784 8010
Fax: (30) 788 3193

Martin Nagele manufacture and distribute Klaus Block's furniture. Klaus Block's furniture pieces "happen" as a by product of his work as an architect. He designs them and one of his friends, a cabinet maker, makes the prototypes. These are then sent to furniture fairs and exhibitions in Germany, Europe and Japan, and then marketed on their return.

Storage: p. 133/**9**

Carl F. Petersen
See *Doors* p. 174

Quattrocchio Srl
Via Isonzo 51
15100 Alessandria
Italy
Tel: (131) 445 361
Fax: (131) 68745

US outlets:
Zero US Corp
Industrial Circle
Lincoln
RI 02865
Tel: (401) 724 4470
Fax: (401) 724 1190

Zero Showroom
89 Grand Street
New York
NY 10013
Tel: (212) 925 3615
Fax: (212) 925 3634

An established bicycle manufacturer by 1919, Quattrocchio turned to modular fixtures for stores and exhibitions and more recently introduced a collection of complementary free-standing storage systems for the home.

Storage: p. 134/**8**

Rosenthal Einrichtung
Wittelsbacherstrasse 43
PO Box 1520
8672 Selb
Germany
Tel: (9287) 72507
Fax: (9287) 72228

US outlets:
European Interiors
Interform
200 Lexington Avenue
Suite 512, New York
NY 10016
Tel: (212) 685 4959
Fax: (212) 685 9117

Massini
Pacific Design Center
8687 Melrose Avenue
Los Angeles
CA 90069
Tel: (310) 652 1060
Fax: (310) 652 2208

Rosenthal Design
Showroom Inc D-Cota
1855 Griffin Road, Suite B-408
Dania
FL 33004
Tel: (305) 922 7234
Fax: (305) 925 5019

Rosenthal's functional and esthetic furniture designs are characterized by three intentions: to serve the needs of hospitality; to combine functional design with artistic expression and to create furniture for living and working.

Storage: pp. 124/**3 & 4**, 133/**8**

Rosenthal Furniture
See *Rosenthal Einrichtung*

Salvado and Sole
See *Disform*

Sawaya & Moroni SpA
Via Manzoni 11
20121 Milano
Italy
Tel: (2) 8646 3066
Fax: (2) 8646 4831

US outlets:
Adesso
200 Boyloston Street
Boston
MASS
Tel: (617) 451 3628

Diva
8818 Beverly Boulevard
Los Angeles
CA 90048
Tel: (213) 274 718
Fax: (213) 274 7189

Domus Design Center Inc
215 East 58th Street
New York
NY 10022
Tel: (212) 2800

Modern Age
41 East 11th Street
New York
NY 10003
Tel: (212) 674 5603

Postmark
333 Bryant Street
San Francisco
California
Tel: (415) 243 9780

Stilnovo
370 Altara Avenue
Coral Gables
FL 33146
Tel: (305) 441 9007
Fax: (305) 441 1185

Founded in 1984 in Milan by interior designers William Sawaya and Paolo Moroni, the company bases its production on contemporary design commissioned from different cultural backgrounds and within different design concepts. This accounts for the individual character and presence of each of their pieces. The result is a furniture collection – divans, tables, chairs, shelves – and a line of small decorative products.

Storage: p. 132/**6**

Tebong
See *Lighting* p. 179

Tecta
Sohnreystrasse 10
3471 Lauenfoerde
Germany
Tel: (5273) 7006
Fax: (5273) 8410

US outlets:
Unit
Bauhaus Gallery
7301 Melrose Avenue
Los Angeles
CA 90046
Tel: (213) 933 8391
Fax: (213) 650 3711

Nuovo Melodrom
60 Green Street
New York
NY 10012
Tel: (212) 219 0013
Fax: (212) 431 3931

Tecta produces some of the classic designs of the Bauhaus movement, together with contemporary furniture like the storage systems and kitchen "tree" by Stefan Wewerka.

Lighting: p. 126/**5**

Tonelli Srl
Via della Produzione 16
61025 Montelabbate (PS)
Italy
Tel: (721) 481339
Fax: (721) 481291

US outlets:
Roche Bobois
585 Commercial Street
Boston
MA 2109
Tel: (617) 742 9611
Fax: (617) 742 9630

Roche Bobois
9947 Harwin Suite I
Houston
TX 77036
Tel: (713) 977 1444
Fax: (713) 789 6049

Roche Bobois
8850 Beverly Boulevard
Los Angeles
CA 90048
Tel: (213) 273 4886
Fax: (213) 273 6517

E.G. Cody
80 NE 40th Street
Miami
FL 33137
Tel: (305) 374 4777
Fax: (305) 576 4060

Roche Bobois
One Henry Adams Street
San Francisco
CA 94103
Tel: (415) 626 8613
Fax: (415) 626 7647

Roche Bobois
1002 Western Avenue
Seattle
WA 98104
Tel: (206) 622 7166
Fax: (206) 682 7841

The Tonelli collection has made an impact on the international market over the last few years as the company's high technical production stardards have been recognized. Products have been commissioned from well-known designers such as Isao Hose, De Pas D'urbino Lomazzi, Bruno Munari and Luigi Serafini.

Storage: pp. 124/**1 & 2**, 125/**9**

Zanotta SpA
See *Walls and Ceilings* p. 170

Zerodisegno
See *Quattrocchio Srl*

Bathrooms

Agape Srl
Via Ploner 2
46038 Frassino (MA)
Italy
Tel: (376) 371738
Fax: (376) 374213

US outlet:
Water Colors Inc
Garrison on Hudson
New York 10524
Tel: (914) 424 3327
Fax: (914) 424 3169

Since 1973 Agape have produced and distributed elements to furnish the bathroom. Characteristics of their products, which range from sinks to bathroom accessories like mirrors with built-in halogen lights and dimmers, are quality design, functionalism and precision finishes.

Bathrooms: pp. 147/**2**, 150/**9**

Amtico Co. Ltd
See *Floors* p. 170

Borma
C.N. Borma AS
Chr Nielsens Veu 3
Post Box 279
DK-8700 Horsens
Denmark
Tel: (75) 64 59 00
Fax: (75) 64 59 01

Lighting p. 174
Bathrooms: p. 148/**9**

Cesana SpA
Via Dalmazia 3
20059 Vimercate
Milan
Italy
Tel: (2) 608 2441
Fax: (2) 661 166

US outlet:
Cesana Inc
Shore Pointe One
Selleck Street
Norwalk
CN 06855
Tel: (203) 853 3678
Fax: (203) 855 1360

Among the first bathroom hardware manufacturers to convert the production of fireclay to a porcelained fine "gres" comparable to porcelain, Cesane markets two collections worldwide: the one exploiting the craft fascination of the ceramic art, the other since 1966 promoting enameling.

Bathrooms: p. 144/**2-4**

Daryl Industries Ltd
Alfred Road
Wallasey
Wirral L44 7HY
England
Tel: (051) 638 8211
Fax: (051) 638 0303

Daryl Industries manufacture shower enclosures and bath screens, using safety glass and fiber/white/gold anodized frames.

Bathrooms: pp. 140/**1**, 144/**5**, 145/**7 & 9**

Aloys F. Dornbracht GmbH & Co. KG
Koebbingser Muehle 6
D-5860 Iserlohn
Germany
Tel: (2371) 4330
Fax: (2371) 433232

US outlets:
The Baths Beyond
135 Mississippi Street
San Francisco
CA 94107
Tel: (415) 552 5001
Fax: (415) 552 0714

Community Home Supply
3924 North Lincoln
Chicago
ILL 60613
Tel: (312) 281 7010
Fax: (312) 935 7465

Davis & Warshow Inc
57-22 48th Street
Maspeth
NY 11378
Tel: (718) 937 9500
Fax: (718) 786 9771

Hardware Designs Inc
135 New Dutch Lane
Fairfield
NJ 07004
Tel: (201) 808 0266
Fax: (201) 808 0207

Snyder Diamond
100 South Robertson Boulevard
Los Angeles
CA 90048
Tel: (310) 859 1702
Fax: (310) 274 3125

Dornbracht is well-known worldwide for its design-orientated plumbing products. The company combines unique European design with quality German precision and engineering to produce luxurious bathroom fixtures, and over the past half century has established world standards for decorative brass fixtures.

Bathrooms: pp. 136/**3**, 137/**4**, 148/**1 & 7**, 149/**18 & 19**

Duravit AG
See *Storage* p. 179

Eljer
Department PB
901 Tenth Street
PO Box 37
Plano
TX 75074

Bathroom fixtures

FIR Rubinetterie SpA
Via M. Gioia 64
20125 Milan
Italy
Tel: (2) 6880249
Fax: (2) 6880791

US outlet:
FIR America Inc
1323 South 30th Avenue
Hollywood
CA 33020

Established in the late 1950s, FIR Rubinetterie initially produced traditional faucets and valves mainly for worldwide export from Italy. In 1970, the commercial and production trend changed completely, and FIR now concentrate on creating "top quality, designed and colored faucets," studying technical solutions to ensure the greatest efficiency and durability.

Bathrooms: pp. 148/**3, 4 & 6**

Frog Design
34 South 2nd Street
Cambell
CA 95008

Bathroom fixtures

Gruppo Metals
See *Rubinetteria F.lli Fantini*

Gruppo Novellini
See *Novellini Diffusion Srl*

Ideal-Standard Ltd
PO Box 60
National Avenue
Kingston upon Hull HU5 4JE
England
Tel: (0482) 46461
Fax: (0482) 445886

Ideal-Standard works with leading designers from around the world to create its wide range of bathroom equipment, including suites, individual baths, faucets and mixers, showers, furniture and accessories. Precision engineering, high-quality materials and superb detail combine in a comprehensive range renowned for its durability.

Bathrooms: p. 142/**3**

Inno
See *Inno-Tuote Oy* under *Storage* p. 179

Kartell SpA
Via delle Industrie 1
20082 Noviglio
Milan
Italy
Tel: (2) 900 121
Fax: (2) 905 3316

US outlet:
I.L. Euro Inc
Ivan Luini
900 Broadway, Interior 902
New York
NY 1003
Tel: (212) 477 3188
Fax: (212) 477 4862

Kartell, founded in the 1950s, is today a leader in the production of plastic furnishings, distinguished from others by collaboration with some of the most famous international designers, including Matteo Thun's mirror collection.

Bathrooms: p. 150/**7**

Laufen
See *Oespag Laufen*

I.P. Lund Trading ApS
Axel Kiers Vej 12
8270 Hojbjerg
Denmark
Tel: (8629) 1444
Fax: (8629) 2459

US outlet:
Kroin Incorporated
180 Fawcett Street
Cambridge
MA 02138
Tel: (617) 492 4000
Fax: (617) 492 4001

I.P. Lund produce Vola faucets. Made in Denmark, they are a hallmark of architectural design, the spout being simplified to simulate a stream of water. Created in 1968 by one of the world's leading architects, Arne Jacobsen, the Vola design is a unique combination of designer skills and fine craftsmanship. Today Vola faucets are installed throughout the world.

Bathrooms: pp. 148/**2**, 168/**6**

M & Z Rubinetteria
Via Casale 37
28010 Bolzano Novarese (No)
Italy
Tel: (322) 982086
Fax: (322) 982226

A manufacturer of sanitary fixtures with 20 years' experience, M & Z Rubinetteria makes bath

and kitchen faucets in different colors and finishes by world-famous designers.

Bathrooms: p. 149/**14**

Milldue Arredi SpA
Via Balegante 7
31039 Riese Pio X (TV)
Italy
Tel: (423) 485041-2
Fax: (423) 456319

Milldue, specialists in the production of bathroom furniture, was founded in 1977. From the start, its aim was to market top designs, while not forgetting the final cost to the customer. Materials used range from walnut to polyester lacquer and maple, with counters supplied in polyester lacquer, marble or granite.

Bathrooms: p. 138/**7**

Novellini Diffusione Srl
Via della Stazione 2
46030 Romanore Borgoforte (MN)
Italy
Tel: (376) 64911
Fax: (376) 648267

Combining Italian design with the highest quality requirements, Novellini is a leading Italian manufacturer of shower screens in laminated safety glass and of acrylic whirlpools.

Bathrooms: p. 142/**2 & 5**

Oespag Laufen AG
Goethegasse 3
1015 Wien
Austria
Tel: (222) 51597-0
Fax: (222) 51597222

US outlet:
Burgess & Association
34480 Goddard Road
PO Box 335
Romulus
MI 48174-0335
Tel: (313) 941 0092
Fax: (313) 941 1288

Laufen is one of Europe's leading ceramic manufacturers with factories located all over the world. Throughout all Laufen's various design and manufacturing divisions which include production of bathroom fixtures, wall and floor tiles, tableware, chimney stacks, insulators, and roof tiles, the company's philosophy is quality, design and functionality. Their sink, toilet and bidet all designed by F.A. Porsche, operate as a furnishing scheme rather than separate fixtures, unified within a base cabinet, allowing combinations of components on a modular system.

Bathrooms: pp. 141/**6**, 145/**6**

Carl F. Petersen
See *Doors* p. 174

Rapsel SpA
Via Volta 13
20019 Settimo Milanese
Milan
Italy
Tel: (2) 3285851/5
Fax: (2) 3287997

Hastings Pavement Co Inc
30 Commercial Street
Freeport
NY 11520
Tel: (516) 829 3500

In the 1970s Rapsel began marketing first textiles, then bathroom fixtures from Scandinavia with Vola faucets. Since 1978 they have commissioned designs for tubs and sinks stylish enough for the streamlined faucets, producing the "washmobil" by Berger and Stahl, then "Euclide" by Finn Skoedt, Philippe Starck's sink in 1985, "Rapsody" by Berger and Stahl and in 1990 "Pan" by Turi and Gagliardi.

Bathrooms: pp. 139/**6**, 147/**6 & 7**, 150/**4**

Rubinetteria F.lli Fantini
Via Buonarroti 4
Pella
Novara
Italy
Tel: (322) 969 127
Fax: (322) 969 530

Rubinetteria F.lli Fantini produce Gruppo Metals' innovative faucet designs, including the "Giro tondo."

Bathrooms: pp. 148/**8**, 149/**11-13**

**Rubinetterie "Chantal 27,"
"Ondatris 29," "Time 95"**
See *FIR Rubinetterie SpA*

Rubinetterie "Toscane Ponsi"
See *Tosca & Ponsi Rubinetterie SpA*

Sieger faucet
See *Aloys F. Dornbracht GmbH & Co. KG*

Societé André
24 Rue de Colmar
94170 Le Perreaux
France
Tel: (48) 72 20 21

Societé André manufactures bath fixtures, including the Andrée Putman sink designed with Ecart, an interior design firm she launched in 1978. Her individuality, for which she is famous in France and the USA, is based on sobriety and rigor. Her aim is a controlled space in which serenity comes from purity of

lines and harmony of materials, and a look that is modern, yet timeless.

Bathrooms: pp. 137/**7**

StudioLine di Lena A. & C. SnC
Via Torricelli 16
Fontane di Villorba ZI (TV)
Italy
Tel: (422) 608044
Fax: (422) 608166

StudioLine's range of complementary accessories in many materials from ceramics and metal to wood and marble allows a choice of fittings and fixtures in the bathroom to provide the best use of available space.

Bathrooms: p. 150/**1**

Studio Rapsel
See *Rapsel SpA*

T & S Brass and Bronze Works
Route 4, Old Buncombe Road
Travelers Rest
SCA 20690

Bathroom fixtures

Toni
See *Toni Armatur A/S*

Toni Armatur A/S
Rodovre
Denmark
Tel: (317) 01422

Denmark is a serious challenge to Italy in the manufacture of bathroom hardware favored by modern architects.

Bathrooms: p. 149/**16**

Tosca & Ponsi Rubinetterie
Via Volta 2
55049 Viareggio (LU)
Italy
Tel: (584) 46131
Fax: (584) 46117

US outlet:
Great Western Kitchen and Bath Inc
16140 Raymer Street
Van Nuys
CA 91406
Tel: (213) 873 8365

Since 1935, Ponsi have designed and manufactured faucets and bathroom accessories. Production, from the foundry to despatch, is carried out in Tuscany. The greatest care is taken in esthetics, quality and reliability.

Bathrooms: p. 149/**17**

"Vola" faucets
See *I.P. Lund Trading ApS*

Kitchens

Alessi
See *F.A.O. SpA* under *Heating* p. 176

Allmilmo
See *Milewski Mobelwerk Zeil KG*

Alno Moebelwerke GmbH & Co. KG
Postfach 1160
D-7798 Pfullendorf
Germany
Tel: (7552) 210
Fax: (7552) 213400

Since 1930, Alno have made kitchens, in wood – solid oak or modern laminate combinations – or with a high-gloss finish. Styles range from traditional fronts and detailing to streamlined modernity. The largest independent kitchen manufacturer in Europe, Alno gives priority to recyclable materials and renewable resources, using only local wood.

Kitchens: pp. 153/**5**, 159/**4 & 5**, 160/**4**

Avonite Inc
1945 Highway 304
Belen
New Mexico 87002

Avonite is a modified polyester sheet material for counters produced in the USA, available in a choice of 15 eye-catching granite and marble-effect colors and shaped to individual design and specification.

Kitchens: pp. 166/**3**, 167/**9**

Barking Grohe Ltd
See *Friedrich Grohe*

Blanco GmbH & Co
Postfach 1160
D-7519 Oberderdingen 1
Germany
Tel: (497) 045 440
Fax: (497) 045 44299

US outlet:
Blanco America Inc
Village of Pine Run
Commerce Center
1001 Lower Landing Road
Suite 607
Blackwood
NJ 08012
Tel: (609) 228 3500
Fax: (609) 228 7956

For more than 40 years, domestic sinks and appliances from Germany's Blanco GmbH & Co have set standards for design, quality and innovation. Blanco manufactuers sinks for every size and style of kitchen in stainless steel and Silacron – a durable composite material developed in Blanco's own laboratories. Their range of appliances includes refrigerators, freezers, dishwashers, ovens, cooktops and exhaust hoods.

Kitchens: pp. 167/**7**, 168/**7**

Boffi Arredamento Cucina SpA
Via Oberdan 70
20030 Lentate sul Seveso
Milan
Italy
Tel: (2) 562881
Fax: (2) 565077

Boffi Arredamento Cucina are known worldwide for their kitchen design with products displayed at the Triennale, the Museum of Modern Art in New York, and the Universal Exhibition Expo 85 in Tsukuba in Japan. Since 1940, Italian Boffi have launched several innovations: the first colored polyester door finish, the first door without a pull grip, and also the first door to be made with vertical wood strips.

Kitchens: pp. 161/**9-11**, 164/**1**

Robert Bosch Hausgerate GmbH
Hochstrasse 17
8000 Munchen 80
Germany
Tel: (4989) 4808 00
Fax: (4989) 4808 2418

US outlets:
Exclusive Distributors Inc
312 South Catalina Avenue
Redondo Beach
CA 90277
Tel: (213) 274 1678
Fax: (213) 372 1188

Kevin Inc
11 Prospekt Street
Madison
NJ 07940
Tel: (201) 593 0303
Fax: (201) 593 0302

Represented around the world, Robert Bosch's kitchen design employs the latest technology, elegantly clad in a wide variety of door fronts, cabinet types and finishes to make an individual kitchen that lines up with their extensive range of dishwashers, as well as refrigeration, cooking and home laundry appliances.

Kitchens: p. 163/**11**

Bulthaup
Systemmobel Industrie
D-8318 Aich
Germany
Tel: (8741) 800
Fax: (8741) 80309

US outlet:
Bulthaup
153 South Robertson Boulevard
Los Angeles
CA 90048
Tel: (213) 288 3880
Fax: (213) 288 3885

The name Bulthaup is well known internationally for top design and innovative technology in the quality built-in kitchen industry, and the company has received many awards. Since Gerd Bulthaup took over the management of the company from his father in the 1970s, strong Bauhaus and Ulm school influences have become evident in all aspects of Bulthaup's design management and philosophy. Simplicity and practicality in conjuction with truth to materials form the basis of Bulthaup's design philosophy resulting in functional, individual and timeless solutions to kitchen planning. Nearly 150 different colors and a wide variety of wood and laminate finishes are used.

Kitchens: pp. 154/**1**, 165/**8**

Chicago Faucet Company
2100 South Clearwater Drive
Des Planes
IL 60018
Tel: (708) 803 5000
Fax: (708) 298 3101

The Chicago Faucet Company is a leading manufacturer in the United States of top-quality, stylish kitchen and bathroom faucets and fixtures. Headquartered in Des Planes, Illinois, the company distributes its products throughout North America and Europe, an alliance which inspired the company's most recent and exciting bathroom faucet introduction, the "Illusion Collection (R)," which combines old-world workmanship in brass with modern style.

Ciatti a Tavola SpA
Via Valentini 8/D
50047 Prato (FI)
Italy
Tel: (574) 22106
Fax: (574) 40654

Bulthaup
Systemmobel Industrie
D-8318 Aich
Germany
Tel: (8741) 800
Fax: (8741) 80309

US outlet:
In'Italia Ltd
205 Vanderbilt Street
Brooklyn
NY 11218
Tel: (718) 871 8177
Fax: (718) 228 0558

Ciatti, a leading manufacturer of top-grade, complementary kitchen furniture, is renowned for innovative design and versatility: Italian country pieces reinterpreted in light and airy beech, sturdy but elegant chairs and stools, and the revolutionary Axis free-standing system for the smaller kitchen.

Kitchens: p. 166/**1**

Colorcor
See *Formica Corp*

Corian
See *Du Pont*

Dacor
950 South Avenue
Pasadena
CA 91109
Tel: (818) 799 1000

Dacor is a manufacturer of high-quality, innovative, domestic kitchen cooking equipment and ventilating systems. Products include electric and gas cooktops, electric built-in ovens and ranges and downdraft and overhead ventilation systems.

Kitchens: p. 164/**4**

Du Pont
Market Street
1007 Wilmington
DL 19898
Tel: (302) 774 1000

Du Pont produce Corian, a high-performance, solid-surface material well-known for its robust performance. Corian is non-porous, highly resistant to damage and can be molded to form integral sinks and basins. It is available in a wide range of plain colors and natural granite and marble effects.

Kitchens: pp. 159/**4**, 164/**5**

Ecart International
See *Lighting* p. 177

Effeti SpA
Via B. Cellini 174
50028 Tavarnelle VP
Florence
Italy
Tel: (55) 8070007-9
Fax: (55) 8070085

Guaranteed by in-house production standards in the finest tradition of Tuscan carpentry, the Effeti kitchen brings vigor to inspired design, and innovative styling, like turning corners with curvaceous cabinets fitted with specially curved cooking appliances.

Kitchens: p. 156/**2 & 3**

F.lli Ferretti di Ferretto SpA
Via Volterrana 60
56033 Capannoli
Pisa
Italy
Tel: (50) 587 639111
Fax: (50) 587 609146

The Ferretti family control one of Italy's leading companies in the production of built-in kitchens, manufacturing under three brand names; "Ferretti," "Gandi," and "Belcari & Bulleri."

Kitchens: pp. 157/**7**, 162/**7**, 167/**12**

Formica Corp
Oak Hill Park
1680 Route 23 North
Wayne
NJ 07470
Tel: (201) 305 9400
Fax: (201) 305 1095

The Formica Corporation's global group of companies manufacture high-pressure decorative laminates. Formica's international team of designers work with color, pattern, texture and reflectivity to create visual features or background effects. The ranges are tuned to trends in decor, established and anticipated, at home and overseas.

Kitchens: p. 167/**6**

Franke Ag
4663 Aarburg
Switzerland
Tel: (62) 433 131
Fax: (62) 416 761

US outlet:
Franke Inc
Kitchen Systems Division
212 Church Road
North Wales
PA 19454
Tel: (215) 699 8761
Fax: (215) 699 7464

With factories in 14 countries worldwide, Franke claims to be the world's largest sink manufacturers. Their range includes both stainless steel, enamel and various synthetic materials and is complemented by an international range of faucets, accessories and other sink-related items to the highest specifications.

Kitchens: pp. 166/**5**, 167/**8**, 168/**2 & 3**

Friedrich Grohe AG
Hauptstrasse 137
Postfach 1361
D-5870 Hemer
Germany
Tel: (2372) 53-1
Fax: (2372) 53322

US outlet:
Grohe America Inc
900 Lively Boulevard
Wood Dale
IL 60191
Tel: (708) 350 2600
Fax: (708) 350 2615

The European sanitary-ware industry has been decisively influenced for decades by Friedrich Grohe, not only as its largest manufacturer of faucets, offering a large variety of articles and producing over 30,000 valves daily, but also as a company whose trend-setting technology and product designs have won it international recognition and respect throughout the industry worldwide.

Kitchens: pp. 168/**1 & 5**

Marshall Erdman & Associates Inc
500 South Division Street
Waunakee
WI 53597
Tel: (800) 356 8400

Marshall Erdman and Associates is an architectural and building firm that also designs and manufactures Techline furniture and cabinetry, closet and office systems. This high-quality system features sophisticated design, precision engineering, durability and versatility. The laminate, modular components include options for the bedroom, office, kitchen and for entertainment, dining and all kinds of storage.

Storage: p. 128/**6**
Kitchens: p. 159/**3**

Miele & Cie GmbH & Co
Carl Miele Strasse 29
W-4830 Gutersloh
Germany
Tel: (05241) 890

US outlets:
Miele Appliances Inc
1900 South Norfolk Street
Suite 101
San Mateo
CA 94403
Tel: (415) 571 9074
Fax: (415) 571 9188

Miele Appliances Inc
22D World's Fair Drive
Somerset
NJ 08873
Tel: (908) 560 0899
Fax: (908) 560 9649

The name Miele is synonymous with quality kitchens throughout the world. The company first made high-quality appliances, expanding in the 1970s to make cabinets to house them. Their design and production technology combines in a wide range of stylish kitchens in wood, laminate, lacquer and high-gloss finishes and the company offers the architect a range of services covering design, costing and installation.

Kitchens: pp. 154/**2**, 155/**5**, 163/**12**

Milewski Mobelwerk Zeil KG
Postfach 1180
D-8729 Weil Am Main
Germany
Tel: (49) 952 4910
Fax: (49) 952 49925

Established in 1965, Milewski Mobelwerk Zeil found early international success with a range of built-in kitchens with revolutionary new designs and a folding door system which is still unique today. The company has consistently pursued an innovation strategy, concentrating on finding out exactly what the kitchen buyer wants and needs.

Kitchens: p. 158/**2**

Neff GmbH
Hochstrasse 17
8000 Munich 80
Germany
Tel: (89) 4808 2837
Fax: (89) 4808 2911

Neff is synonymous with the finest cooking appliances and the Circotherm cooking system. Stylish, modern and innovative are words used to describe Neff's 150 energy-saving and environmentally-friendly features.

Kitchens: pp. 162/**2**, 163/**12**, 165/**9**

Pegler Ltd
St Catherine's Avenue
Doncaster
South Yorkshire DN4 8DF
England
Tel: (0302) 368 581
Fax: (0302) 367 661

US outlet:
Pegler Ltd
Operations Office
PO Box 59986
Dallas
TX 75229
Tel: (214) 406 9007
Fax: (214) 406 8947

Pegler Ltd is one of the world's leading manufacturers of plumber's brassware and heating controls. The Pegler range includes faucets, mixers and showers for specialist as well as domestic use, comprising fixtures, brass and bronze valves, radiator valves and a full range of domestic and commercial heating and hot water controls.

Kitchens: p. 168/**4**

Philips Whirlpool
See *Whirlpool International BV*

Poggenpohl GmbH & Co
Herringhauser Strasse 33
Postfach 2455
D-4900 Hertford
Germany
Tel: (05221) 381-0
Fax: (05221) 381321

US outlet:
Poggenpohl US Inc
5905 Johns Road
Tampa
FL 33634
Tel: (813) 882 9292
Fax: (813) 888 8218

For almost 100 years Poggenpohl have manufactured kitchens in Hertford. Although many changes have occurred in the production processes, the company's objectives have remained the same: high quality and precision of their custom-built kitchens, together with contemporary and highly functional design. Over many decades and in over 40 countries worldwide, Poggenpohl has gained a high reputation.

Kitchens: pp. 155/**6**, 156/**5**, 157/**11**, 160/**3 & 5**, 161/**12**, 162/**8**

Salima/Tecnoarredo Srl
Via Mazzini 154
Chiusi Scalo (FI)
Italy
Tel: (578) 20350
Fax: (578) 227459

The aim of the Salima factory is to satisfy customers who do not want a mass-produced article. Salima only needs three days to custom-build particular designs.

Kitchens: pp. 160/**1**, 165/**10**

Scavolini SpA
Via Risara 60/70
61025 Montelabbate (PS)
Italy
Tel: (721) 4431
Fax: (721) 482366

Scavolini, a leading Italian kitchen producer, creates warm and rational kitchens that represent the best of Italian design. Accurate targeting and marketing of Scavolini assures the best possible service to customers and its products are distributed worldwide with increasing success.

Kitchens: p. 156/**1**

SieMatic Mobelwerke GmbH & Co
August-Siekmann Str. 1-5
D-4972 Loehne 1
Germany
Tel: (05732) 67-1
Fax: (05732) 67 297

SieMatic, designers and builders of kitchens since 1930, are responsible for many innovations under the watchful eye of the founder's heir, August Siekmann. Distributed throughout Europe and the USA, their 34 designs offer high-gloss lacquer finishes, combined with polished chrome or brass pulls and strong color. They have introduced a brilliant red to their 2002G, 400RG and 9009PR ranges.

Kitchens: pp. 155/**8**, 157/**8**, 161/**13**, 167/**10-11**

Siemens Electrogeriate GmbH
Hochstrasse 17
D-8000 Munchen 80
Germany
Tel: (4989) 480809
Fax:

Kitchens: p. 162/**8**

Smeg SpA
Via Circonvallazione Nord 36
42016 Guastalla
Reggio Emilia
Italy
Tel: (522) 825241
Fax: (522) 838384

North American outlets:
Conwest Wholesale Ltd
12185 86th Avenue
Surrey
British Columbia
Canada
Tel: (604) 594 1688
Fax: (604) 591 9141

Dajon Electromenagers Inc
1645 Autoroute Laval
(440 Ouest)
Chomedey, Laval
Quebec
Canada
Tel: (514) 381 8013

Energy Saving Appliances
390 Tapscott Road
Scarborough
Ontario
Canada
Tel: (416) 291 2143
Fax: (416) 291 3454

From the first automatic gas ranges to the latest electronic built-in ovens, the development of electrical household appliances over the last 35 years by Smeg SpA has brought the company to the forefront in the built-in oven sector in both Italy and the world. From the 1970s, the company has pursued a policy of innovation in all sectors of electrical household goods, putting a series of appliances, both built-in and free-standing, onto the market, that are not just technologically perfect, but also well designed and attractive.

Kitchens: pp. 162/**5**, 165/**11**

Strato SnC
Via Nationale 65
23012 Castione
Sondrio
Italy
Tel: (342) 358 116
Fax: (342) 358 525

Strato was established in 1987 by Marco Gorini and Gianna Farina. A policy of continual research and technological updating has enabled Strato to design and produce high-quality kitchens which meet with exceptional criteria of esthetics and functionality.

Kitchens: pp. 153/**6**, 155/**7**, 161/**8**

Tantoflex
Birches Industrial Estate
Imberhorne Lane
East Grinstead
West Sussex RH19 1XG
England
Tel: (0342) 328166
Fax: (0342) 410353

Tantofex is Britain's largest privately owned brass foundry, manufacturing faucets and mixers; the company sells bathroom accessories. In addition to producing traditional lines, Tantofex manufactures modern fixtures such as single-lever mixers as well as Victorian-style fixtures.

Kitchens: p. 168/8

Techline Furniture
See *Marshall Erdman & Associates Inc*, under *Storage* p. 180

Villeroy & Boch AG
Faiencerie Mettlach
Postfach 10140
D-6642 Mettlach
Germany
Tel: (6864) 811
Fax: (6864) 81405

US outlet:
Villeroy & Boch Tableware
41 Madison Avenue
New York
NY 10010
Tel: (212) 683 1747/8

Villeroy & Boch, manufacturers of fine ceramics for 250 years, produce a range of efficient kitchen sinks, combining modern design with superior quality in ceramic or the new synthetic materials. Villeroy & Boch's kitchen sinks are curved and organic, octagonal (to fit across corners), rounded or squared in a wide choice of sizes.

Kitchens: pp. 166/**4**, 168/**5**

"Vola" faucets
See *I.P. Lund Trading ApS*, under *Bathrooms* p. 181

Whirlpool International BV
Administrative Center
2000 M-63
Benton Harbor
MI 49022
Tel: (616) 926 3315
Fax: (616) 926 5486

Whirlpool International is the wholly owned subsidiary of Whirlpool Corporation, the world's leading manufacturer and marketer of major domestic appliances. Created in early 1989, the company represents a joint venture with Philips of the Netherlands to manufacture, market, sell and service major domestic appliances in western Europe. Whirlpool International's European domestic appliance brands are Philips Whirlpool, Bauknecht, Ignis and Laden.

Kitchens: pp. 162/**3**, 164/**2**

Woodstock Furniture
23 Pakenham Street
London WC1X 0LB
England
Tel: (071) 837 1818
Fax: (071) 837 1852

In a world where interiors are too often treated as objects of fashion rather than function, Woodstock remain dedicated to designing and building real furniture. Renowned for the quality of its kitchen furniture, the company build in the traditional manner, constructing each cabinet from solid wood as an individual piece of furniture.

Kitchens: p. 154/**3**

Zanussi Elettrodomestici SpA
Via Giardini Cattaneo 3
33170 Pordenone
Italy
Tel: (434) 394660
Fax: (434) 394035

Part of the Electrolux Group, Zanussi is Europe's leading manufacturer of "white goods." Design and innovation are the basic tools of its product strategy, and the "Wizard" collection of white goods styled and finished in matte black have won the company international awards.

Kitchens: pp. 152/**2**, 162/**6**, 164/**1, 6 & 7**

Zerowatt SpA
Via Busa 19
24020 Nese
Italy
Tel: (35) 514646
Fax: (35) 513251

The best-known products of Zerowatt are washing-machines, washer-dryers, and dryers. Space saving is their aim. Zerowatt has integrated the high technology of a 5 kg/front-loading washing machine in a slim-line appliance with a depth of only 17 inches. This saves about 30 percent of the space required for a standard 5kg washing-machine. In 1989, Zerowatt launched the Spaziozero 33 washing-machine, which has a depth of only 13 inches. Another famous product is the 1007 Electronic, the only appliance which can wash and dry automatically 4kg of laundry, compared with the 2kg or 2.5kg which can be done by any other washer-dryer.

Architects & Designers

Tadao Ando Architect and Associates
5-23 Toyosaki 2
Chome Osado-Ku
Osaka
Japan 531
Tel: (6) 375 1148

Introduction: p. 11/**4**
Walls & Ceilings: pp. 19/**4**, 30/**5**
Stairs: p. 90/**7**
Storage: p. 130/**2**

Armstrong Associates
2 Hinde Street
London W1 5RN
England
Tel: (071) 935 6389
Fax: (071) 487 4056

Walls & Ceilings: p. 25/**11**
Doors: p. 55/**11**
Stairs: p. 80/**2**

Aukett Associates
Albert Bridge House
127 Albert Bridge Road
London SW11 4PL
England
Tel: (071) 352 0142
Fax: (071) 924 1125

Stairs: p. 83/**5**

Pierre d'Avoine Architects
Tapestry Court
Mortlake High Street
London SW14 8HJ
England
Tel: (081) 878 9455

Introduction: p. 10/**2**
Walls & Ceilings: p. 27/**11**
Stairs: p. 77

Albert Bardawil
6-28 Hyde Park Gardens
London W2 2NB
England
Tel: (071) 262 6415
Fax: (071) 402 2855

Stairs: p. 90/**1 & 2**

Benn-Gurleyik Design Studio
Markgroningerstrasse 61/1
D-7000 Stuttgart 40
Germany
Tel: (711) 870 2105
Fax: (711) 870 2106

Heating: p. 98/**2**

Cecilia & Ottorino Berselli
Via Luzzago 6
Brescia
Italy
Tel: (30) 58 139
Fax: (30) 24 20 886

Stairs: p. 89/**6**
Kitchens: p. 166/**2**

Klaus Block
Sieglindestrasse 5
Berlin 41
Germany
Tel: (30) 851 8548
Fax: (30) 851 7083

Storage: p. 133/**9**

Cini Boeri
Via Giovannino de Grassi 4
20123 Milan
Italy
Tel: (2) 875 531

Lighting: p. 116/**5 & 6**

Jacques Borris
154 West 18th Street
New York
NY 10011
Tel: (212) 243571

Walls & Ceilings: p. 26/**1**
Storage: p. 127/**10**

Ron Brinkers & d'Soto
Engine Room
Spring House
10 Spring Place
London NW5 3BH
England
Tel: (071) 267 3857

Walls & Ceilings: p. 20/**5**
Floors: p. 37/**7**

Mrs A. Brinitzer
Saalgasse 16
Frankfurt
Germany

Doors: p. 56/**2**
Stairs: p. 79/**4 & 5**, 88/**1**

Butler and Radici
X Warehouse
Metropolitian Wharf
Wapping Wall
London E1
England
Tel: (071) 480 6564

Heating: p. 94/**1**

Michael Carapettan
c/o Jake George
Flat 8
1 Linden Gardens
London W2 4HA
England
Tel: (071) 727 3763

Stairs: p. 78/**1 & 2**
Bathrooms: p. 138/**4 & 5**
Kitchens: p. 160/**6**

Gianfranco Cavaglia Architect
Via Giolitti N.11
19123 Turin
Italy
Tel: (11) 548 168

Walls & Ceilings: p. 21/**6**
Doors: p. 59/**7 & 8**

Chassay Last Architects
90 Westbourne Terrace
London W2 6QE
England
Tel: (071) 402 3233
Fax: (071) 262 1475

Walls & Ceilings: p. 19/**3**

David Chipperfield Associates
1a Cobham Mews
Agar Grove
London NW1 9SB
England
Tel: (071) 267 9422
Fax: (071) 267 9347

Walls & Ceilings: p. 19/**5**
Floors: p. 39/**8**
Windows: pp. 69/**7 & 8**, 71/**6**, 75/**8**
Stairs: pp. 80/**3**, 85/**7**, 87/**6**, 90/**4**
Heating: p. 95/**7**
Storage: pp. 122, 129/**10**, 131/**5**
Kitchens: pp. 159/**8**, 164/**3**

Nobby Clarke & Partners
See *Charles Rutherfoord*

David Connor
Plato Place
72 Dionis Road
London SW6 4TU
England
Tel: (071) 736 9337

Jo Crepain
De Pretlann 3
Kapellen 2080
Belgium
Tel: (3) 666 4916

Walls & Ceilings: p. 25/**7**
Doors: p. 57/**5**
Windows: p. 73/**5**
Heating: p. 98/**1**

Gary Cunningham Architects
2700 Fairmount/200
Dallas
TX 75201
Tel: (214) 855 5272
Fax: (212) 871 3307

Walls & Ceilings: p. 31/**7 & 11**
Floors: pp. 36/**6**, 42/**4**
Windows: p. 73/**7**
Lighting: p. 120/**4**
Bathrooms: pp. 136/**2**, 150/**2**
Kitchens: p. 163/**10**

Lynn Davis Architects
13 Harnet Street
Sandwich
Kent CT13 9ES
England
Tel: (0304) 612089

Doors: p. 57/**9**

Stephano de Martino
26 Roupell Street
London SE1 8TB
England
Tel: (071) 928 7754
Fax: (071) 401 2107

Walls & Ceilings: p. 24/**2**

**Din Associates Ltd
Design Consultants**
6 South Lambeth Place
London SW8 1SP
England
Tel: (071) 582 0777

Windows: p. 73/**9**

Epton Studio
Via Cernaia 1
10121 Torino
Italy
Tel: (11) 513 734
Fax: (11) 532 230

Floors: pp. 38/**5**, 42/**1-3**
Doors: p. 52/**1 & 2**
Lighting: p. 114/**11**

Luigi Ferrario
Via Castelfidardo 10
20100 Milano
Italy
Tel: (2) 657 2806

Stairs: p. 79/**3**

Frank Fitzgibbons
443 South Pedro
Los Angeles
CA 90013
Tel: (213) 624 8383

Walls & Ceilings: p. 20/**4**
Stairs: p. 87/**7**
Heating: pp. 100/**5**, 102/1

Terry Flowers
See *Stephano de Martino
Architects*

Steven Forman Architect
160 East 48th Street
Studio 12-0
New York
NY 10017
Tel: (212) 486 0352

Doors: p. 60/**2**
Stairs: p. 90/**5**

Future Systems
See *Jan Kaplicky*

GMW Partnership
PO Box 1613
239 Kensington High Street
London W8 6SL
England
Tel: (071) 937 8020

Doors: p. 52

Alexander Gorlin
380 Lafayette Street
New York
NY 10003
Tel: (212) 228 9000
Fax: (212) 979 6876

Windows: p. 69/**6**

Michael Graves
341 Nassau Street
Princeton
NJ 08540
Tel: (609) 924 6409
Fax: (609) 924 1795

Heating: p. 92/**3**
Lighting: pp. 114/**1**,
116/**1, 3, 4 & 7**, 117/**15**

Johnny Grey
Fyning Copse
Rogate
Petersfield
Hampshire GU31 5DH
England
Tel: (0730) 821 424
Fax: (0730) 821 717

Gruppo Metals
Via Lanza 4
20123 Milan
Italy
Tel: (2) 861 649
Fax: (2) 861 662

Gwathmey Siegel & Associates
475 Tenth Avenue
New York
NY 10018
Tel: (212) 947 1240
Fax: (212) 967 0890

Walls & Ceilings: pp. 24/**5**, 27/**10**
Windows: pp. 66/**1**, 70/**1 & 2**, 71/**8**
Stairs: p. 87/**3**
Heating: p. 92/**2**
Storage: p. 129/**9**
Bathrooms: p. 138/**3**, 140/**3**,
141/**4 & 5**
Kitchens: p. 159/**7**

Steven Holl Architects
133 West 19th Street
New York
NY 10011
USA
Tel: (212) 989 0918

Walls & Ceilings: p. 18

Michael Hopkins & Partners
27 Broadley Terrace
London NW1 6LG
England
Tel: (071) 724 1751

Walls & Ceilings: p. 26/**5**

Arata Isozaki & Associates
6-14 Akasaku 9
Chome Minato-Ku
Tokyo
Japan
Tel: (3) 405 1526-9

Introduction: p. 11/**7**
Windows: p. 71/**7**
Bathrooms: pp. 138/**1**, 145/**8**

Franklin D. Israel
South Robertson Boulevard
Suite 205, Beverly Hills
CA 90211

Walls & Ceilings: pp. 23/**10**, 26/**7**
Doors: p. 60/**1**
Windows: p.75/**11**
Storage: p. 127/**7**
Lighting: p. 111/**11 & 12**

Charles & Maggie Jencks Architects
19 Lansdowne Walk
Holland Park
London W11
England
Tel: (071) 727 8216

Stairs: p. 88/**2**
Heating: p. 92/**3**

Eva Jiricna Architects
7 Dering Street
London W1R 9AB
England
Tel: (071) 629 7077
Fax: (071) 491 3370

Introduction: p. 11/**8**
Walls & Ceilings: p. 24/**6**
Doors: p. 61/**4**
Heating: p. 96/**3**
Storage: pp. 124/**5**, 126/**6**, 127/**9**
Bathrooms: pp. 142/**4**, 144/**1**
Kitchens: pp. 161/**7**, 167/**6**

Jan Kaplicky
27 Whitfield Street
London W1P 5RB
England
Tel: (071) 323 1272

Floors: p. 43/**6 & 7**
Doors: p. 53/**6**
Heating: p. 94/**4**
Lighting: p. 119/**12 & 13**
Bathrooms: p. 142/**3**

Ben Kelly
10 Stoney Street
London SE1 9AD
England
Tel: (071) 378 8116

Doors: p. 60/**3**
Heating: p. 96/**8**

Liz Kitching
Glenwhelt Farm
Greenhead
Carlisle CA6 7HF
England

Floors: p. 46/**6**

Malcolm Last
See *Chassay Last Architects*

Lake/Flato Architects Inc
311 Third Street
Suite 200
San Antonio
TX 78205

Mark Marcinik
272 St Charles Street
San Francisco
CA 94132
Tel: (415) 992 3227

McBride and Associates
560 Broadway
Suite 501
New York
NY 10012
Tel: (212) 941 0818
Fax: (212) 274 1856

Stairs: p. 83/**9**

Mark McInturff Architects
4220 Leeward Place
Bethesda
MD 20816

Vico Magistretti
Via Conservatorio 20
20122 Milan
Italy
Tel: (2) 7600 2964

Walls & Ceilings: p. 22/**2**

Rick Mather Architects
121 Camden High Street
London NW1
England
Tel: (071) 284 1726
Fax: (071) 267 7826

Windows: p. 69/**5**
Stairs: pp. 81/**11**, 89/**7**

Ingo Maurer GmbH
Kaiserstrasse 47
8000 München 40
Germany
Tel: (89) 334 364
Fax: (89) 337 959

Munkenbeck & Marshall Architects
113-117 Farringdon Road
London EC1R
England
Tel: (071) 833 1407

Floors: p. 43/**9**
Lighting: p. 105/**5**
Storage: p. 125/**11**
Bathrooms: p. 149/**10**

One Off Ltd
62 Chalk Farm Road
London NW1 8AN
England
Tel: (071) 284 4963

Doors: p. 60/**1**
Stairs: pp. 80/**4**, 90/**3**

Outram Cullinan & Co Ltd
Kings Buildings
Smith Square
London SW1
England
Tel: (071) 834 7447

Doors: p. 55/**9**
Kitchens: p. 163/**12**

John Pawson
77 Bond Street
London W1Y 9DB
England
Tel: (071) 495 1212

Introduction: pp. 2 & 3, 11/**5**
Walls & Ceilings: pp. 20/**1 & 2**, 27/**8**
Doors: p. 54/**1 & 2**
Windows: p. 66/**2 & 3**

Lighting: pp. 106/**4 & 5**, 112/**5**
Storage: pp. 123/**5**, 131/**6**
Bathrooms: pp. 135/**1**, 140/**2**, 142/**1**, 143/**7**, 146/**1**, 147/**3**
Kitchens: p. 159/**6**

Jochem Poensgen
Poststrasse 7
4000 Dusseldorf 1
Germany

Windows: p. 73/**6**

Powell-Tuck Associates
Plato Place
72 Dionis Road
London SW6 4TU
England
Tel: (071) 736 9337

Introduction: p. 1
Doors: p. 52/**3**

Sergio Puente
Calle del Carmen 34
Colonia San Benabe
Ocotepei
Magdalena Cantreras
Mexico DF 10300

Floors: pp. 40/**1**, 43/**8**
Doors: p. 53/**4**
Kitchens: p. 162/**1**

Andrée Putman
Introduction: p. 10/**3**
Windows: p. 70/**4**
Storage: p. 130/**3**
Bathrooms: pp. 137/**7**, 150/**5**
Kitchens: pp. 158/**1**, 160/**2**

Patrick Ross-Smith
Moss End
Gore Bridge
Midlothian EH23 4NL
Scotland

Windows: p. 73/**8**

Richard Rogers Partnership Ltd
Thames Wharf Studio
Rainville Road
London W6 9HA
England
Tel: (071) 385 1235
Fax: (071) 385 8409

Introduction: p. 14

Michael Russum
Birds, Portchmouth, Russum
Shoreditch Studio
44-46 Scrutton Street
London EC2A 4HH
England
Tel: (071) 377 2777
Fax: (071) 377 5439

Heating: p. 93/**4**

Charles Rutherfoord
51 The Chase
London SW4 0NP
England
Tel: (071) 627 0182

Architectural interior designer who makes special fixtures for clients' houses and is renowned for his theatrical wall finishes.

Walls & Ceilings: p. 23/**8**

Schmidt-Lackner Design
Marktplatz 2
6900 Heidelberg
Germany
Tel: (6221) 163 280
Fax: (6221) 163 780

Sieger Design
Schloss Harkotten
4414 Sassenberg 2
Germany
Tel: (5426) 2796
Fax: (5426) 3875

Claudio Silvestrin
Studio 42
69 Chancery Lane
London WC2A 1AF
England
Tel: (071) 323 6564
Fax: (071) 404 1084

Introduction: p. 2 & 3
Walls & Ceilings: p. 27/**8**
Doors: p. 54/**1 & 2**
Windows: p. 66/**2 & 3**
Bathrooms: pp. 136/**1**, 140/**2**, 143/**7**

Dr Hermann Simsch
Saalgasse 18
Frankfurt
Germany

Floors: p. 41/**11**
Windows: p. 70/**3**
Lighting: p. 107/**9**
Bathrooms: p. 137/**6**
Kitchens: p. 154/**4**

Stanton Williams
Studio 9A
17 Heneage Street
London E1
England
Tel: (071) 247 3171

Lighting: p. 107/**10**

Philippe Starck
Rue de Dion
Montfort-l'amoury
Paris 78490
France
Tel: (1) 34 86 84 74
Fax: (1) 34 86 09 74

Introduction: p. 14
Heating: p. 101/**9 & 10**

Stuart-Silk Architects
1932 First Avenue
Seattle
WA 98101

Ingrid Stegmann
Odenwaldstrasse 8
2000 Hamburg
Germany
Tel: (40) 490 4042
Fax: (40) 511 8535

Tsao & McKnown
Suite 1610
41 East 42nd Street
New York
NY 10017
Tel: (212) 697 0980

Stairs: p. 83/**6**

Charles van den Hove
15 Rue Saint-Pierre
Leige 4000
Belgium

Stairs: p. 88/**3-5**

Christine van der Hurd
41 East 11th Street
11th Floor
New York
NY 10003
Tel: (212) 353 3450
Floors: pp. 46/**5**, 47/**10**

Von Gerkan, Marg and partner
Elbchaussee 139
2000 Hamburg 50
Germany
Tel: (40) 883 0070
Fax: (40) 880 778
Stairs: p. 82/**1**

Walz Design Inc
141 Fifth Avenue
New York
NY 10010
Tel: (212) 477 2211
Fax: (212) 677 3780

Bathrooms: p. 148/**5**

Ian Wall
979 Third Avenue
16th Floor
New York
NY 10022
Tel: (212) 758 5337

Andreas Weber
Nymphenburgerstrasse 79
8000 Munchen 19
Germany
Tel: (89) 123 4551

Storage: p. 122/**1**

David Wild Design & Build
44 Rochester Place
London NW1
England
Tel: (071) 267 7126

Introduction: pp. 3, 10/**1**
Walls & Ceilings: pp. 20/**3**, 23/**7**
Floors: p. 44/**1**
Doors: p. 58/**3**
Windows: pp. 66, 68/**1 & 2**
Stairs: pp. 83/**7**, 85/**5**
Heating: pp. 98/**6**, 99/**9**
Lighting: p. 113/**12**
Storage: p. 128/**8**

Peter Wilson
Studio 3
5 Thurloe Square
London SW7
England
Tel: (071) 589 7560

Walls & Ceilings: pp. 28/**8**, 29/**9**
Windows: p. 72/**1**
Stairs: p. 87/**4 & 5**
Lighting: p. 110/**1**
Bathrooms: p. 139/**9**

Chassay Wright
Chassay Architects
90 Westbourne Terrace
London W2 6QE
England
Tel: (071) 402 3233

Stairs: p. 87/**4 & 5**
Bathrooms: p. 139/**9**

John Young Architect
c/o Richard Rogers Partnership Ltd
Rainville Road
Thames Wharf
London W6 9HA
England
Tel: (071) 385 1235
Fax: (071) 385 8409

Introduction: pp. 8 & 9
Floors: p. 35/**4**
Doors: pp. 56/**4**, 58/**1**
Windows: p. 67/**4 & 5**
Stairs: p. 84/**3 & 4**
Heating: p. 92
Lighting: p. 109/**7**
Storage: p. 123/**6**
Bathrooms: pp. 136, 137/**5**
Kitchens: p. 156/**4**

Index

INDEX

Bibliography

Billcliffe, Roger
Charles Rennie Mackintosh,
The Complete Furniture,
Furniture Drawings and
Interior Designs
John Murray
1979

Calloway, Stephen
The Elements of Style
Mitchell Beazley
1991

Coad, Emma Dent
Spanish Design
and Architecture
Studio Vista
1990

Collins, Michael,
Papadallis, Andreas
Post-Modern Design,
Academy Editions
1989

Glancey, Jonathan
New British Architecture
Thames and Hudson
1989

Glancey, Jonathan
Bryant, Richard,
The New Moderns
Mitchell Beazley
1990

Huygen, Frederique
British Design,
Image and Identity
Thames and Hudson
1989

Isaacs, Reginald
Gropius, An Illustrated
Biography of the Creator
of the Bauhaus
Bullfinch
1986

Jencks, Charles
Architecture Today
Academy Editions
1988

Jencks, Charles
The New Moderns
Academy Editions
1990

Julier, Guy
New Spanish Design
Thames and Hudson
1991

Mauries, Patrick
Fornasetti,
Designer of Dreams
Thames and Hudson
1991

Moor, Andrew
Contemporary
Stained Glass
Mitchell Beazley
1989

Neuhart, John and Marilyn
Eames, Ray,
Eames Design,
The Work of the Office of
Charles and Ray Eames
Thames and Hudson
1989

Pasca, Vanni
Vico Magistretti,
Elegance and Innovation
in Postwar Italian Design
Thames and Hudson
1991

Pawley, Martin
Eva Jiricna,
Design in Exile
Fourth Estate
1990

Rogers, Richard
Richard Rogers
and Architects
Academy Editions
1985

Sudjic, Deyan
The Lighting Book
Mitchell Beazley
1985

Sudjic, Deyan
New Directions in
British Architecture,
Norman Foster, Richard
Rogers, James Stirling
Thames and Hudson
1988

Tapert, Annette
Swid Powell
Objects and Architects
Thames and Hudson
1990

Westphal, Uwe
The Bauhaus
Studio Editions
1991

Acknowledgments

Author's acknowledgments

Thank you to Hilu Ginger for her invaluable assistance with research, to Graham Bell for the Directory computer program and to my sons, James and Oliver Niesewand, and my husband, Christopher Ward, for their help and support.

Thank you to all the manufacturers, agents and designers who generously submitted an excellent range of material for selection. Finally, I would like to thank everyone at Mitchell Beazley.